NEGOTIATING THE DIVINE

SOUTH ASIA INSTITUTE, NEW DELHI BRANCH
HEIDELBERG UNIVERSITY
SOUTH ASIAN STUDIES NO. XLI

NEGOTIATING THE DIVINE

Temple Religion and Temple Politics in Contemporary Urban India

URSULA RAO

MANOIIAR
2003

First published 2003

ISBN 81-7304-515-1

Published by
Ajay Kumar Jain for
Manohar Publishers & Distributors
4753/23 Ansari Road, Daryaganj
New Delhi 110002

Typeset by
A J Software Publishing Co. Pvt. Ltd.
New Delhi 110005

Printed at
Lordson Publishers Pvt. Ltd.
Delhi 110007

Contents

Illustrations

Acknowledgements

There are many people who have helped make this study possible—too many to thank all of them. But let me mention at least a few. I wish to offer special thanks to all the people in Bhopal who allowed me to take part in their life and did everything to facilitate my research. I owe gratitude to the Kali and the Durga Temple Committees who welcomed me and extended their full support throughout the long months of fieldwork. I am also particularly indebted to Dr. Ishwar Dass and his wife Meera Dass, who accepted me into their house and treated me like a family member during my fieldwork. Their friendship and support helped me carry on with my work, even in difficult times.

My academic interest and the turn it took was influenced by Prof. Richard Burghart. I profited from his tuition and I am indebted for the support he gave me. After his tragic death, Prof. Klaus-Peter Koepping carried on his work and became my academic advisor. I want to particularly thank him for the interest he took in my research and the patience he showed. His suggestions were of great help to me, showing me new angles to the interpretation of my material. Prof. Monika Boehm-Tettelbach, of the Department of Indology in Heidelberg, was always ready to listen to my problems and extended her help during all the years of my work. I also thank Prof. Schiffauer of the Department of Anthropology at the University of Frankfurt/Oder for his revision of my thesis and the helpful comments he made, both during its production as well as afterwards. During the process of rewriting my Ph.D. thesis, Prof. Dr. William Sax of the Department of Anthropology in the South Asia Institute, Heidelberg, has been of great help. I thank him for the patience he showed while going through my script in detail and for the suggestions he made for its improvement.

I also wish to thank academic institutions in India for extending their support. My special thanks go to Prof. Veena Das from the Delhi School of Economics, Delhi University who helped me make sense of my experience in the field and translate them into academic reflections. I would like to thank members of Bhopal University and especially its Vice-Chancellor, Prof. Chakravarty.

There are a number of friends in Heidelberg whose academic advice and personal support I enjoyed. It is impossible to name them all. I am particularly grateful to Alexander Henn, Martin Fuchs, Antje Linkenbach, and Aditya Malik for helping me clarify my ideas, supporting me in my search for literature, and encouraging me whenever I lost hope and patience.

All this work would not have been possible without the financial support of the Cusanuswerk and the DFG (Deutsche Forschungsgesellschaft). The Cusanuswerk supported me over a period of two years including the time spent on my trips to Bhopal. Since October 1999 I have been the recipient of a grant from the DFG, in the form of a research fellowship, as well as several travel grants. I also thank the Institute for Anthropology in Heidelberg for technical and material support.

URSULA RAO

CHAPTER 1

Introduction

The study set out with the question of how the idea of the divine is realized by Hindus in contemporary India. The focus of observation is the temple, which provides the centre for the description and analysis of the way religious beliefs and practices take shape in a modern urban environment.[1] The aim is twofold. First, the study offers an introduction into the institution of Hindu temples. It gives examples of how they are built and managed and discusses the way they are shaped as sacred territory by human activities directed towards the divine. Secondly, the study presents a discussion of religious politics rooted in the daily practices of a wide range of people.

Integrating these perspectives, the study strives to contribute to an understanding of contemporary forms of Hinduism, both in their devotional orientation as well as their political dimension. It takes seriously the claims of believers about the existence of non-human agents, whom they turn to for orientation and protection, and investigates the ways deities become present in the lives of devotees through mutual communication in the temple. Simultaneously, it also looks at oppositional forces as well as the opinions and stances of those who deny the possibility of divine intervention, or see other motivations at work during the construction of temples and their (socially determined) realization as sacred territory. The aim is to understand the practices of temple religiosity in the larger context of urban negotiations about an appropriate place for the divine in the human world.

In this context, religious practices are understood as political in two ways. First, they take shape within a field of human negotiations in which exist many different ways of creating reality and acting upon it, in competition to one another. They are political in the sense that they contribute to overall power struggles. Secondly, religious activities are meaningful for the making and unmaking of leaders, and for the assessment of their contribution to the welfare of society. They are influential in a discourse socially delineated as political, in which

[1] The material was collected in Bhopal during 16 months of fieldwork in the years 1996-9.

religious attitudes and activities are important markers of positions in a field of oppositional ideologies.

By investigating the everyday religious practice of people in terms of their affinity to power struggles, the analysis is situated in an area left void by those studies that investigate the politics of religion from the point of view of religious ideologies or party strategies. There are many interesting and detailed studies of the histories of Hindu organizations and parties (for example, Basu et al. 1993; Graham 1990; Hansen and Jaffrelot 1998; Jaffrelot 1996; Lele 1995) the rhetoric and symbolism of Hindu nationalism (Ludden 1996; Pandey 1993; Sarkar and Butalia 1995; van de Veer 1994) and about the logic of Hindu-Muslim riots (Brass 1998; Kakar 1995; Nandy et al. 1995; Pandey 1990; Panikkar 1999; Sarkar and Butalia 1995). However, few of these studies pay attention to the orientation of citizens outside the political limelight, their framing of religious practices, their shaping of religious concepts and the influence they have on the religious discourse.[2] It is this latter perspective which I have chosen here.[3]

Thus, this work is not about Hindu nationalism. It is rather about the activities of diverse groups of people who shape urban temples through their activities and concepts. This, however, is relevant to the study of religious politics—also in the sense of party politics—because it offers explanations of how religious issues involve worshippers, temple activists, priests, ascetics, beggars, political leaders and administrators in a shared discourse. I do not focus on any one of these groups, but offer an analysis of their interactions in the concrete setting of the temple. Central to the study is the analysis of the various contexts of communication between agents and the way social behaviour and reflexive activity is oriented, shaped and changed in actual situations.

While presenting a detailed analysis of the situated practices of a wide variety of people, I do not intend to submerge the descriptions of society under an endless enumeration of single events. Although people act contextually, they do not act at random. Their perceptions are pre-structured through culturally available standard narratives, which are available to them as 'cultural capital' (Bourdieu 1984) and are selected

[2] Exceptions, where studies have concentrated on the multiplicity of view points, are: Brass 1998; Das 1990b; Hansen 2001; Kakar 1995; Pandey 1991b.

[3] This perspective is also influenced by the works of the Subaltern Studies group, which in an effort to recover the subaltern in history and as such departs from a historiography that has concentrated on elite politics and focused on the beliefs and practices of those who constitute the silent majority. No doubt there are also problems with a view that constructs society as consisting of two independent domains: the elite and the subaltern. These will be discussed at some length in Chapter 6. In spite of all criticism, it is the achievement of Subaltern Studies to have opened up new directions of investigation by reorienting established ways of seeing.

and adjusted in accordance with context. The notion of narrative orientations counters the idea of the existence of one objective truth and points towards the multiplicity of possible interpretations and perspectives. Yet it also shows the limits of an individual understanding of reality, by establishing that every interpretation is embedded in a cultural context which produces explanatory frameworks and gives them plausibility.

This formulation of the research problem is informed by contemporary debates on culture in its overarching anthropological meaning, according to which I understand social systems to be made up of a multiplicity of interconnected and competing discourses. The complexity of a culture—as an intersection of many competing fields of cultural discourse—comes to us with particular force in the urban environment, where life is characterized by the interaction of many actors who have access to different interpretative frameworks. In any concrete situation people will find reasons to draw boundaries and actively maintain the truth of certain ideologies. But their effort to grasp the logic of the social sphere is undermined by social practices that constantly shift frames and dislocate ideologies. Open to interpretation and in no way pre-determined through any given 'cultural core', all categories have to be constantly re-negotiated. In every situation, social actors have to recreate reality by subjecting it to an interpretation set in particular contexts (see Bauman, Richard 1989; Baumann, Gerd 1996: 9-30). These contexts are constructed through the actors themselves and through their selection of relevant elements. Comaroff and Comaroff have suggested a definition of culture that emphasises its fluidity:

> Culture always contains within it polyvalent, potentially contestable messages, images, and actions. It is, in short, a historically situated, historically unfolding ensemble of signifiers-in-action, signifiers at once material and symbolic, social and aesthetic. Some of these, at any moment in time, will be woven into more or less tightly integrated, relatively explicit worldviews; others may be heavily contested, the stuff of counterideologies and 'subcultures'; yet others may become more or less unfixed, relatively freefloating, and indeterminate in their value and meaning. (Comaroff and Comaroff 1992: 27)

This description of culture points towards its variability as well as its stability. Culture comes to life in a variety of contexts to which more or less pre-conceived notions of 'reality' are applied. Yet an analysis of culture cannot rest with the description of actions, interpretations and contexts and their relation to each other, but must also take note of the powers that support the structuring of reality. These powers derive not only from social agents but also from 'non-agentive' force fields like constraints, conventions and values (Comaroff and Comaroff 1992: 28).

To meet the requirements of this multi-dimensional definition of culture in my study of religious meaning, I have anchored my discussion in one particular place, investigating the contextual activities of people, which are then analysed in relation to debates and networks of power that have meaning also beyond the temple and its surroundings. Each of the first four chapters concentrates on one aspect of temple life and investigates the way people's interactions with the divine as well as their mutual appreciation or rejections of certain forms of belief contribute to the structuring of human relations and the shaping of social concepts. Chapter 6 sums up the findings in terms of their relevance to debates on tradition and modernity, as well as to subalternity and resistance. It points to the limits of dichotomous constructions of reality and shows how people's practices in the religious sphere transcend various conceptual boundaries by constantly overstepping and thereby changing them. Therefore, this study is an undertaking in understanding the concrete life world of the temple in its social embeddedness, as well as a contribution to conceptual debates which aim at capturing the logic of the organization of human social activity.

Chapter 2 will set the scene. It introduces the reader to the history of the Kali and Durga Temples, the main sites of observation in this study. Both temples are situated within the old town of Bhopal and rank among the larger and more popular temples. Both have a history of conflicts between Hindus, Muslims and the city administration. The narration of the incidents leading to the construction of these sites will allow a first encounter with two important themes within social negotiations that run through the work. How should urban territory be managed in the light of the competing interests expressed by many groups and the idea of divine intervention? In which context should the construction and management of temples be understood as religious, in which as political, and who should be allowed to claim authority over its procedures? Beyond these more general questions, Chapter 2 follows the joint activities of people who bring a temple into existence, and shows how a temple in its function as a symbol for, and religious core of social groups—here of the Khatik caste and the Hindu community—supports the physical and conceptual integration of a community.

Chapter 3 narrows the perspective and concentrates on the temple as a sacred place that is set apart from other places in the city through the presence of the goddess. It shows how the temple is created as divine territory through the transformative activity of worshippers, who secure the divine presence and its benevolent impact on their lives through ritual activities. The characterization of the temple as sacred territory marks an important point of departure with relevance to the overall discussion on religion, because it shows ways in which the belief in non-human agency is realized in this world.

Returning to the larger urban scene in Chapter 4, the reader is introduced to the ways the temple is embedded in political processes. How it serves social groups and individual leaders to nurture their constituencies, stage their importance, and increase their social status. The interconnections between urban citizens and their leaders are analysed in the context of temple festivals and discussed with reference to the careers of selected politicians. In connection with this, the need for a demarcation of the domains of religion and politics as well as the knowledge of their inseparability in practice becomes an issue of reflexive debates. The vigour and urgency with which it is followed up has to do with people's knowledge about the many ways religion is manipulated for the realization of vested interests. Yet it is also informed by the realization that all social activities, even religious ones, are part of ongoing power negotiations.

The controversial debate about an appropriate place for religion in modern society is continued in Chapter 5, which discusses the way the administration of the city becomes involved in temple matters. The focus is on questions of management and corruption, as well as on urban territory and 'illegal' temple construction. Although the state is said to intervene only in the secular aspects of temples, such as when it determines where a temple can be built and how its finances should be managed, it encounters resistance from some believers, who perceive deities as being independent agents whose activities cannot and should not be constrained by state laws. Most temples are built without state permission. They are defended in terms of the religious needs of the people, the constitutional right to freedom of religious expression, and the self-manifestation of deities. Here we encounter another aspect of the discourse of religion, set against the background of struggles over the organization of urban territory, which finds expression in debates about modernity and tradition, scientific rationality and religious beliefs.

The conceptual antithesis between tradition and modernity provides the point of departure for the theoretical discussion in Chapter 6. Here the dichotomy is deconstructed by placing the constructs of tradition and modernity in relation to social practices, which encompass both taken-for-granted knowledge as well as reflexive awareness. The temple is described as a place of both tradition and modernity, where traditions are remembered, realized, re-worked and invented with reference to the requirements of modern life. The chapter shows how religious beliefs and practices associated with the forefathers are re-adjusted to contemporary life through their conceptual integration into scientific rationality. As a place that encourages resistance to both the idea of a secular society and the negation of divine actors—also by integrating and submitting to ideas of modernity and rationality into its own domain—the temple becomes a space for alternative projections of the social order. Thus, Chapter 6 closes with a review of the rhetoric of resistance, especially in its usage among the members of the Subaltern Studies group, and asks in which way the activities of believers transcend the dichotomy between elite and subaltern and blurs distinctions between dominance and resistance, as well as between persuasion and collaboration.

This study is about ideology as much as it is about performance. It analyses the intersection of belief and practice, of action and reflection, and shows how they are mutually shaped through the integrated activity of people. Yet there are also moments when things appear to fall apart, when people get carried away by activities that appear no longer sanctioned by their convictions, or where no amount of reflection can make certain actions or beliefs intelligible. There are moments when plans are undermined, when views have to be re-evaluated in face of new developments, and when stereotypes are countered by experience. All these moments prove that life is invested with many uncertainties. It forces all actors to constantly re-adjust their ideas and strategies of actions to situations as they unravel and are given a shape as events.

Thus, when I talk in this study of worshippers, temple activists, bureaucrats, and politicians, these are not fixed categories, but social constructs that provide relevant classifications and help people to orient their behaviour without determining it. In fact, there are many cases where people behave at odds with established stereotypes. By considering the multiplicity of orientations displayed in performance, the study shows the dynamic of cultural processes. The identification of ideologies that shape and explain actions, is set within the discussion of the many moments in which different ways of narrative ordering meet and overlap, thereby supporting alternate ways of structuring and understanding reality.

THE ETHNOGRAPHIC SETTING

The study is located in Bhopal, a middle sized city that is the capital of Madhya Pradesh. Its history is marked by its importance as a centre of Muslim culture before Independence, which to this day influences the religious discourse in the city. Founded in 1722 by the invader Dost Mohammed Khan, Bhopal was until 1947 the capital of a small Muslim kingdom of the same name. However, the power of the Muslims was broken when Bhopal joined the Indian Union in 1947. Consequently the city underwent rapid growth through the migration of people from all over the country, including a large number of refugees from Sindh. This development was amplified when the city was declared the capital of the newly founded Madhya Pradesh in 1956. With a population of around 100,000 inhabitants in 1951,[4] the city has today grown to an estimated 1.7 million. As a state capital with a majority Hindu population,[5] Bhopal has become a stronghold of Hindu politics, with new political forces shaping the city in conscious demarcation from its Muslim past.[6]

This also happens with reference to religious buildings. Hardly anyone failed to complain to me that during the Muslim reign, temple construction was banned in the city centre. From written sources I later learned that Hindus had indeed been prevented from publicly celebrating their festivals and from erecting *shikharas* (the typical pyramid-like roofs of North Indian temples) on their temples inside the walled city during the second half of the nineteenth century. This is why, even today, the majority of temples in the city centre are of a *haveli* (mansion) type, which means that they were built inside the houses and are not visible from the outside. In the light of this historical legacy, the construction of temples after Independence, particularly in the old town, became a symbolic act, demonstrating the new 'Hindu dominance'. Especially large temple projects are realized in conscious competition with the religious buildings of the Muslims, who in turn increase the height and size of their mosques.

I decided to take this dimension of growing Hindu self-assurance into account in my selection of temples,[7] as it seemed central to the

[4] The exact figure according to the Census of 1981 is 102,333. Census of India of 1981. Series II, Madhya Pradesh Part II-A. General Population Tables. K.C. Dubey (ed.): 174. The last exact data exists for 1991, for which the number of inhabitants is given as 1,062,018.

[5] According to the census of 1991, religious affiliation is distributed as follows: Hindus 67.36 per cent, Muslims 27.76 per cent, Jains 1.33 per cent, Christians 1.45 per cent, Buddhists 1.31 per cent, Sikhs 0.76 per cent.

[6] For the history and general socio-economic data of Bhopal see: Ashfaq Ali 1987, 1990; Gazetteer of India, Madhya Pradesh, Bhopal State 1995 [1908]; Gazetteer of India, Madhya Pradesh; Sehore and Bhopal 1989; Malhotra 1964; Mittal 1990; Nawab Shahjahan 1876; Singh, J.P. 1994; Shrinivastav and Guru 1989; Verma 1984.

[7] In order to be able to make a decision for particular sacred sites, I surveyed a large number of temples and collected data on their histories and social settings. For an initial overview, I selected city quarters with differing characteristics and surveyed all the temples therein, asking about the history and social setting, sometimes spending one or two days observing the social and religious activities. I included in my survey: Shivaji Nagar, residential area for highly-placed bureaucrats; Barhkairi, residential area for the lower middle and working classes; the City, bazaar area and middle class residential area (here one finds most of the *haveli* temples); BHEL, Piplani, a middle class residential area. Here I surveyed the numerous temples erected by different migrant communities. They have been built in this area in large numbers, because in the 1960s the government provided different migrant communities with land in this new township to build their own temples.

way the religious discourse in the city takes shape. (1) By settling for the Durga Temple right in the middle of the old town and the Kali Temple at the margin of the city centre, I found two temples representing, each in a different way, an opposition to the dominance of Muslims in a locality. (2) The temples were also selected for their size. Amongst the largest in the city, they attract a particularly great number of devotees and are thus highly suitable for the study of the social setting in a temple. (3) They were further chosen in their function as community centres. Both temples were—as is typical of most temples in Bhopal—constructed and managed by a group of people, in one case a caste group, and in the other, a business community. In preferring a typical community-managed temple, I was interested in investigating the social dynamic that prevails among the different social groups engaged in temple matters in a particular locality, thus capturing the local politics of religion. (4) Finally, I opted for the Durga and Kali Temples because of their recent construction, thereby enabling research into the controversial process of their history. With the founders as well as their opponents still alive, the creation of sacred places and their reappropriation through different historical tales became part of my focus.

It was rather by accident that I found myself working in two temples that were both dedicated to Devi (Goddess, here in form of Kali and Durga). There again, thinking back to my experiences among believers in Bhopal, this seems fairly unsurprising. The goddess is considered by many to be more powerful than her male counterparts and Devi temples have become highly popular. There is also scriptural evidence for the enormous power of the various incarnations of the Goddess. The most popular and well known reference in the sacred texts occurs in respect of Durga who, according to the Devi-Mahatmya,[8] was created jointly by numerous male deities (among them Vishnu, Shiva, Yama, Vayu) and invested with all their powers in order to defeat the demon Mahisha. In her fights Durga is fierce and powerful. On the field she creates the goddess Kali, who is said to have sprung from her forehead, embodying her anger[9] (Kinsley 1984: 145-8, 1986: 95-131; see also Coburn 1984; Pintchman 1994). Recently, however, depictions of Kali and Durga have become less fearful and have been adjusted to an increasingly unified style of representation of the divine. This development is coupled with

[8] The Devi-Mahatmya is part of the Markandeya Purana and is dated to the sixth century AD.

[9] This story is evoked in the hymns sung during the daily ritual of *arti* in the Kali and the Durga temples, in which the goddess's victory over the demons is mentioned.

numerous efforts to domesticate the goddesses by creating families for these originally celibate divinities.[10]

In the minds of believers in Bhopal, the goddess bore only a few features of a fearful deity. She was considered a mother, to whom people may turn in times of trouble. The mother here was viewed as the nurturing and ever-giving figure, in contrast to the father who is seen as the disciplining force (see McDermott 1995: 59). Thus, worshippers had their own reasons to congratulate me on the selection of my research topic. They were convinced that the study would be a success, since for them it was a form of Devi *bhakti* (showing devotion to the Goddess). They were sure that the goddess would help me complete my task to the satisfaction of all.

Although this was alien to my way of thinking, I have to admit that the enthusiasm, with which people welcomed my work and my presence in the temple and replied to my questions, helped me to complete my task quickly. It is thanks to the support of all those who were connected with the temples I investigated, that my selection of research sites served to draw me into discussions and helped me understand religious practices and beliefs.

PRODUCING ANTHROPOLOGICAL KNOWLEDGE: REFLECTIONS ON METHOD

With the focus on selected temples and the events surrounding their construction and management, I committed myself to a methodology which, following Gluckman, has been called an 'extended-case-method' in which particular cases and the social constellation they demonstrate are used as an entry point to the analysis of more general social conditions (Gluckman 1954, 1968, see also Mitchell 1956, 1983; van Velsen 1967; Turner 1957, 1967; Kapferer 1983, 1987, 1997). Yet, unlike the classical studies, I do not treat specific cases as concrete realizations of unified and fixed social structures. They are moments of social practice in which structure as a fluid entity is created and re-created through the application of memory to new contexts. I assume that events call upon a cultural repertoire that is used to structure action and experience, while at the same time being context-bound activities in which agents have constantly re-adjusted their perceptions and actions. Thus, I would call them in Bourdieu's words moments of 'regulated improvisations' (Bourdieu 1987: 107).

[10] Kinsley 1986: 95, 116; Masilamani-Meyer and Vogelsanger 1993: 113, 116; see also Babb 1975: 217-46; Hawley 1996; Mookerjee 1988: 61-9; for a discussion of attitudes towards Kali see the analysis of forms of devotion to Kali in Bengal by McDermott (1995, 1996) and the personal account of a believer, Harding (1993).

In order to capture the complexity of social situations, I follow specific events, the practices that bring them about, the negotiations that shape them, and the reflections that give them meaning. They bring to life the temple as a socio-religious institution before the inner eye of the reader. They are further used to formulate more general statements on the discourse of religion in contemporary urban India that crystallizes around the temple. I treat my conclusions not as timeless truths, but as time- and context-bound interpretations. They offer the chance to get acquainted with people's situated actions and opinions. However, departing from the concrete involvement with real people, they also provided a chance to enter into a search for 'similarities in human experiences' (Wikan 1993: 186, see also Kapferer 1997: 11).

What I present is my perspective of things. It is a construction that takes place at the point of conjunction of my involvement with ethnological theory and my encounter with people in the field and is shaped through a situation that Hastrup called the 'performative paradox' (Hastrup 1995: 4-8) of an ethnologist. While engaging in constant efforts to grasp the others' points of view through participation and dialogue, the researcher nevertheless looks at situations from an outsider's point of view whose understanding is guided by an interest in theoretical generalizations:

> It is a particular epistemological position in which we renounce continuity between our own worlds, conceptions, theories and conventions of representation and those of the people studied [...] From the position of the radical other, anthropology may help the world realize the extent to which local cultures are mutually implicated while also allowing for a recognition of difference and points of resistance. [...] By its double vision, and through its speaking from the perceived periphery rather than the self-declared centre of reason, anthropology challenges received wisdom. Thus, it enables us to make the world new rather than to get it right.[11] (Hastrup 1995: 7-8)

Such a formulation of the anthropologists' work has its basis in the method of fieldwork proposed by Malinowski (1961 [1922]), in which he gave priority to recording people's own opinions while simultaneously aiming at formulating (scientific) generalizations about a culture. However, in modern anthropology, observations are no longer believed to take place from an 'objective' point of view. The anthropologist is instead, situated in a particular social constellation from which she offers her own interpretation of the world.

Although I believe that the anthropologists' work is an invention, I do not conceive of it as a fiction. I clearly distance myself from projects like that of Tyler (1990), who wishes to evoke an ultimate human

[11] Cf. Rorty 1991: 44.

experience through a text that has no author and no structure and is a 'collection of indexical anecdotes'. Tyler hopes that through his escape into the world of 'fantasy' he can dissolve perspectivity and abstain from exercising power over other people and their representations. My objections to such a project do not only arise from the belief that it is impossible to escape perspectivity. Worse, Tyler's efforts to abstain from expressing his own opinion forces him also to retreat from the claim to offer a critical evaluation of existing discourses—in his own or the other society (compare on this point also Schiffauer 1997a: 170, Koepping 1994a and b).

In my work the ethnographer does not vanish into the collective of the literary authors, nor do I pretend to abstain from exercising power over (the representations of) others.[12] Instead, I purposefully engage in my own constructions of reality, knowing well that the undertaking takes shape from the specific point of view of a concrete social agent. I believe in trying to come to grips with my own position in relation to the people in the field as well as to the text produced here, fully aware of the fact that there are many aspects that escape my attention and numerous parameters I cannot control (see Fardon 1990: 21-4). I thereby commit myself to what Gouldner called a 'reflexive sociology' in which the researcher strives for 'knowledge as awareness'—which he contrasts to 'knowledge as information'—derived from the sociologist's involvement with people and their reflection on their own position (Gouldner 1970: 493-7).

Like Geertz, I see no option but to take on the 'burden of authorship' (Geertz 1988: 146). Writing here becomes an ethical project that offers new ways of looking at things, with the hope to facilitate mutual understanding and communication (see Koepping 1994a). To make one's viewpoint explicit also means to take seriously people's own efforts to come to terms with their life worlds. Actors themselves strive to connect the bits and pieces of their lives to (their own) logical tales, mapping the universe in order to gain an orientation. As I got involved with people in the field, they in fact expected me to take a stance and explain how things appeared to me. After helping me to grasp their standpoint, they wanted me to divulge mine. I do this extensively now in this work by integrating the new visions that people in the field provided me with into my own cognitive frame.

In spite of presenting my own viewpoint, I insist on *representing* because my writing stems from the involvement with real people in their real life situations. I am accountable in the first instance to those who provided me with my materials. This is important, for it makes a

[12] See also Koepping 1997: 56.

difference whether I reflect on the predicaments of life, or whether I sympathize with actual people in their search for answers to dilemmas and conflicts. Inventing reality in this context does not mean to make it up or to fabricate it, but it means to offer an alternative interpretation, to add a new perspective to the currently available narrative structures, which has the potential to change reality by changing perception.

The aim here is not to exoticize, but to accompany people in their struggle to make sense of their life which shows so many similarities to my own. Such a contribution depends on an attitude that accepts people in the field as the subjects of their own life world with the same right to make their own constructions of reality and their claims to truth (Bauman 1992: xxi-xxii). Every effort has to be made to understand the many conflicting points of view by listening and accepting every perception as real.[13] It is the basis for an honest dialogue in which all opinions qualify to be taken equally seriously, and as a result could also be criticized from a different vantage point.

Aiming at a dialogue, I also handed out my initial written thoughts to some of the literate informants in order to provoke a reaction to *my* interpretation of *their* world. The joint reading of the text started off long and controversial discussions during which I could find my own however contested point of view in the discourse. There were other, more subtle, contexts in which my position came to the fore. People accepted me as a friend and helper. They prodded me repeatedly to tell them about my own religious feelings and beliefs, they pressed me to take a stance on social conflicts, and they gave new directions to my thoughts by openly criticizing my work. In all these situations, I was asked to open up to become a *real* person, a member of *their* discourses which now started to also become mine. I took up the challenge and got involved when I felt it appropriate. In other situations, I explained why I was not able or ready to take a stance. I am convinced that it is due to my efforts to be honest and accessible to people that they were also ready to open up to me and to allow me glimpses of their lives.

Koepping characterizes the work of an anthropologist—consisting of data collecting and writing—as a process of authentication and emancipation. The authentication results from the fieldworker's involvement with people with whom she shares some of their life

[13] Koepping calls this attitude towards the subjects of one's research, in extension of Kurt Wolff's (1976) concepts, 'surrender', which he explains 'does not entail a "giving up"... of self or a "merging" of self and other. Surrender rather implies the attentiveness with which we listen to musical performances, or that is characteristic of lovers' relationships, these relationships which lead not to a losing of self but to finding of it' (Koepping 2002: 259).

experiences, which gives her the authority to speak. Such an engagement fosters emancipation, as it teaches the anthropologist new ways to see the world, enabling her also to find a new (critical) standpoint in relation to both the people she has studied as well as to her own society (Koepping 1987, 1999). It is with this attitude that I undertook my work in Bhopal, listening carefully to people, presenting here a critical appraisal of what I have learned from them by integrating their views into my frame of thinking.

CHAPTER 2

Temples in a World of Changing Communities

How is a public temple built? And under what circumstances is it erected? How are the finances mobilized and the construction supervized? These were my initial questions when surveying the vast number of shrines and temples in Bhopal. Collecting basic data on a great variety of temples, I soon realized that the majority of them resulted from the joint effort of a whole group of people who for various reasons had joint religious interests. The only exception seemed to be those temples that were founded by an individual ascetic in search of a place to stay and a religious institution of his own. Most others were backed by caste groups that wanted to see their caste-deity enshrined, people from a neighbourhood who saw the need for a temple in close proximity, members of a business community who hoped for divine patronage, or local members of a national or international religious organization starting a local branch.

While I observed temples being shaped by groups, I also realized that groups were shaped or re-shaped through joint efforts in construction and management. The wish to build a temple served as a common goal that forced people to organize support networks. Once built, the temple provides the community with a religious centre and a symbolic representation. The first chapter will introduce the reader to case-studies that demonstrate this two-sided process through which a temple is constructed and a social group transformed. I first investigate the history of the Kali Temple and the effect its erection had on the Khatik caste. Then the discussion moves to the Durga Temple and shows how an imagined Hindu-community comes to life in Bhopal. Both issues aim at showing how in contemporary urban India, local actors, by engaging in religious activity, set a process in motion through which social communities are shaped and transformed.

THE KHATIK CASTE AND THE ORIGIN OF THE KALI TEMPLE

In the centre of Bhopal, on an arterial road connecting the city centre of old Bhopal with the posh middle class living areas of new Bhopal, lies the Kali Temple, easily visible to any visitor. Although still under construction—there has been a continuous process of extending the building since its foundation thirty years ago—its structure is imposing. Some worshippers boasted that the temple is even known in America, recollecting the fact that exchange students from an American University had asked about the Kali Temple which had been mentioned to them as a landmark that would help them locate their partner institute in Bhopal.

The temple has been built by Khatiks, a Scheduled Caste of (former) fruit and meat sellers, considered to be of very low status. Although today Khatiks work in a wide range of occupations and many are successful businessmen, politicians or professionals in government offices, they are still confronted with an image that builds on their traditional occupation as butchers and depicts them as crude, ruthless, and indeed simply 'butcher-like'. Independent of the actual situation of individual members, as a group Khatiks are still known as a 'criminal lot' with an 'aggressive character'. Countering this image, the Kali Temple has helped to establish Khatiks as also religiously minded 'social workers', devotees of the goddess, and brave pioneers in the fight for the Hindu cause. As one of the most popular religious sites in the city, the temple helped improve the image of the caste. As an institution, it has facilitated the meeting of Khatiks from all over the state and supported the extension of social networks through which Khatiks are able to realise their growing aspirations.

In order to understand the contribution the Kali Temple made to the transformation of a caste, a detailed analysis of its history is needed. It will bring to light that the construction of a temple and the re-construction of a caste are deeply entwined processes, in which changes in the urban landscape influence social dynamics and the transformation of social relations has a bearing on the organization of urban space.

The Kali Temple started as a small wayside shrine in 1968, when a congregation of Khatik men decided to construct a new temple for their caste goddess outside the crowded lanes of their residential quarter, Budhvara. They chose an open space adjoining their neighbourhood, near the Chota Talab (Small Lake), which has served them as festival ground for the yearly celebration of Hariyali Amavas,[1] a religious celebration during which all male members of the caste jointly offer a blood sacrifice to their caste goddess. Instead of erecting a new

[1] This festival is not an official holiday. It is celebrated by Khatiks in Bhopal on the first day of the new moon of the lunar month of Shravana (July/August). On this day all male Khatiks assemble at the lower lake a little outside of Budhvara (the spot where today the Kali Temple is situated) to offer an animal sacrifice to Kali. Formerly, the celebration used to last till the early morning with everyone sharing a non-vegetarian meal and alcohol, both considered to be *prasad*, as they were the returns from the sacrificial offering

provisional shrine every year, they considered it more prestigious and powerful to build a permanent temple which could be used the year round. The construction was well planned, and took place within one night, the night before Ganesh Chaturthi.[2] This date had been carefully selected because the Khatiks were determined to build the temple without state permission, which they did not think would be easy to receive for a temple near the lake in a predominant Muslim area, and moreover in the crowded area of old Bhopal. Instead of entering into complicated negotiations with the city administration they preferred to follow the common tactic of 'illegal' temple construction.[3]

In order to hide their intention, the Khatiks first set up a tent at the site on which they pretended to hold readings of sacred texts, but actually prepared the ground for the construction. Meanwhile the elements of the building were made: the Kali statue, four pillars, and a roof. During the night these were brought to the spot and the shrine assembled. The tent was removed and the temple became visible on the festival day. The state was unable to intervene because processions crowded the streets and charged the city with a religious atmosphere. Most of the parades passed the new shrine on their way to the Bara Talab (Big Lake), so it became popular within one single day. Thereafter state intervention became practically impossible. Also, the protest of Muslim neighbours, who were not willing to accept a temple directly opposite a mosque in a pre-dominantly Muslim living area, soon petered out, since it lacked support from the police officers in charge.

This outline allows for an initial analysis of the way Khatiks construct their identity in the modern urban environment of Bhopal. Narrating the events on the foundation day, Khatiks emphasize their fearless support of the caste goddess, in spite of anticipated opposition from the administration and from Muslims. It is a story that reinforces an image of Khatiks as brave fighters who know no fear, as well as estab-

---

Since the construction of the Kali Temple, the celebration has changed somewhat. The temple is now a vegetarian place (like most other temples). While in all other festivals animal sacrifices—if they are considered necessary—are substituted through the offering of pumpkins, Hariyali Aamavas still sees the sacrifice of real goats. Today, however, the meat is not consumed inside the temple; it is distributed among the participants who take it home and share it with their families.

[2] This festival takes place on the fourth day of the lunar month Bhadrapad (August/September). Prior to this day provisional shrines with clay images of Ganesh are set up everywhere in the city and special rituals are performed to the deity. On the day of Ganesh Chaturthi, the clay images are taken in processions to a water resource (in Bhopal to the Big Lake), where they are immersed (for further details see Gupte 1919: 54-8; Gnanambal 1967: 10-11).

[3] For further discussions of the question of illegal temple construction see Chapter 5.

lishing their caste as a community that is concerned about religious issues and committed to furthering the Hindu cause. This latter point is of particular importance to Khatiks, since as former 'untouchables' they still suffer from discrimination. By erecting a public shrine in a central and predominantly Muslim location—where most people would never have dared to build a temple—they proved their worth as Hindus.

The construction of the temple, however, created friction within the caste. They lead to internal power-struggles through which individual members of the caste tried to gain power over the temple and subsequently over the caste. This gave important impulses for the transformation of the Khatik caste from a locally organized caste-group to a trans-local heritage community (see also Rao 2002a).

THE KALI TEMPLE AND THE COMPETITION FOR POWER

In order to comprehend the friction that characterizes relationships within the Khatik caste today, a return to the narration of the origin of the Kali Temple is instructive. There are subtle but important differences in the various versions, which indicate the ways in which power over the temple and the caste is contested. The majority of the caste members familiar with the history of the Kali Temple emphasize that its construction has been a joint effort of the whole caste. It is said to have been the idea of a whole group of men and realized with the help of all caste members. Large numbers of Khatiks are said to have been present during the night of its instalment. In fact, there is hardly anyone who could not name some relative who is said to have attended the consecration, conducted by a Brahmin priest.

Bagware, the president of the Kali Temple Trust, gives a significantly different version of the events. He insists that the idea for the temple came up among the members of the 360 Gautriya Kshatriya Navayuvak Bundele Rajput Sangh, an organization which consisted of educated young Khatiks, founded and headed by Bagware himself. During their frequent quarrels with Muslim neighbours, the young men are said to have made a vow to Kali to erect a new temple in her honour in order to protect the women from harassment by Muslim boys and to prevent the building of a mosque on the same spot. Once the vow was taken, the young men could not back out, even when they realized that they lacked support in their caste group. Bagware relates that initially only his father was ready to support the idea. Others only joined later, once the project started to take off. According to Bagware, another surprise was in store for them on the night of the instalment. The project was

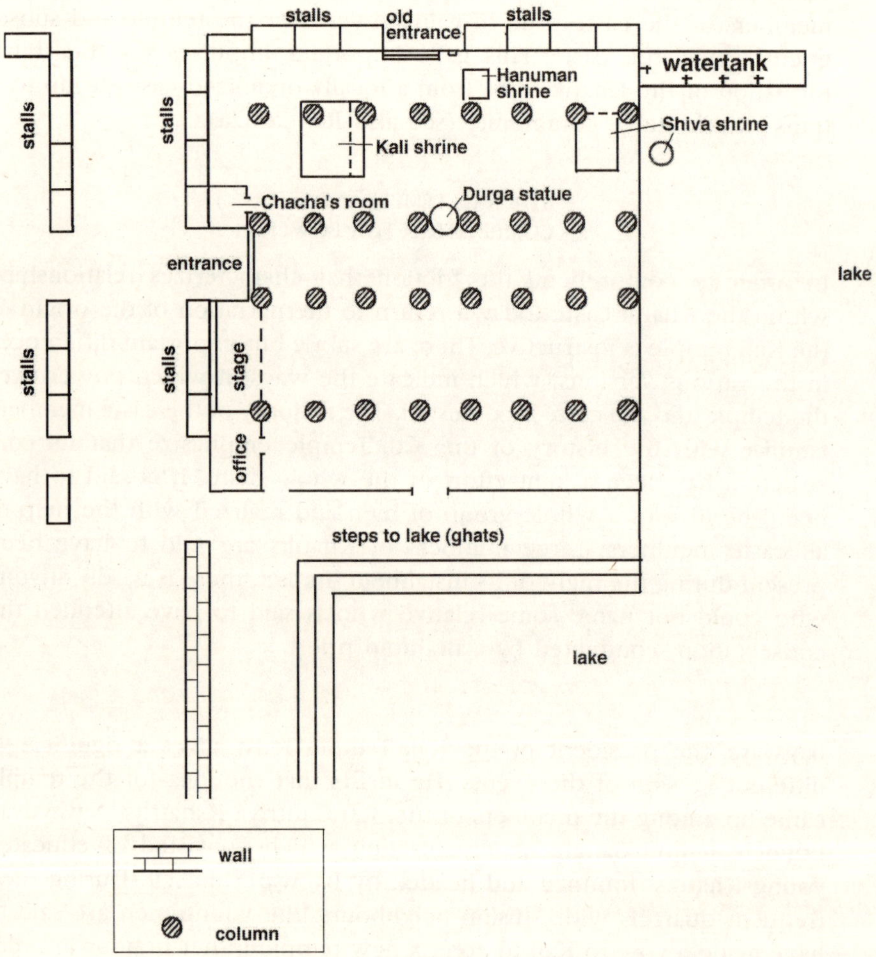
stalls
old entrance
stalls
watertank
Hanuman shrine
Shiva shrine
Kali shrine
stalls
stalls
Chacha's room
Durga statue
entrance
lake
stalls
stalls
stage
office
steps to lake (ghats)
lake
wall
column

Kali Temple

endangered one more time because the priest who had been called to perform the necessary rituals failed to turn up. Bagware claims that in his desperation he himself took up the ritual duty and consecrated the image through an improvized *puja*, during which he raked his memory for all his knowledge of Sanskrit from his schooldays.

These two versions of the temple's history indicate the basic split of the caste into two competing factions. One is made up of Bagware and his supporters from all over the state, while the other consists of a large and influential group of local Khatiks, who can rely on the support of the traditional caste authorities (*patel* and *barhkul*).[4] Bagware bases his claim to a leading position in the caste on his university education and his position as an officer of the State Bank of India. He believes that through his career he has risen beyond the 'ignorance' that he perceives to be characteristic of the majority of the caste members, at least in Bhopal. He feels that his strong dedication to his group of origin predestines him for the function of 'father' and 'patriarch' of his caste, whose duty it is to help his fellow caste members to 'grow up' and prosper, and to help modernize the structure of the caste group to make it fit for the future. In this context he sees the temple as a transformative agent that gives importance to the caste and imparts discipline and religious values to its members. By asserting his outstanding contribution during the days of construction, he underlines his claims to leadership.

Bagware's claim is contested by the active members of the caste-*panchayat*,[5] and the elders of the local caste group, who fight for the maintenance of their traditional authoritative status and the survival of the traditional caste structure. Their emphasis on the community aspect of the temple construction serves their interest in protecting the caste as a local solidarity group. This conflict between two factions is the result of a generation change in the caste that now pits traditional authorities against ambitious younger men, and increases the competition between all those who want to replace the elders. How did this generation change take place, and what role did the temple play in facilitating it?

The temple, once built, was of great importance to the whole caste. Only a short time after its erection, rules were passed that forced every Khatik marriage party in the state and every Khatik household in the city to contribute financially to its maintenance and extension. In order

[4] Both these titles—*patel* and *barhkul*—are inherited and mark the traditional caste-headmen in the Khatik caste in Bhopal. In other areas other titles are used, such as *mukhiya* or *mate*.

[5] According to the tradition in the Khatik caste, the *panchayat* encompasses all male members of the caste group in a specific locality.

to manage the income and organize the necessary work a meeting was called in 1974, with the aim of setting up an official temple committee:

> Since the matters of the temple had not been managed satisfactorily, some bright young men from the caste organized elections at the Guffa Temple, which were held under the presidency of the *barhkul*. The following office-holders were elected for the year 1974-75 for the sake of the development of the temple and the construction work. (Maljoniya 1984: 3, my translation)

What follows is a list of nine office-holders and eleven additional members,[6] among them three from the group of 'young educated men'. Against the traditional way of constructing history and understanding politics as always dominated by the elders, here the *young* men appeared as the idea-givers, and were subsequently also able to capture some of the positions in the prestigious temple committee. However, leaders of the next generation did not yet dominate the scene. The *barhkul* was called to preside over the meeting and was also elected president of the first official management board, in which older men formed the majority. Interestingly, these were the brothers, fathers or uncles of those who appear in Bagware's account as temple founders. This supports the assumption that the young men inspired the temple construction but depended on the elders to provide the necessary authority for the realization of the project.

But the power of the elders eroded further with the proposal that the caste should register a Temple Trust. For this work the illiterate elders had to rely on the 'bright young men', who had a university education and were able to understand legal procedures. Bagware fought at the forefront of this venture. Even his opponents admit that during the days of registration he was requested to help with the legal formalities. Bagware drew up a trust deed that addressed the challenge of carefully balancing the wish of the traditional authorities to retain their importance and the growing ambitions of the next generations, first and foremost his own interests. Initially the Kali Temple Trust[7] was registered with eleven members, among them the *patel* and the *barhkul* as well as three of the young men. Bagware himself became life-time president. He justified this departure from the tradition of leaving the highest position for one of the elders by emphasizing that he had been personally appointed to organize the communication between the caste and the state authorities.

Parallel with the foundation of a Temple Trust, Bagware also registered

[6] In Bagware's version of the same event *ten* office-bearers are mentioned, including his own name for the post of the chief advisor, which is omitted in Maljoniya's report (Bagware 1996: 2). It again demonstrates the intra-caste competition for status positions that is similarly supported by the claims made about the history of the temple.

[7] The official name of the trust is Kali Temple Religious Trust, Kali Ghat.

a state-wide caste society called '360 Gautriya Kshatriya Samaj'.[8] By this means he wished to give the caste a modern outlook and to create a forum through which the caste could survive in the changing urban environment. Again, Bagware reserved the highest position of life-time chief advisor for himself. He also created positions for the traditional authorities, the *patel* and the *barhkul* who became chief advisor and advisor respectively. Bagware hoped that this state-wide organization would in time replace the older form of local caste *panchayat*s, which had no official standing within the legal frame of independent India, and did not appear dynamic enough to adapt to the new requirements of modern society. By coupling the membership of this new organization with that of the Temple Trust, he established a close link between the temple and the caste, thereby increasing the attraction of the caste organization and demonstrating the centrality of the temple for the caste.

CHANGING CASTE STRUCTURES

The temple became the most important institution of the Khatik caste. With its growth in size, popularity and income, it is the wealthiest institution the caste has ever managed. But Bagware's grip over it is not quite as firm as the trust deed and the status of the society might suggest. There is substantial opposition to his domination, which is organized from the platform of the *panchayat*. While the claim of his opponents is to save old traditions, the authority structure of the *panchayat* has been re-worked and turned into a powerful weapon to curtail Bagware's influence, and formulate political alternatives to his projects by ambitious competitors from his age group. Yet these efforts seem to be in vain: with the representatives of the *panchayat* on the defensive, they appear to have very limited influence over the majority of caste members. This became clear during a fight which culminated in the excommunication of Bagware from the caste and his subsequent re-admission.

The fight started as a conflict over temple finances. Bagware, exercising what he saw as his duty as temple president, called upon all Khatiks to account for the financial grants they had received for organizational purposes as members of the various working committees. At the same time, he also started a state-wide call for membership to the trust and fixed a date for new elections. When the members of the informal working committees failed to submit receipts and did not become

[8] The name indicates that some Khatiks conceive of their caste as a Kshatriya case. A status from which they are said to have fallen due to their low level of sophistication and education.

members of the trust, he dissolved the committees and removed the office-holders from their posts by letter.

Bagware's opponents felt humiliated and unwilling to accept him as the final arbitrator of temple matters. They called a meeting of the local *panchayat* and had Bagware removed from the post of chief advisor and president, and subsequently excommunicated. Knowing that he could not be removed by people who were not even members of the organization he headed, Bagware countered the attack by publishing an official refutation. In order to regain authority he sent a second call for membership, giving a new deadline for registration which he even extended one time. When no-one from the Khatik caste in Bhopal registered, he drew a final boundary between the temple trust and the *panchayat*, withdrawing power from all those who had not joined his organizations.

His opponents reacted by looting the donation boxes and replacing the locks in order to bring the temple money under their control. Thereafter Bagware registered a criminal offence and personally replaced the locks. At this point communication between the two factions came to a standstill. Things only started to move again when Khatiks formerly from Bhopal but now living outside the city stepped in as arbitrators. Their arbitration worked in favour of Bagware, who is known and respected among Khatiks all over the state for his work on behalf of the Kali Temple and the caste community. While the promoters of the caste *panchayat* had based their claim for authority on their influence on the local Khatik community, Bagware had—with his commitment to a modern Khatik organization—made an effort to unify the caste in the state. To achieve this, Bagware relied on changes in caste relations in a modern urban environment.

A number of Khatiks—especially of those born after independence—took advantage of the new job opportunities offered in the state capital. Their entry into prestigious jobs in banks and government institutions was facilitated by reservations for members of Scheduled Castes. Khatiks also ventured into new fields of business, opening hotels, starting transport companies, etc. Many of the successful caste members moved out of the dense neighbourhood of Budhvara and built their houses in the new colonies outside the old city. Diversity of occupations and the scattered residential situation loosened the connection between caste members. The *panchayat* lost more and more importance as its authority over the caste members weakened. As a result, regular *panchayat* meetings were discontinued. Now Khatiks meet only occasionally when important issues are on the agenda.[9]

[9] When asked on which occasions the *panchayat* is called, Khatiks in Bhopal said that the most important work of the *panchayat* was the preparation of caste celebrations and arbitration between warring members.

This progressive loosening of local caste ties is paralleled by an increase in translocal caste relations. Caste relations were never limited to the locality. Khatiks in Bhopal were always connected with the hinterland through marriage alliances and business partnerships. However, traditionally these relations were limited in range. This changed in recent years because more and more Khatiks are now in a position to avail of quick transport. Today marriages are often arranged in distant places. An increase in migration and the frequent transfer of state employees has further widened the radius of caste relations. Some business partnerships now extend far beyond the surrounding countryside and link up industrial enterprises in a number of cities.[10] In short, the relationships of Khatiks steadily spread beyond the locality.

Bagware's answer to these developments was the registration of a caste society that recruited members from all over the state. Membership is, of course, voluntary and is not meant to intervene in people's personal lives but to create a network of families of the same origin and with overlapping interests. Through this venture, Bagware hoped to modernize the social institutions of the caste in such a way that they could be meaningful and therefore survive in an urban environment. His efforts have made him known throughout the state, where he is respected as activist in caste matters.

This is also the reason why the excommunication of Bagware by the local Khatik community had little effect on him. As a manager at the State Bank of India and an active member of various organizations, he is financially independent and also respected outside the caste. Due to his commitment to a state-wide caste organization, his relations reach far beyond the locality to Khatiks who did not accept the ban effected by the local *panchayat*. In fact, it seems that it actually worked against those who imposed it, for example when Bagware continued to be invited to marriage parties all over the state, while those who had excommunicated him were asked to eat separately if they objected to his joining the meal. Thus, when Khatiks from outside Bhopal demanded Bagware's re-admission, the *panchayat* had little option but to follow the request. Secretly, many were relieved that this outside interference provided them with an excuse to normalize relations, since they had realized that banning Bagware had actually cut them off from an important source of patronage.

It is apparent here that in a modern setting caste has little ability to effectively control people's conduct. No longer a tightly knit face-to-

[10] The growing tendency of castes to form supra-local solidarity groups is not unique to Bhopal. It can be shown to occur in many castes throughout India and traced back to colonial times (Pandey 1990; B. Cohen, 1968; Dirks 1989a, 1989b; Rudolph and Rudolph 1960, 1967).

face community, caste now turned into a rather loosely organized trans-local community of people of the same origin,[11] in which caste members support each other out of a feeling of belonging (Rao 2002b). Of course, this transformation is not complete, but it has started to give caste a new meaning.[12] In this situation, the temple has become of central importance. In the absence of an organization that represents all Khatiks, the temple functions as a symbol of integration, as a visible sign of Khatik solidarity and as a religious centre, hosting the caste goddess. Even before the construction of the new Kali Temple, Khatiks called a small Kali shrine in the middle of their residential area their own. But this shrine never created anything resembling the excitement the new temple generated.

The new temple was different because it worked on the imagination of the ambitious young men and because it stood at a place where it was visible to everyone. An atmosphere developed in which the temple became more than just a holy site. It stood for the caste itself, its power, its bravery, and its devotion. It became a meeting ground for Khatiks that replaced the lost neighbourhood and developed into the focal point of a 'modern' caste identity that reaches beyond the locality. Some of the developments in the history of the temple as well as the community involvement that occurs during important rituals will be able to prove this point.

THE KALI TEMPLE AND FORMS OF CASTE SOLIDARITY

While on the one hand the temple was a site for power struggles between rivals, it also served to unify the caste, especially in times of crisis and during festivals. Khatiks remember two occasions when they had to defend their temple against the city administration and the Muslims neighbours. The trouble with the administration started in

[11] In this context it is not possible to talk of a caste structure in which all castes are ranked (in accordance with their purity) in a clear hierarchy, as Dumont (1972) has described, claiming this to be a universal feature of Indian society. Dumont has been variously criticised for his a-historical view of India that fully disregards context (see for example Chatterjee 1989; Fuller 1997; Gupta 1991; Mencher 1991; Quigley 1993; Searle-Chatterjee and Sharma 1994). But even a more localized approach would not bring any ranking to light, since people measure their relationships not by caste, but by a number of other criteria (wealth, employment, religious affiliation; see Holmstroem 1972). There are also no ritual activities in the city that involve castes in joint celebrations, ranking them while simultaneously strengthening solidarity between them, such as are reported for many villages (see Brubaker 1979).

[12] For the description of similar developments in other castes see: Anderson 1992; Freitag 1989; Lynch 1969; Rudolph and Rudolph 1960; Fuller 1997; Shah and Desai 1988.

1986, when Bagware received a note from the Municipal Corporation, saying that the temple hall, which had been added to the initial shrine, was illegal and would be torn down.

While Bagware admitted to me that they had no official permit when starting the construction of the hall in 1985, he still viewed the activity as legal because he had submitted the plans to the administration beforehand. Bagware thus wrote a reply to the official notice, reminding the officers that the plans had been submitted and pointing out the importance of the temple to the city of Bhopal. He also threatened to mobilize the public if no understanding could be reached, which he did simultaneously by publishing a press note denouncing the planned act of 'blasphemy'. Bagware further ensured political patronage for the cause by informing the local Member of Parliament, a member of the Hindu nationalist party BJP, who could be expected to support a religious demand. Subsequently a meeting was arranged between the Khatiks and the Chief Minister, who, after listening to the grievances of the community had the notice cancelled, and the temple—which despite the fact that a trust had been registered, had constituted the illegal possession of public land—legalized.

This incident united the two factions of the Khatik caste who joined hands in their fight during a time when they were actually entangled in major differences. Bagware, who as temple president claims the right to supervise all activities undertaken in the temple, was enraged when one of the informal working committees started with the construction of the hall in the dark of night without informing anyone. Remembering this incident, Bagware wrote:

> In this difficult situation when the Trust made intense efforts to ensure that the ground would be allotted to the temple, some trouble-makers illegally began work right then, on 7th July 1985, and in the name of the construction committee, on a construction that deviated from the plans. (Bagware 1996: 3, my translation)

Although Bagware opposed the construction activity initiated by his competitors, he took the lead when defending it before the city administration, thereby risking that the credit for extending the building would go not to him but to his opponents. When called to meet the Chief Minister, the Khatik men stood together, reaching his residence in a joint protest march of about 200 to 300 people in order to add force to their demands. This angered the Chief Minister who wanted to maintain a low key. A second meeting had to be arranged during which only a few leading men were asked to come. A small congregation of seven important men (among them Bagware) went, overcoming for the time being their personal antagonisms for the sake of their religious site.

Shortly after the temple had been legalized, the Muslim neighbours made their presence felt. They were afraid that the temple would continue to grow now that the city administration had given up its opposition. During the night of 24 January 1988 they planted a green flag on the narrow land strip between the temple and the lake. Seeing that the flag was fixed in concrete, the Khatiks reported the incident to the police, pointing out that the place where the flag was situated belonged to the temple. Access to the lake was necessary for the performance of numerous rituals. The controversy simmered for two months and found a solution only when the state authorities called a meeting on 19 March 1988, during which the antagonistic parties agreed that the flag would be removed and no further Muslim construction undertaken on the disputed site. As a concession, the Khatiks had to settle for the limitation of the temple space as well as to accept that the steps leading to the lake would not be part of the temple and should remain accessible to the general public.

Just like the conflict with the administration, this incident created solidarity among the antagonistic factions of the Khatik community as well as between the low caste Khatiks and the Brahmin Hindu leaders of the city. In this case, it was built on a constantly simmering feeling of antagonism between Muslims and Hindus, here especially between Khatiks and Kasais (Muslim butchers), who traditionally shared the same occupation and locality. More than just defending a caste institution, the Khatiks here rushed to protect their version of Hinduism.

Both incidents drew the caste members closer together, but not on the bases of their everyday life or an agreement on caste issues. Khatiks were mobilized in defence of an institution that was central to contemporary caste politics and formed the religious core of their community. It was also an action in defence of the goddess herself. After all, the temple had been built with the explicit purpose of providing a new home for Kali. The (young) men had given a vow to provide their goddess with a new earthly abode, and Khatiks claim that it is due to her divine help that they succeeded. Her presence in the centre of the community is a blessing for all Khatiks, a reminder of their common origin, and a sign of the caste's joint contribution to the welfare of the urban (Hindu) community.

The temple, in its function as divine core and religious centre, is particularly visible during the celebration of religious festivals. It is the ritual observance during festivals that provides occasions for the celebration of Khatik solidarity. In times when caste is fast disintegrating as an institution that regulates people's everyday life, Khatiks still place major importance on the joint observance of religious festivals and marriage celebrations. For Khatiks, especially in Bhopal, all these moments of heightened excitement have become associated with the Kali Temple. The temple is a place where they can meet, worship their goddess, and have their children married.[13]

[13] Even among those who have their children married individually, there are

The two periods of Navratri[14] are especially highly regarded among the religious festivals, for they centre on the different aspects of Devi, among them Kali, who during this time is worshipped by people of all backgrounds. In comparison to the other goddess temples in Bhopal, the Kali Temple is one of the largest and most popular places. Daily, people crowd the temple, lining up to touch the divine image inside the sanctuary, which is opened to the public only during the days of Navratri. They anoint, decorate and bath the goddess and offer sacrificial gifts and prayers. Khatiks feel a special obligation to participate in the Navratri celebrations, since it is *their goddess* who is celebrated and *their temple* that is the centre of attraction. Khatiks also use the festive days for lengthy meetings with their caste fellows, from the city and outside relatives. Day and night, Khatiks can be seen sitting in front of the temple enjoying each other's company and refreshing their memory of caste affairs.

The celebration reaches its peak on the ninth day. In the evening, the temple is teeming with worshippers, that it becomes difficult to even put a foot on the ground. Devotees bring donations, attend the rituals, and offer private prayers. The stream of visitors only starts to thin out

---

many who rent the hall of the Kali Temple for the celebrations. During the marriage season, hardly a month goes by without the celebration of at least two Khatik marriages in the Kali Temple.

[14] Navratri is celebrated twice a year: once during the first nine days of the lunar month Ashvin (September/October), the second time exactly half a year later during the first nine days of the lunar month Chaitra (March/April). The celebration in autumn is larger and more popular, as the goddess is not only worshipped in her temples, but also in provisional shrines that are erected all over the city, showing the goddess in her different (nine) forms. In the morning people attend the temple, while they roam the city in the evening to offer their prayers at various shrines. On the tenth day (Dashara) the clay statues are taken in large processions to a water resource, where they are immersed. The spring festival of Navratri does not see the erection of additional shrines (even though some rich business people in Bhopal have now started this 'tradition' in a few central places in the city).

The celebrations in the temple during the two periods of Navratri do not demonstrate any differences. People stream to the temple on nine consecutive mornings to wash and anoint the goddess, because during these days the sanctuary is opened for the public to enter and actually touch the goddess (in the more orthodox Durga Temple people are not allowed inside the sanctuary, instead an additional statue of Durga is installed. This may well be the reason why attendance at the Kali Temple is higher during the festivals, because there are no restrictions here). People also come in the evening—when entry to the sanctuary is closed—in large numbers to offer their prayers. The period of celebration is ended by a fire sacrifice (*havan*) in the night after the ninth day and the distribution of special *prasad* to virgins (*kanya bhoj*) during the morning of the tenth day (for further details refer to Gnanambal 1967: 13-15; Gupte 1919: 181-8; Östoer 1980; Thomas 1984: 4-7).

towards midnight. After that, only Khatiks and a few regular temple servants remain to perform the fire sacrifice (*havan*), which forms the climax of the festival and ends the cycle of the nine day celebration. Every year, a discussion ensues whether interested non-Khatiks should or should not be allowed to join the group of sacrificers. Usually no restrictions are imposed.[15] Thus, in the end Khatiks from all factions and all age groups (young men predominating) sit together with a few other devotees to sacrifice together.

Holi[16] and Rangpanchmi[17] provide other occasions for displaying vigorous caste solidarity. On these days groups of Khatiks swarm out over the city visiting each others' houses. It is of special importance to visit those families who have lost a member during the previous year through death. The festivities have come to mark the official end of their period of mourning, when they are readmitted to full ritual status. Nowadays any such celebration will also include the temple. It has become the major meeting ground and starting point for groups touring the city.

A third major festival, and the one that most explicitly includes Khatiks from all over the state, is the yearly celebration of a mass wedding ceremony. Since 1991,[18] this new tradition has become identified with the Kali Temple in Bhopal. Each year, on the occasion of Akshay Tritiya[19] (April/May), Khatiks from all over Madhya Pradesh are called to sign up their children for the mass marriage service at the Kali Temple in Bhopal. This practice began—also among other castes—to reduce marriage costs and to end the practice of dowry. Above all villagers take advantage of it and travel to Bhopal accompanied by their relatives to have their sons and daughters married for a nominal fee.

[15] The only restriction enforced in all temples is that women are not allowed to perform. Bagware though has reformed this rule for the Kali Temple and allowed couples as participants for the first time in 1997.

[16] Holi, often referred to as the festival of colours, is celebrated on the day of the full moon day in the month Phalgun (February-March). This day is marked by people throwing coloured powder and water at each other and embracing each other. Humans meet as equals, regardless of their status in normal life. Strangers are treated like friends and the relationships to friends and relatives are renewed (for more details Gnanambal 1967: 20-1; Gupte 1919: 88-93; Thomas 1984: 7).

[17] A festival similar to Holi celebrated five days after Holi, on the fifth day of the dark half of the month of Phalgun. In Bhopal this day is marked by a procession in which all participants (only men)—regardless of their status in normal life—mix freely, throwing colours at each other.

[18] Some sources give 1990 as the initial year.

[19] Traditionally this day—the third day in the month of Vaisakha (April/May)—marked the beginning of the agricultural season, which was celebrated in many parts of north India (Gnanambal 1967: 7-8; see also Gupte 1919: 5). In Bhopal mass marriages are all held on this auspicious day.

The temple is large enough to accommodate them all, and thus for three days every year it turns into a shelter for hundreds of Khatiks, who witness the marriage of 50 to 100 boys and girls from their caste. There are plans to extend the celebration by organizing a large get-together of families with marriageable children approximately half a year before the mass marriage, in order to facilitate match-making.

Meeting and celebrating together in the temple reinforces the idea that the caste provides for a vivid community. Festivals are occasions to experience the solidarity of Khatiks from different social backgrounds, factions and localities. Caste solidarity here becomes real. It is experienced in the moment of the heightened enthusiasm generated by the celebration as well as later by their memory. It is renewed and strengthened through the refreshment and the visualization of trans-local relationships, which become identified with the temple as its physical centre.

To describe the communication that exists during the special times of rituals, festivals, pilgrimages as well as oppositional movements, Turner has developed the concept of communitas, which describes the 'direct, immediate, and total confrontation of human identities' (Turner 1969: 131). He contrasts it with structure which he sees prevailing in everyday life, and which separates people through status, positions, or occupations. Sandria Freitag has applied Turner's concept to the religious sphere of colonial India and emphasizes the importance of joint celebrations for the formation of a translocal Hindu community in British India. She argues that celebrations like the Ramlila,[20] in which competing castes, neighbourhoods and city quarters united into one single procession and a joint celebration,' had a lasting effect on the minds of people for whom the Hindu community became visible, palpable by experience, as well as identified with a particular territory (Freitag 1989).

Yet the explanatory power of the notion of communitas appears to be limited in the context of Khatik religiosity.[21] While I do not question that the enthusiasm generated during the celebrations provides the participants with an experience of community, their identities do not

[20] The Ramlila is celebrated all over north India during the Dashara holiday, usually starting in late September (the lunar of month Ashvin) and lasting for several days or even weeks. On this occasion the Ramayana is enacted in plays and processions (Freitag 1991; Hess 1983; Hein 1972, 1975; A. Kapur 1984, 1991; Lutgendorf 1991, 1992, 1994; Niehus 1905).

[21] There are others who question the usefulness of Turner's concept of communitas, especially in the context of pilgrimage. Sax, for example, points to the fact that central to the experience of pilgrimage is not the transformation of human relations, but interaction with places with particular qualities and persons with special powers (Sax 1991: 12).

merge, neither in the form of an unstructured 'existential communitas', as the spontaneous experience of direct human communion, nor in the form of a 'normative' or 'ideological communitas', as a structured social system that has at its base the ideology of human equality. The data from the Kali Temple in Bhopal suggest, rather, that festivals not only provide a meeting ground of equals, but are also symbolically loaded forums for the renegotiation of caste relationships, in which claims to particular positions are made, which also have implications for the status of a person after the celebration. Contrary to Turner's theory, festivals here seem particularly prone to becoming the scene of fights and renewals of friction, since the importance a person evinces during celebrations grants particular effectiveness to claims that are made in front of a large audience and in a religious atmosphere that lends them authority.

The question of how religious festivals establish and renew the authority of individual people will be discussed at length in Chapter 4. Here I shall confine myself to one example: how the fight between the two factions of the local Khatik caste was heightened and made visible during one of the Navratri celebrations.

As mentioned above, the period of Navratri culminates in the celebration of the *havan*, attended mostly by Khatiks. Traditionally, males offer the sacrifice while women and children watch. A few weeks before each celebration a discussion takes place concerning who among the Khatiks will be granted the honour of occupying the position of main sacrificer. As temple president, Bagware claims this prestigious position for himself, a claim other Khatiks can hardly oppose with success. Even during the ritual in October 1996, when Bagware was officially excommunicated, he acted as main sacrificer. The only way for his opponents to express their dissent was to avoid participation altogether. Fearing that an open fight might break out during the celebration, the number of visitors was substantially reduced that year. Those who attended spent most of their time gossiping about the tension prevailing in the caste.

Half a year later during the next Navratri, Bagware had been re-admitted to the caste, yet only reluctantly and due to pressures from outside the local group. Since memories of hurt feelings were still fresh and the re-established relationships still fragile, Bagware avoided participating in the *havan*. Instead he called upon his caste fellow Amarchand to take the lead in the ritual. Amarchand is a man of little education and with no political ambitions, whose aim is recognition as a great *bhakta* of the goddess. Yet, although Bagware abstained from active participation, many worshippers still feared a controversy and they came in even smaller numbers—which of course was also partly due to the fact that the April celebration is considered less important.

Although Bagware did not take part in the actual sacrifice, he came to the temple during the night, just like Maljoniya, one of his opponents. Both watched the ritual from a distance, sitting far enough apart to avoid contact, a fact that did not go unnoticed. The atmosphere was very tense, which found direct expression when some of the youngsters sitting at the *havan* aimed some sacrificial objects at Amarchand, instead of throwing them into the fire. Enraged, Amarchand broke his vow of silence, which he observes during every Navratri period, in order to vent his anger and loudly denounce this rude behaviour. This incident was considered to be extremely inauspicious by all those present, and was told and retold many times, even after the festival.

This example shows that not every celebration passes off to the satisfaction of all, culminating in a feeling of common brotherhood. Instead the fights taking place in the local community continue during the preparation and the actual celebration of a festival. In their symbolic transformation within a religious context they might even gain momentum. A case in point is the *havan* of May 1997, when instead of being shown special reverence, the goddess was the butt of insults from youngsters.

Even if a celebration passes off without any major disruption, the positioning of people in the sacrificial space, the presence or absence of individuals and the interaction between those present, all indicate the current power situation in the caste. They are noticed by all those present, discussed and measured in their symbolic value and their effectiveness in influencing relationships. As people establish connections between the things that happened during the festivals and those that occur in everyday life, they transgress the boundaries and transport the effectiveness an action has in one domain into the other, so that the dichotomy between structure as characteristic of everyday life and communitas as typical of the liminal period of celebrations has to be called into question.

In this context I would like to note the value of the remark Sallnow made after trying to apply the concept of communitas to his data on Christian pilgrimages in the Peruvian Andes. His efforts failed, whereupon he stated that it is not communitas but rather egalitarianism that prevails:

> Egalitarianism, however, is not necessarily the same as communitas. Equality–no less a cultural invention than its converse–may manifest itself through competition, that is the attempt to generate differentials between opponents regarded as evenly matched, or through reciprocal exchange, either in a sacred or a secular context, as well as through the conjunction implied by communitas. (Sallnow 1981: 176-7)

This view acknowledges that communication between participants in a pilgrimage contains expressions of both unity and competition.

Even in Bhopal, the declaration of difference and conflict were coupled throughout with a wish for unity, even harmony. This is apparent in the joint presence of Bagware and Maljoniya during the 1997 *havan*, which could be seen as an effort to normalize relations and re-establish communication. Even Bagware's withdrawal from the position of main sacrificer can be interpreted as an effort to keep tensions low, and avoid provocation of the other side now that there was hope for a re-integration of his person. How important caste unity is for Khatiks, both in secular times and during religious celebrations, became overtly clear during the preparation of the 1997 mass-marriage that followed shortly after the disastrous *havan*. During this period every effort was made, by people in and outside of Bhopal, to curtail plans for the organization of two parallel mass-marriages, organized separately by the respective leaders of the two factions. The re-admission of Bagware earlier in the year was part of this effort to prevent the final break-up of the caste and to allow it to continue as a single unity with competing factions.

Summing up, we can say that the temple serves as a centre for the organization and representation of the Khatik caste. It creates a place of communication between the dispersed members of a community, now including Khatiks from all over the state, as well as presenting a picture of caste unity and strength to the outside world. But the moment the caste finds a new form of existence and expression through the temple, its boundaries also become blurred. During their fight against the Muslims and the administration, Khatiks were supported by a large number of worshippers of diverse origins. Devotees of the goddess share the everyday life in the temple with Khatiks and join in their celebrations. In the presence of the goddess, all caste differences are transcended. And it was not surprising for me that I could listen to Khatiks dream about an extension of the mass marriage programme to include other castes. Thus, paradoxically, the assertion of Khatik identity takes place within a larger framework of Hindu solidarity in which caste identity is thought to be secondary. It becomes visible and palpable through joint efforts in temple building, temple management and ritual communion.

KHATIKS AS HINDUS

Khatiks do not seem to have any doubts that they belong to the Hindu community. This is not self-evident since there is a large number of former 'untouchables' in India who resist being counted as Hindus, arguing that the (political) assertion of a Hindu community is an effort to perpetuate high caste hegemony.[22] The Khatiks in Bhopal have gone

[22] For an extensive discussion of the relationship between Hinduism and the

in the opposite direction. Instead of opposing high caste dominance, they trace their origins to high caste status.

Bagware is the head of this interpretative venture. By making efforts to (re-)unite the caste under the label of a society called the 360 Gautriya Kshatriya Samaj, he suggests a Kshatriya origin for Khatiks.[23] He sees it as his mission to lead the caste 'back to lost glory', not only by re-uniting it, but also by reforming caste practices along orthodox ideals of religious and social behaviour. A war was opened on 'bad habits' like drinking, gambling and meat eating. Admonitions for modern education are heard and Brahmanical forms of religiosity supported. This is a classic example of towards Sanskritization or Brahmanization, which Srinivas (1955/56, 1962) describes as a common strategy all over India among castes wishing to rise in the local hierarchy.

So far, this middle class venture to convince Khatiks of their Kshatriya origin and to divest them of 'bad habits' has been only partly successful, although there are more and more Khatiks who have adopted this new ideology, which is also visible through the frequent inclusion of the title, Singh, in the names of the young. Outside their own group I could not find anyone who identified Khatiks as Kshatriyas. This, however, is no hindrance for their integration into the cultural project of a unified Hinduism, which takes place—at least in this case—independently of the question of caste origin. Today a large number of Khatiks can be found who support or have joined organizations that stand for an aggressive Hinduism and the struggle for the realization of a Hindu nation. Khatiks have accepted many of those forms of worship that today constitute the standard repertoire of Hindu religion (e.g. the centrality of temple worship, the popularity of a canon of sanskritized gods and goddesses, the general appeal of certain national pilgrimage sites). Both these tendencies, brahmanization as well as the unification of Hinduism, are supported by the temple.

'untouchable' castes, see Mendelson and Vicziany 1998, see also Ayrookuzhiel 1995; Herrenschmidt 1989; Rudolph and Rudolph 1967: 132-54; or the personal account of a Dalit who in his book resists any inclusion in the Hindu fold (Ilaiah 1996).

It is interesting to note that Ambedkar converted from Hinduism to Buddhism because he saw no chance for the equality of 'untouchables' within the framework of Hinduism, of which he believed the suppression of lower castes to be an intrinsic property (see Mendelsohn and Vicziany 1998: 114-17).

It has frequently been noted that religious traditions among 'untouchables' are quite distinct from those among high castes (B. Cohen 1975). Khatiks confirmed this when they explained to me that they (as 'untouchables') used to be unable to perform the 'correct' rituals, which they learned only after the construction of the new Kali Temple.

[23] Bagware also used the terms Thakur and Rajput as interchangeable.

The construction of a temple is in itself a visible sign of Khatik membership in the Hindu fold, which is claimed to transcend boundaries of caste, region and group affiliation. Considering the fact that until the middle of this century 'untouchables' were not even allowed to enter temples[24] in most parts of India, it comes almost as a revolution that one of the most popular goddess temples in the city has been built and is administered by a Scheduled Caste.[25] In the Kali Temple, Khatiks worship side by side with caste Hindus, who do not object if they are attended to by voluntary temple servants from a Scheduled Caste. In this sense, the Kali Temple realizes a new unified Hinduism in which caste barriers no longer present an obstacle to common ritual observance, and in which everyone has the same chance of entry into a number of ritual roles. Caste here has to a great extent lost its meaning as a discriminating feature, and given way to the integration of a wider community that includes all devotees of the goddess.[26]

Within this community Khatiks can claim the position of brave fighters for the Hindu cause. This image has been strengthened by the fact that Khatiks were the first who had the courage to build a temple in the old town of Bhopal, an area generally identified with Muslim culture. The construction of the temple has established this caste as the spearhead of an aggressive Hinduism.

What emerges is the paradox that the temple reasserts caste at the same time that it starts integrating it into a greater solidarity of Hindus. In this context, caste does not primarily stand as a discriminatory institution of India's social life, but as a descent group that marks people who are otherwise part of a larger community. But the integration of the Hindu community is not complete. The feeling of Hindu unity can at any time give way to internal struggles between castes, classes and gender. The strategists of the Hindu nationalist movement are well aware of this fact, and it is for this reason that they support events and projects that will refresh the memory of Hindu unity and serve as a medium for the crystallization of Hindu identity. The incidents surrounding the construction of the Durga Temple in Bhopal are a case in point.

[24] See on this matter for example Bailey 1996, Fuller 1984a: 150, 154.

[25] Bagware exploits this new situation by claiming a right to the membership of all major religious institutions in the city in the name of reservations for Scheduled Castes.

[26] I do not wish to claim that the equality of all devotees of different castes is perfectly realised in the Kali Temple. There are situations in which a clear distinction between Brahmins and non-Brahmins is made. But the democratic setting in the temple has blurred the majority of these distinctions and in most contexts made them secondary (see also Chapter 3).

THE ASSERTION OF HINDU IDENTITY AT PIR GATE

Situated at Pir Gate, one of the major crossings in old Bhopal, is a temple dedicated to 'Our Lady of the Curfew' (*Darbar Curfew Mata Ka*). It is one of the most popular and best known temples of the city. This is not only due to its central location and its beauty, but also a result of the controversy that surrounded its construction in the middle of a territory so far identified with Muslim culture. From the beginning, the construction of a Durga Temple at Pir Gate was motivated both by devotion to the goddess and the wish to mark the presence of Hindus as a powerful community in the heart of the city. The temple changed the atmosphere in the locality, transforming a former Muslim locality into a major politico-religious site, where ritual activities, Hindu nationalist propaganda and everyday politics overlap and blend. The history of the temple acted on the images of the Hindu and Muslim communities. It appeared to confirm a narrative order that establishes them as potentially antagonistic groups, and effected the ordering of space according to this perception. An interpretation of the history of the Durga Temple thus has to take into account the political and the religious dimensions of the activity and its relation to a discourse of communalism.

In 1972 the city administration had selected Pir Gate as the site of a new crossing that would absorb the ever increasing traffic in the area and act as a junction of the new arterial roads leading through the city. As a result, many houses in this old Muslim neighbourhood had to be pulled down. However, the effects of the new spacious crossing were destroyed when ten years later Hindus began illegally to construct a Durga Temple right in the middle of Pir Gate crossing. The city administration was concerned that the new religious building would obstruct the traffic, and feared that the temple in an area with a large Muslim population would increased Hindu-Muslim tension in the locality. This fear was accentuated by the fact that the temple occupied a spot at the centre of the city's three largest and most important mosques. As such it formed an intrusion into a territory marked as the symbolic and religious heart of 'Muslim Bhopal'. Opposition from the Muslim quarters also mentioned that it was not for the sake of a Hindu place of worship that members of their community had given up their houses in the locality, but rather as a contribution to the improvement of the traffic situation.

In spite of the protests, Hindus insisted that their community needed a place of worship and a representation of their community in old Bhopal, near the main bazaar where many of them managed successful businesses. They were determined to change the symbolic weight and the social atmosphere of the location. Pir Gate was intended to become the home of Hindus. One of the activities formulated:

> We were a group of ten to twelve men who spent their evenings together in Chowk[27] or at the platform on Pir Gate. We always had difficulties with the Muslims. The neighbourhood was in their hands.They always teased us [...] The Muslims in this area are notorious. [...] They are the reason why we decided to build a temple that would strengthen and unite the Hindus.

Many others supported this view and felt that the area was not save for Hindus. A temple was to remedy this situation. Plans for the construction of a goddess temple took shape in the year 1981, when the festival committee in charge of constructing a provisional Durga shrine for the nine days of the Navratri festival in autumn installed a Durga statue of marble, rather than the normal mud image, on the concrete platform in the middle of the street. It was clear that they had no intention of removing the shrine after the nine days, as was the custom, but planned to retain the Durga image as a foundation for a larger temple. Over the following nine days the committee went ahead with the construction, so that by the end of the festival a permanent Durga Temple stood right in the middle of Pir Gate crossing.

The committee members knew that their project would not be acceptable either to Muslims in the locality or to the city administration. This is why they had deliberately chosen the days of the festival for the construction, because they knew that the police could not intervene during this period without endangering the peace of the city. The year of its construction was also carefully chosen. Since in 1981 both the Collector and the Superintendent of Police were newly posted in Bhopal, the committee members expected that the administration would be weak and thus refrain from intervention. To further secure their position, the builders had informed all Durga Committees in the city—which were in operation during the time of Navratri—about the plans for a Devi Temple at Pir Gate and asked them to plant saffron flags near the shrine to show their support, and to mark the territory as a Hindu area. In turn, the Muslims who felt threatened by this 'invasion' of their territory lodged a complaint with the city authorities, who promised to intervene as soon as the festival was over. And indeed, the night after the tenth day marked the beginning of open and sometimes virulent antagonism.

When the Durga statue was not destroyed after the festival, the Collector intervened at night and had the statue removed and the temple torn down. An ordinance was passed restricting the right to assemble at Pir Gate crossing. Ignoring this directive, a large Hindu

[27] This is the name of the place right at the centre of the walled city, where the Jami Masjid is situated. The place is within walking distance from Pir Gate (ten minutes by foot).

crowd gathered at Pir Gate the next day to show their protest through open prayers and the singing of *bhajans* at an improvized goddess shrine, which was reinstalled at the same place where the temple had stood. Again the police intervened and had the crossing cleared. Once more their efforts were frustrated when the policemen, now trapped in the middle of the crossing, were attacked by Hindus who had fled into the adjoining houses and lanes. Locked in this strategically disadvantageous position, the policemen feared for their lives and there appeared to be no other solution than to clear the lanes with force and impose a curfew. One of the officers still remembers the operation vividly:

> At 7:45 p.m., we got the order to clear the crossing. We assembled 250 men. The Collector took one street, I took another. It was night and the operation was difficult. With a jeep [...] we entered the lane [...]. The [police] men followed us in a jail van. This way they felt secure. We cleared one barricade after the other and secured the area and returned to Pir Gate. It was like war. It was difficult to keep the men under control. A boy, for example, threw a stone. Some men then pulled him out from the house and started beating him. In the end we had to save the boy. Then there was Mishra, my right-hand man, he wanted to be extra brave and got hit on the head by a stone. After that the police went wild. They were afraid [...] Besides the fear the policemen are all religious so you have to convince them that the operation is necessary. But fortunately in Bhopal the troops are mostly secular [...] That time I had an excellent gunman, Amar Singh. After I got out of the jeep someone threw a rock, and he jumped and pushed me aside. The rock then landed on his foot and he had to be rushed to hospital. That was a dangerous situation, not that I would have got killed, but... By 9:40-10:00 p.m. we had cleared the lane.

As soon as the crossing was cleared, negotiations began between the Durga Temple Committee, the Muslim leaders, representatives of the administration and the police, and several leading politicians. The officers suggested that a place somewhere else in old Bhopal be assigned for the construction of the temple, but the Hindus insisted on Pir Gate. After long and heated discussions, the parties agreed that the temple should remain on the crossing, although not in the middle of the street but to one side.

A space equivalent to four shops (10 times 12 feet) was allotted for the Durga Temple. As compensation for the destruction of the original temple, the Municipal Corporation agreed to prepare the foundations for the new building. They also consented that the statue should not immediately be taken to the new spot. Instead it was to be re-installed in its original place at the middle of the crossing, from whence the committee members would transfer it to the new ground. In return, the Durga Temple Committee agreed to restrain from any further agitation and to help restore an atmosphere of peace and good will in the city (Agreement signed on 11 October 1981).

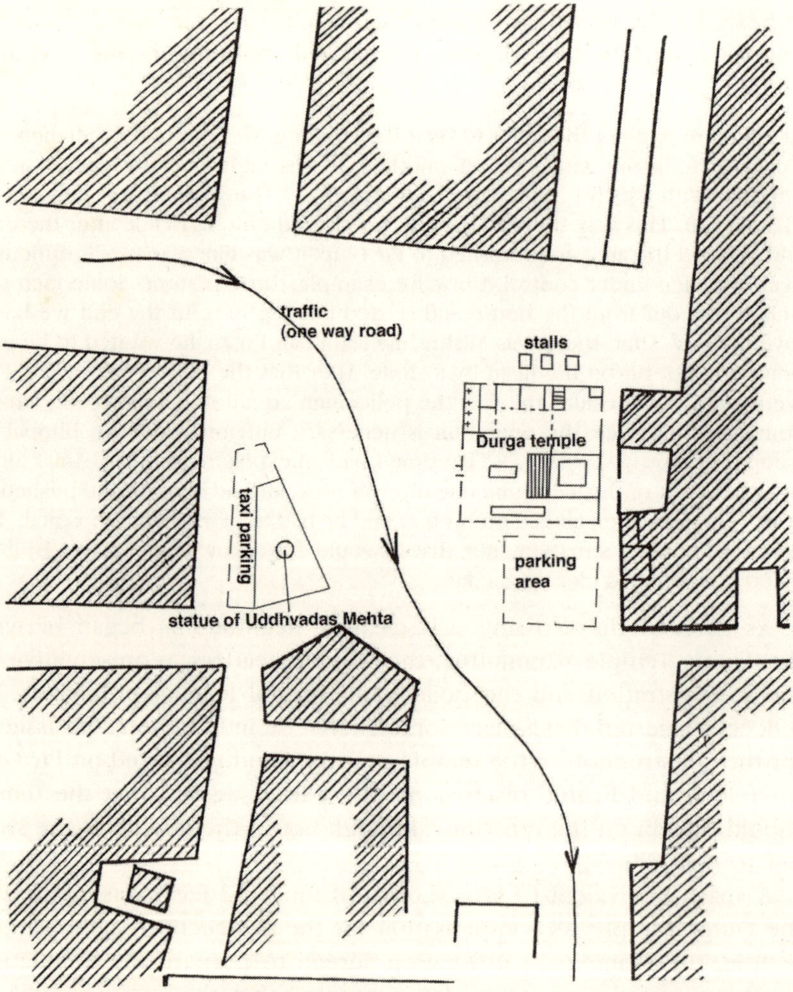

Pir Gate Crossing

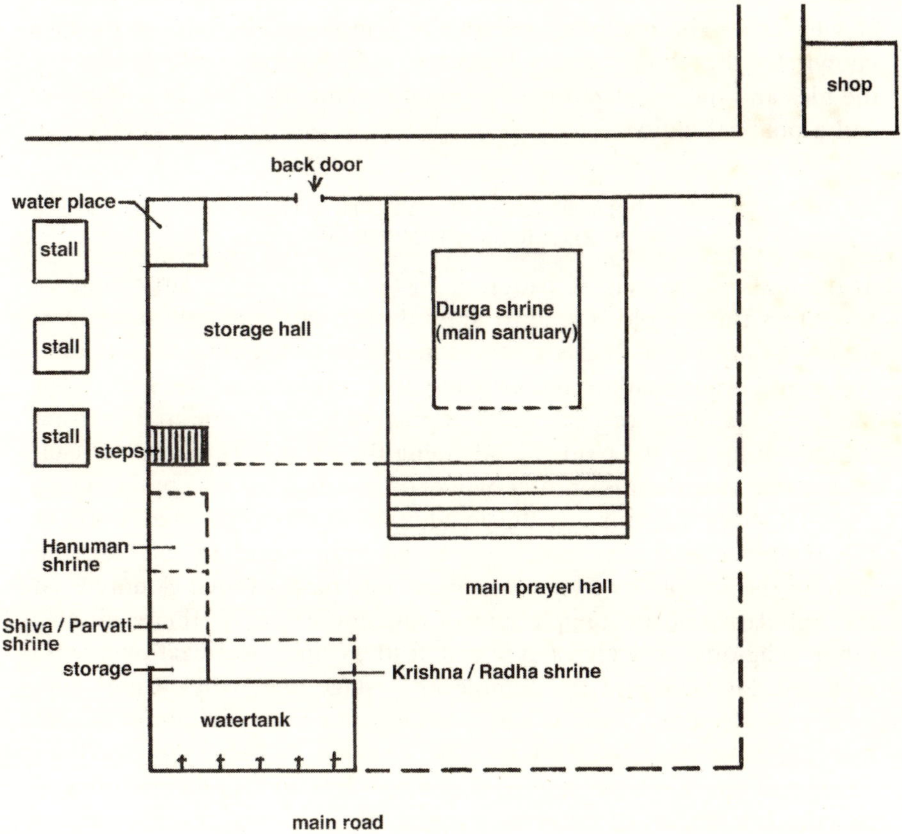

Durga Temple

On 15 October 1981, the temple was officially inaugurated and it stands as a sign of the benevolence of the 'Lady of Curfew', and as a symbol of the strength of a Hindu community, representing a 'victory' against the secular administration and the Muslim neighbours. Its impact is so powerful that no further objections were ever raised, even when the temple started to outgrow the officially allotted space of 11 times 12 feet. It has become one of the most popular temples in the city and has changed the religious and political landscape of old Bhopal. Now Pir Gate is a popular place for informal politics and an important centre for the organization of large religious functions and political rallies, especially those with Hindu nationalist overtones. The history as well as its contemporary use of the Temple at Pir Gate—now also known by the Hindu names Somvara or Bhavani Chowk—promotes the idea and the organization of a Hindu community, both as a religious and a political entity.

PIR GATE AND THE FORMATION OF RELIGIOUS COMMUNITIES

At the basis of the transformation of Pir Gate today is the large number of visitors the temple is able to draw during daily opening hours and on festive occasions. It has given prominence to the religious building and symbolically marked the crossing as a Hindu area. The success of the temple is not pure chance. Its popularity is partly due to its central location at an arterial road and adjoining the main bazaar, lending itself to a quick visit before or after work, on the way to an appointment, during a shopping tour etc. But in addition to this come the efforts of the Temple committee, which works all year round to increase the fame of the temple by frequently organizing mass events. Counting on the popularity of the temple and in turn increasing it, there are also other religious as well as political leaders and organizations, who welcome Pir Gate and the Temple as a 'stage' that will ensure them maximum attention. There is hardly a religious procession in old Bhopal that does not pass by Pir Gate. The crossing is frequently used for devotional music events (*jagaran*), sermons by famous religious leaders, and the celebration of religious festivals. Most of these events address Hindus, who often come in great number to attend the programs, worship their goddess and celebrate the festivals. In turn, Muslim religious celebrations in the location are much fewer in number. There are parades during big Muslim festivals like Muharram which cross Pir Gate and for a moment return to the Muslims a territory that used to be considered theirs.

At the same time that Pir Gate has turned into a dominant place for the display of Hindu devotion, it has also become a popular place for political negotiations and events. The place is frequented by political leaders who appear at the religious festivals or at other times, when they meet informally over tea to discuss current affairs, strategies and programmes with friends and subordinates. Although Pir Gate has not fully replaced the older meeting ground at Chowk, a place at the centre of the bazaar next to the Jami Masjid, it has nevertheless re-centred informal politics by shifting many meetings to the new locality. The potential of Pir Gate as a political centre is further realized by the frequent rallies, *dharnas* and protest marches that are organized, which more often than not carry Hindu nationalist messages. They take up the topic of cow protection, are organized on the occasion of electoral victories of the BJP, give moral support to other temple movements, etc. Most of these events integrate the temple into their programme and thereby add a devotional element to their agenda and a political meaning to the temple. Organized around the goddess and addressing Hindus as community, they have brought about the transformation that has turned Pir Gate into a stronghold of political Hinduism.

The effects that the change in the physical environment at Pir Gate has had on the social landscape are not only local by nature. They are part of a social process through which Hinduism is defined and a Hindu community organized and made palpable as a political entity. In order to understand the way the transformed Pir Gate works on people's imaginations, it is important to take into account the intertwining of political events and ritual actions there, which fosters an integration of religious beliefs and political ideologies. From a religious point of view the Durga Temple has marked the crossing as divine territory possessed by the goddess. This is also manifested by the banishing of the polluting presence of a non-vegetarian restaurant and a liquor shop from the area. In the light of the divine occupancy, the place has become a religiously loaded area in which every conceivable activity can be justified as being willed by the goddess or as serving to protect her, irrespective of the motivations named by individual actors. Any economic undertaking or political event can from another angle be seen as a devotional act that has the goddess as its centre and *raison-d'être*.

This is not to say that people may not criticise the content of the programmes organized at Pir Gate. It is rather to assert that they have at their disposal an explanation that is able to justify any activity rallying around a divine centre as sanctioned by a higher authority, based on the belief that divine actors are willing and able to intervene in this world. The presence of a temple in the most unlikely area of the city—the symbolic heart of 'Muslim Bhopal'—itself seems like proof of this assumption. Furthermore, it is the continuing presence of large number of devotees on Pir Gate that strengthens the belief that the deity reigns here.

When every activity gets organised around the divine as the power centre, the boundary between religious, political and economic enterprises gets blurred, so that the celebration of a religious festival can well be perceived as a political assertion of Hindu nationalist forces. In the same way, the activity of the local representative of the BJP who inaugurated a toilet near the temple to serve the needs of the devotees and visitors of the bazaar can be seen as a devotional activity when the sudden success of this long planned enterprise is interpreted as a result of the benevolent presence of the goddess in the area.

Such a framework of interpretation, which makes a connection between religious devotion and political message, opens a discursive field in which the meaning of any performance that takes place at Pir Gate is subject to conflicting interpretations, which offer different perspectives on the interconnection between religion and politics. The organization of the sacrifice (*havan*), which is celebrated twice a year on the occasion of Navratri, may serve as one example. The celebration takes place during the evening hours of the ninth day of goddess worship and generates great enthusiasm in the area, with thousands of Hindus crowding around Pir Gate. There are many among the audience who recall the event as an intense experience of the divine presence, as a feeling of 'Hindu communion', and even as an entertaining evening programme. Many participants also considered it a laudable form of preserving Hindu traditions in modern India. Furthermore, those familiar with the locality recall the way the celebration of Navratri allows the Durga Temple Committee, leading priests and political leaders to stage their importance. Depending on the intimacy of the knowledge people have of the power struggles, they acknowledge the ways in which the celebration is used as a forum for the performance and negotiation of status positions, and the effect it has had on power equations in the area.

Not everyone may be aware of all these meanings that are attached to the celebration, nor does everyone agree with every given interpretation, but many people acknowledge different levels of meaning and are aware that a religious event can simultaneously be an entertaining programme, an act of devotion, and part of a political struggle. The connection between Hindu devotional acts, political messages and economic enterprises in modern India has been discussed by many scholars, and especially discerned in the context of Hindu nationalist agendas that try to organize Hindus into a politically potent religious community (see for example Hasan 2001; Jaffrelot 1996; Ludden 1996; McKean 1996; Pandey 1993; van de Veer 1994). Kapur (1993) gives one example of how changes in the iconography of Ram instil a particular political message into a religious image. She shows that in the process of the fight for a Ram Temple in Ayodhya, the depiction of Ram changed from the traditional portrait of a graceful and benevolent god into a crusader fighting for the Hindu cause. Ram was later also shown as an infant in need of human protection. Both these depictions contain an exhortation to Hindus to line up behind their god to defend him and their community interests.[28]

There are other studies which have taken up the theme of processions and shown how the aim of unifying and politicizing Hindus and demarcating them from Muslims is realized during religious processions or political parades laden with religious imagery.[29] Davis (1996), for example, examines the ways in which political intentions and religious messages were combined in the 1990 *rath yatra* organized by the VHP (Vishva Hindu Parishad) and the BJP. The parade was part of a larger campaign by the Sangh Parivar to gain political strength by forging an aggressive and violent movement for the realization of a Ram Temple in Ayodhya, directed against Muslims. During the procession the BJP leader Advani was carried in a chariot, designed as a copy of the mythical vehicle of Ram. The resulting merging of political and religious imagery and the identification of Advani with god Ram was not only acknowledged but also applauded by the organisers, who knew that people came also in devotion to the god. In this situation opposing the movement became a tricky question, because acting against the procession did not only mean to stand up against a certain party, a particular ideology or a movement that was anticipated to turn violent. But it was also interpreted as an act against the Lord Ram Himself (Davis 1996).

Many references made by Hindus in the city support the thesis that the events at Pir Gate can and must be seen in the perspective of a religio-political movement that actively identifies Hindu religious practices with a movement designed to strengthen the political representation of Hindus by organizing them into a potent majority community and brining them into opposition to Muslims and other religious groups defined as 'the other'. The political dimension of the Durga Temple became overtly clear when in 1996 a statue of the late Hindu leader Uddvadas Mehta was fixed across the temple in the middle of Pir Gate crossing. Mehta is known as a great supporter of the Hindu nationalist project and remembered as the first person who

[28] For details on the controversy in Ayodhya see Gopal 1991; Jaffrelot 1996; Nandy et al. 1995; van de Veer 1994.

[29] More on processions in the context of the Hindu nationalist movement can be found in Jaffrelot 1998. For historical evidence see Cashman 1970; Freitag 1989, 1991; van de Veer 1987; Yang 1980.

fought elections for the Hindu Mahasabha. He is said to have actively supported the temple as a means to strengthen 'Hindu representation' in the old city of Bhopal.

Yet, opinions remain divided. There are many who do not subscribe to the political project of Hindu nationalism and wish to see the temple as a purely religious project. Especially women were reluctant to understand their fight for a goddess temple in the old town as part of a Hindu-Muslim struggle. They wish to reclaim the temple as a place of religious worship and oppose its politicization through leaders.

However, independent of the intention of individual actors, the different messages associated with the Durga Temple remain inseparable. The success of the movement is also an effect of the merging of religious and political intention, which allowed for the mobilisation of large number of divers actors. This was already apparent during foundation days, when the Durga Temple Committee called upon all Hindus in the city to support their project. Fused with the Navratri celebration the construction of the Durga Temple became part of a large religious festival. The political intentions were pushed to the background in this initial situation. People came to offer their worship to the goddess during their extensive visits of different Navratri shrines. The political struggle started days later, after the celebration was over, in a situation where the temple had already become part of the religious landscape of Bhopal.

The visibility of the Hindus increased during the campaign, and for the duration they were fused into a community in which differences were glossed over by a joint action that created the impression that they all shared a single belief and aim. Independent of the individual motivation and the internal friction between different supporter groups, the high visibility of the Temple movement, as well as the changes it brought about at Pir Gate, strengthened a stereotypical perception of Indian society as split into antagonistic religious communities. As such it is part of a complex institution that ensures the integration of religious movements into a discourse of communalism, with its singular emphasis on Hindu-Muslim conflict. Any other interpretation becomes relegated to the background, in this case the difference between local Hindus and the city administration that was at the back of the confrontation.

In his study on the narrative re-appropriation of violent encounters in North India, Brass (1997) demonstrates how events are given their meaning through a process of negotiating perspectives. Collecting accounts from a verity of actors, Brass realizes that the events has no inner core of truth that would emerge from the narrations. He rather finds a multiplicity of perspectives, which can not be reduced to one another. In keeping with Bauman, he sees an event not as an external referent but a reality that is created and shaped through narrative accounts (Bauman 1986: 5, see also Koepping and Rao 2002). Occurrences become events through their narrative appropriation. They are shaped and reshaped through constant process of re-collection, re-telling and judging. In this process violent encounters become classified as communal violence, caste conflict or police atrocity. Their complexity is reduced in favour of highlighting a certain dimension in preference to others, which are subdued or even forgotten in the course of establishing of a socially authorized standard narrative.

Interestingly, such processes of standardization are not only used by outsiders in their appropriation of an event, but also shape the memory of actual participants (Pandey 1991, see also Das 1990b, 1995). The effect of this process is that communal mobilization works in the form of a self-fulfilling prophesy that brings the expected into existence by applying a certain label to a movement, and thus influencing the course of events as well as their later re-appropriation. The idea that religious communities are well defined, unified and competing entities is a discursive construction, which comes into being through the mutual influence of action and interpretation.

Following this argument it becomes clear why the events at Pir Gate have to be taken seriously as part of the history of Hindu-Muslim antagonism in the city. While many different motivations were at work that summated and turned the initiative for a temple into a success, it was the anti-Muslim bias that became established as the main motivation in public memory. It is part of almost every reference to the Durga Temple and serves as the logic for the massive state intervention. The Collector in charge during the foundation days is praised for his swift and effective action, which is said to have prevented the outbreak of Hindu-Muslim riots.

This logic, which singles out a leading figure as responsible for the occurrence of Hindu-Muslim violence, increases the likelihood that a Hindu-Muslim narrative is applied to incidents by decision makers, who are constantly on the guard to prevent communal encounters. Today Pir Gate is listed among the 'sensitive spots', considered to be a likely location for the outbreak of religiously motivated violence. It has a permanent police post and during festivals extra forces are stationed to make Pir Gate safe for Hindus and Muslims.

Here the temple has become more than a religious building or a political site. It works as a catalyst for the conceptualization of society along the dimension of Hindu-Muslim opposition, which is effective in re-shaping urban relations. Widely accepted as a symbol of an aggressive Hindu polity and part of a larger anti-Muslim project, the temple is singled out and guaranteed constant attention by the local authorities, the political actors, and the media. Consequently it becomes well suited to activities aimed at addressing a larger audience. As a result, the place has in fact become what it was considered to be: a centre for political activities, especially when they are built on a Hindu-Muslim narrative, be they in support of Hindu nationalist ideals or for the creation of communal harmony. The constant presence of leaders with their different political messages also feeds back on the interpretation of religious activities taking place at Pir Gate, which now appear as part of the larger project of Hindu nationalism advertised here. Religious and political activities merge, not necessarily because of the intentions of the actors, but as a result of the confluence of different activities and strategies at one place.

CONCLUSION

This chapter started out to narrate the history of the construction of two temples with the aim of showing how temples are supported by communities and communities by temples. I have argued that the Durga Temple has strengthened feelings of Hindu solidarity. This is due to the interpretation given to the dramatic events that accompanied its construction, which are seen to be a result of perceived antagonism between Hindu and Muslim interests. The ensuing developments at Pir Gate have turned the place into one of the most popular sites for mass political and religious events. Here Hindu solidarity is visible and can be emotionally experienced during the celebration of festivals and the participation in (religious) demonstrations. Associated with a Hindu nationalist project, the temple has encouraged a definition of Hindu community and its demarcation from the Muslim 'Other'.

Although there were also anti-Muslim overtones at play during the construction of the Kali Temple, it is associated not so much with 'the Hindu community' but with a particular caste. Narrations centre on the Khatiks as variously heroic and brave or devious and criminal agents, who took on the Muslims to realize a temple in their territory. The identification of the Kali Temple with the Khatik community is also due to the organizational set-up that confines the membership of the trust to one particular caste and is a result of the organization of religious festivals that focus on the Khatiks, singles them out as owners of the temple, and provides a platform for them to meet. Caste here comes into existence not so much as a social group that shares an everyday life, but as an imagined community based on a common origin. At a time when caste as a category of social specification appears to lose power in urban environments, it is re-created as a descent group centred around the goddess as protector and guarantor of social solidarity.

I therefore conclude that the temple, as a socio-religious place, has a lasting effect on the structure of urban relations. It realizes the interests of certain groups, which search for representation in space. However, in turn the temple also alters the ideas of these groups. On the basis of local face-to-face communities, it supports the formulation of new ideal groups, which exist as reflexive categories that transcend the locality. In case of the Kali and Durga Temple we find the formulation of a state-wide 'Khatik community' and a nation-wide 'Hindu community', which do not arise out of experience of concrete relationships but are, like modern nation states, '*imagined communities*' (Anderson 1992 [1983]). By using the term 'imagined' Anderson does not mean to say that national communities are fabricated and thus false, but draws attention to their character as constructed, since they comprise of members who mostly do not know each other and yet develop a sense of belonging together. Both the idea of 'a Hindu community' and that of a trans-local 'Khatik community' remain fuzzy in the absence of a clear-cut definition of membership. Yet with the existence of temples, that are seen as their representation, they become real and inform behaviour that is directed at people as members or non-members of these communities.[30]

As a place that supports the formulation of socially relevant unities, the temple is simultaneously a place of religion and of politics. It accommodates the divine in the human world and provides the space for ritual communication. It also structures the relations between human beings and gives shape to certain conceptions of the social order. It is a contested field of activity the negotiation are intended to find an appropriate place for the divine in the urban environment. Through the action of believers and the integration and re-collection of their activities in different social discourses, a triangular relationship between urban territory, social imagination and religious activity is created. They are mutually supportive in bringing about the temple as a physical place and as an image that shapes the relations between the human and the non-human world, as well as between different social agents.

I started my account with the description of those moments in the history of the temples where religious beliefs, political ambitions and images came together to bring about new places of worship. To investigate activities through which the temple is instilled with life and moulded into an institution through the ritual, social and political activity of people in the city, I shall increase the radius of observation: starting from the life inside the temple in the next chapter, moving to the festivals celebrated around the temples in Chapter 4, and dealing with the urban negotiations about temples and religion in Chapter 5. By situating the analysis of the temple in various discursive fields, I aim

[30] On the process of formation of trans-local religious communities as 'imagined communities', that started during British colonialism and continues till today see for example Das 1995; Freitag 1989; Pandey 1990.

to show the intersection of different forms of structured and structuring activities that lead to the formation and re-affirmation of religious perceptions. I intend to show how concepts of religion, politics and science entwined, how the discourse of religion is shaped through ideas about modernity and tradition, and how reflections and social concepts are related to the interactional practices of people.

CHAPTER 3

Ritual Life and the Mediation of Authority in the Divine *Darbar*

Where everyday life inside a temple is concerned, politics is not analysed with reference to established social institutions in the city, but is understood in the broad sense of power contests. The latter are an important part of the organization of ritual life because they are the means by which people make sense of the divine will and carry it out. In order to formulate basic traits of the organization of temple life and the social processes through which ritual performances are realized and become effective, I rely for my interpretation on the material on the two temples described in Chapter 2. These represent the two poles of the spectrum of religious orthodoxy. While the Durga Temple is managed by members of high castes, in accordance with Brahmanic ideals of religiosity, the Kali Temple by contrast is perceived as a 'democratic place' in which religious traditions are negotiated between social actors from various backgrounds.

The temple emerged as a loosely organized socio-religious space that leaves considerable room for the re-negotiation of rules and internal hierarchies. What is important is the respect given to the goddess at the centre, a centre that is both over- and under-determined. Its over-determination results from the enormous power that is accorded to the divine, which exceeds all human abilities. At the same time the divine centre is under-determined since the goddess rarely communicates directly, and never in an unambiguous way. Thus there is a constant need for interpretation. Ideas about the correct procedures vary greatly according to the clientele of a temple and may deviate from the social logic that governs life outside. In such cases the temple offers glimpses of an alternative conception of social relations.

THE 'UNIVERSE' OF THE TEMPLE

A visitor entering any of the larger temples in India is overwhelmed by the bustling atmosphere created by the diverse activities of the large numbers of visitors who ring bells, approach the deity, perform individual *puja*,[1] address the priests, sit down in groups to rest, or sing devotional songs. A visitor's attention is also drawn to the children who run around, happy to have escaped from their parents. They jump to reach bells placed far too high for them to reach, enjoy the pleasure of the sweets distributed as *prasad* (divine leavings), returning over and over again to ask for more, and are happy to use the large compound for their games.

Only slowly, through a painful process of familiarization that brought me into close contact with many of the worshippers and priests, did I start to make sense of the many activities. What slowly emerged as a regular feature or common denominator of all the actions is their orientation to the divine centre. Whatever happens in the temple is the result of the deity's presence, which transforms the territory and re-arranges social relations. The following section aims at introducing the reader to the logic that governs temple life by constructing relevant categories of worshippers and rules of interactions. The importance I have given to the detailed description of temple life is a response to the dire state of the present situation in the literature on the temple as a social place. A number of scholars have studied temple life from one particular angle: they have discussed aspects of the ritual life (Fuller 1984a; Kane 1974; Preston 1980), studied the work and organization of priests (Fuller 1982, 1984a, 1984b), and also the organization of a temple's service system (Appadurai and Breckenridge 1976; Roesel 1980).

In contrast to these studies, which all revolve around ritual activity and the groups involved, I wish to look at the temple as a 'total social fact' (Mauss 1969 [1950]: 76) that comes to life through the activities of many different groups of people, including priests, worshippers, voluntary helpers and beggars.[2] Naturally, there is no one way to consider everything that could be said about temple life, and I had to select, leaving out many interesting details and concentrating on what to my mind constitutes the central features, the overall governing

[1] In the literature, *puja* is used in two basically different ways. Scholars who worked in south India, Orissa and Bengal summarize all public rituals under this term (Appadurai and Breckenridge 1976: 192-3; Fuller 1992: 62-3; Mearns 1995: 187-201; Roesel 1980: 185; Good 1987: 7; Ostoer 1982). Conversely, studies conducted predominantly among north Indians use the word to describe private rituals (Humphrey and Laidlaw 1994: 21-31, 3; Nye 1995: 108-9). In order to avoid any confusion, I take *puja* to mean individual (temple) worship, thereby following its usage in the everyday language of the Bhopalis. For all other rituals Hindi terms like *arti*, *dhup arti*, *havan* will be used.

[2] Appadurai and Breckenridge (1976) come closest to accomplishing such a task. They made sense of the temple as an integrated institution by formulating a general governing principle of temple life. Their work will be discussed in some detail below.

principles, thereby creating my own skeleton from the body of life. My narration has come about through a concentration on the social dimensions of temple life, demonstrating how the temple as divine universe is created through the human attendance to the deity. With the intention of providing the reader with a 'map' that may guide their perceptions during the following complex discussion, I have chosen to start with an introduction of the temple as divine territory, then go on to introduce the different groups of people who visit the temple and finally discuss their relationships in relation to their activities in the temple.

THE TEMPLE AS SACRED TERRITORY

At the centre of every temple there is the sanctuary of the main deity. It takes a prominent place in the hall, where it is often only one among a number of shrines, but nevertheless remains the main attraction (Fuller 1988: 51-2). The divine power that is said to be contained in the statues of the different deities transforms the place, sets it apart from its surrounding environment and makes it a sacred territory. This finds expression in people taking off their shoes before entering, sometimes covering their heads in respect, and abstaining from drinking and eating meat.[3] In both of the temples considered in this study, a goddess shrine—Kali's and Durga's—constitutes the sacred centre. People perceive it as a special blessing to be allowed to touch and wash the main image. But during normal days public entry into the sanctuary is prohibited. Worshippers have to conduct their worship from outside the enshrined area, which is open to all.[4]

Central to temple worship is the 'beholding' (*darshan*) of the deity. It is through *darshan* that the worshipper comes into direct contact with the goddess, since viewing is seen as effective in a Hindu context. Through visual interaction with the deity divine substance is believed to be transmitted to the human being. However, it is not the worshipper

[3] The old Kali Temple of the Khatik caste did not have any restrictions on the offering and consumption of meat, since animal sacrifices were an established tradition among Khatiks. However, after undergoing a process of Brahmanization, the caste has now restricted animal sacrifice, especially in the popular new Kali Temple. The taboo on animal sacrifice in the new Kali Temple is only lifted once a year during the performance of Hariyali Amavas, when male Khatiks offer goats in the temple at night to secure the goddess's protection.

[4] Some temples restrict entrance solely to Hindus, especially in famous pilgrimage places (e.g. Vishvanath Temple in Benares, Jagannath Temple in Puri, Pashupatinath Temple in Kathmandu). Traditionally there were also restrictions on the entrance of 'untouchables'. This practice was abandoned by law in 1949. People in Bhopal maintained that the temple is a particularly suitable place for the mixing of all castes, for in the eyes of the divine all people are equal.

who initiates the visual interaction. It is the deity who *gives darshan* whereas the devotee *receives* it (Eck 1981: 6-7, 1986). Brass describes the importance of the devotees' efforts to attract the deity's benevolent gaze during worship as follows: 'visual interaction between deity and worshipper establishes a special sort of intimacy between them, which confers benefits by allowing worshippers to "drink" divine power with their eyes, a power that carries with it—at least potentially—an extraordinary and revelatory "point of view"' (Babb 1981: 388). The temple turns into a preferred place for a communication with a deity, since the image enshrined here permits the transmission of divine substance and allows for an unmediated interaction with the goddess.

How and when this substance is present in the statue was never a question of debate. It was taken for granted. This is remarkable because many scientific writings on temples debate exactly this point. Different theological interpretations are quoted supporting either the argument that the deity is permanently present, or that the divine power has to be evoked anew before every ritual. There is also disagreement over whether it is actually the deity or only the divine power that is thought to be present in the statue (Babb 1981; Eck 1981, 1986; Fuller 1984a: 10; 1992: 60-2; Good 1987: 16).

Whereas most people I interviewed were willing and able to answer direct questions about the relation between the image and the deity, they themselves never engaged in any such theoretical or theological speculations. People simply acted on the expectation that the goddess is permanently present in the shrine, even if the shrine is closed. Asked whether the deity is really inside the statue, they replied that this was a question of faith. If there is someone to believe it, then the deity is also present.[5] Radically formulated, this means that without the believer there is no deity. Seen from another angle, the statement also implies that the divine presence is not actually bound to any temple, but can be manifest in any place (e.g. a stone in the forest) where believers assemble.

Yet, in spite of the boundless presence of the divine, the temple constitutes a special terrain in popular perception as it serves as a (permanent) home for a deity, thus binding the divine's presence to this world. In the temple, a divinity's hall of audience (*darbar*), the deity is permanently and directly accessible. Once installed, the statue of the goddess is considered absolutely immovable. Popular belief has it that any effort to remove the image would provoke divine revenge. In turn, the boundaries of the temple are rather flexible; they can be shifted through the construction or destruction of any part of the building. Especially during festivals they are temporarily extended onto

[5] See similarly the findings of Paul Radin 1956: 15ff.

the streets, incorporating territory not normally considered part of the sacred site. The demarcation of the temple as a physical entity can also be blurred through adjoining landscapes that are incorporated in the divine territory. This happens in the Kali Temple, where the lake and the steps leading down to it are considered part of the sacred site, as they serve important ritual functions.

The belief that the aura of the sacred is not confined within the walls of a temple is also confirmed through the display of respect many people show when viewing a temple from the outside. Nodding towards the temple—or better the deity that is known to be inside—while passing by serves as a form of *darshan*. It is an act of reflection that is set in motion through the site of the temple and becomes equated with physically approaching the goddess. It is the spatial proximity to the deity, the power of imagination and the omnipresence of the divine, that here makes the thought of the goddess an effective *darshan*.[6]

The conceptualization of the temple as a transformed territory that brings to presence divine power has implications for social life, which is organized around the goddess as the imaginary centre. The aim of the following discussion is to show how the temple becomes alive through the interaction between human agents and their relationship to the divine centre. I will structure the discussion by introducing four categories of devotees: religious specialists, voluntary servants (*sevak*s), worshippers (*darshanarthi*s) and beggars. Although these categories are only loosely defined, and membership is contextual and can overlap or differ in accordance with the viewpoint, they may serve as an ideal construction that helps to re-construct the order that governs social relationships in the temple.

RANKING PEOPLE IN THE DIVINE *DARBAR*

Outside a temple, one usually encounters a group of beggars who have settled in front of the religious site. Their placement at the margin of the sacred territory is symbolic of their position in the temple society. They are kept outside, since they are not counted as members of the religious clientele. This impression is supported by the beggars themselves, who rarely offer religious reasons for their presence at the divine *darbar*. Here they are tolerated and can hope to receive generous alms. This, of course, can be and is at times interpreted in religious terms. It is argued that the deity accepts everyone and is concerned also about the well-being of the lowliest of human beings.

[6] See also Humphrey and Laidlaw (1994) for the question of identity between the actual performance of a ritual and its mental reiteration.

Having passed the beggars, the visitor enters the temple and is there confronted with a lot of activity, carried out by a large number of people. The group of persons that stands out most clearly are the officially employed priests, normally situated next to or inside the sanctuary. It is a normal procedure in all larger temples in Bhopal that the managing committee employs one or more Brahmin priests on a salary basis in order to ensure regular and 'correct' ritual observance. Besides the employed priests there are a number of other religious specialists—like unemployed or freelance priests, and ascetics (*sanyasi*s)—who usually mark their claim to a special status through a distinct way of dressing (a *dhoti* and a saffron rope). They offer their blessings and special ritual service, in return for which they are allowed to stay in the temple and live off the deity. Together with the priests they contribute to the attraction of a temple, since they offer an effective mediation between the deity and devotee.

People refer to visitors in general as *darshanarthi*s, those who have come to receive *darshan*. After a few days in the temple one learns to differentiate between occasional and regular devotees, as well as between normal worshippers and voluntary helpers (*sevak*s). While worshippers come to perform a ritual, to rest for a while, or to chat with some friends, *sevak*s attend the divine *darbar* with the aim to serve the goddess through extending a helping hand in the organization of temple matters. They open the temple in the morning and close it at night; they clean and decorate the shrines, distribute *prasad*, attend to worshippers and sometimes perform rituals. Some come for a few minutes to sweep the ground, while others spend almost the entire day performing a full range of duties. No matter how often helpers come or which duties they shoulder, if seen to perform a task in the temple they will be classified as those who have come to do *seva* (service). After a while, I was included in this category as someone who served the goddess by writing about her temple.

Once acquainted with the four categories of *darshanarthi*, *sevak*, religious specialist and beggar, I was soon able to distinguish people according to the purpose of their presence. However, just a few days in the temple also taught me that this general classification was far from clear-cut. The differences between religious specialists and *sevak*s, between *sevak*s and beggars, as well as between regular worshippers and *sevak*s, could be so intricate or minute that confusion would easily ensue. And the distinctions were not so much a result of an observable reality as the outcome of a constant communicative interaction between the temple clientele, through which single visitors received their social identity and could subsequently be placed in a hierarchy of visitors. Generally, people saw priests and *sanyasi*s at the top of the hierarchy, *sevak*s immediately below, followed by regular and irregular worshippers, with beggars ranked the lowest. However, due to the negotiability of categories, this hierarchy also was often put to question. In order to demonstrate these conceptual problems, let me consider the case of Chacha—a Khatik who retired from his job and his family life to settle permanently in the Kali Temple to serve the goddess.

Chacha decided, only a short time after the foundation of the Kali Temple, to resign from his job at the railway. He became an ascetic and dedicated his life to Kali by settling in the newly-built caste-temple. In spite of his membership to a Scheduled Caste, he took over the responsibility for the organization of the ritual routine.[7] By now Chacha has spent nearly thirty years in the temple and is well known to the majority of devotees. He has grown old in the temple, too old now to perform any major duties. Yet, he is highly respected and considered the main authority in the Kali Temple. People come from all over the city especially for his blessing and advice. The importance of his presence became clear when illness forced him to remain absent for a while during the summer of 1996. The atmosphere in the temple changed. Regular visitors stopped coming, many worshippers no longer spent time in the temple after finishing their religious duties, theological discussions discontinued, and the supply of material for the rituals and other donations declined. Normality was only restored on Chacha's return.

Considering the different aspects of Chacha's presence in the temple, he qualifies as priest, as *sanyasi*, and as voluntary worker. Classification seems tricky in his case, since he spent years performing many of the lowest tasks in the temple and has been deprived of all comforts. Yet on the other hand, he has also been involved in the performance of important ritual activities as well as in blessing and healing people, and by now he, without doubt, represents the main authority in the temple. In spite of his debility and inability to enforce, or even clearly voice, his opinion, people respect him out of fear of and respect for the goddess to whom he is believed to be very close. The efficacy of Chacha's blessings and his enduring presence near the goddess proves to visitors that divine authority has been bestowed on him.

This example shows that people in the temple are not only judged according to the tasks they perform and the extent to which they are known, but also in relation to their closeness to the deity. The study of Appadurai and Breckenridge (1976, also Appadurai 1981a) confirmed this connection between status classification and closeness to the deity. In their study of historical South Indian temples, they describe the temple as a redistributive system centred on the deity as paradigmatic sovereign who oversees a pooling and re-allocation of resources. More concretely, this process consists of the giving of goods and services to the deity, their subsequent transformation through a ritual, and their re-distribution to worshippers in the form of divine leavings (*prasad*) and special rights, also known as 'honours'. Through the reception of such honours, people partake in divine authority, which in turn invests them with power in the human domain. What emerges here is that authority is always borrowed as a partaking in divine authority. In the temple people are judged with reference to their relationship with the divine and classified accordingly, which could be different from their normal status.

Seen from this angle, it becomes clear why priests usually receive great respect in the temple, for they are (generally) from a ritually clean caste (Brahmins) and perform an activity that brings them close to the deities. But whether they are actually respected depends on their ability to convince the devotees of this closeness to the divine. Respect is achieved by fulfilling expectations in a ritual performance that is intended to realize the divine presence, a task that is invested with the risk of failure (see also Schieffelin 1996). The evaluation of the status of ascetics and even *sevak*s is of a similar nature. Caste status, employment or education, is of limited help in assessing their standing in the temple. To gain respect they have to demonstrate their dedication to the goddess and prove their ability to serve humans by serving the divine.

Establishing a connection with the divine is also the means for poorer servants of the goddess to distinguish themselves from beggars. Whether someone escapes the stigma of begging depends partly on his physical location in the temple. Does he stay with the other beggars at the margin of the temple or does he choose a place closer to the goddess? What is even more important is the question of gift reception. Whilst a beggar comes to a temple in search of alms, a *sevak* stays there to be near the goddess and to serve her. He lives from whatever she chooses to provide him with. Contrary to the beggars, *sevak*s believe they have a special right to a better share of *prasad* as acknowledgement of their work for the deity.

However, the distinction between those who beg for alms and those who accept only *prasad* is not easy to make. Stories about mistaken identity told in the temple show how often confusions occur. *Sevak*s can spend hours discussing and laughing at incidents where they were mistaken for beggars, which demonstrates the importance given to such differentiation. Problems of classification arise because it is difficult to know how close a person is to the goddess. Such judgements remain vague since no-one has an overview of what each person does, how much he contributes, which gifts he accepts or how dedicated his service is. Any such judgement can only be provisional in character, since social constellations in a temple constantly change and make it impossible to fix a certain person in any one position. The example of Jugnu, a *sevak* and night-watchman at the temple, will demonstrate this latter point.

Jugnu is employed in the Kali Temple as a night-watchman. For many years he has demonstrated his devotion and he has earned himself respect for his religious knowledge, his dedication to the goddess, his simple life style, and the way he cares for Chacha, the aged ascetic. He holds considerable authority and often voices his opinion or intervenes in organizational questions, and bosses *sevak*s, worshippers and sometimes even priests about. In the absence of Chacha he was once even elevated to the status of his proxy, an honour hardly to be matched by anything else.

But even Jugnu is not beyond question. On one occasion he became the main target in a fight over a vanished *lagan* (bundle with offerings and horoscope needed in a Hindu-marriage ceremony). A family had brought the *lagan* in the morning and left it in the sanctuary, to collect it again later, but when they returned in the afternoon the bundle had disappeared. In their anger and frustration the family members accused Jugnu of neglecting his duty as a watchman. Of course they could equally have blamed the priest or the *sevak* who had been in charge of the morning duties. But Jugnu was an easy target not only because it was understood to be his duty as watchman to ensure the temple's safety (omitting the fact that he was actually a *night*-watchman), but also because his status did not match up to that of the priests and *sevak*s in charge of ritual performances.

As the fight heated up, the accusation changed. Initially only abused for failing in this particular case, now general doubts were voiced about his ability to protect the temple. If today a *lagan* could disappear, then maybe tomorrow the statue itself will be stolen, without anyone noticing. This allegation was particular effective in undermining Jugnu's status, since his authority depended on his visible devotion to the goddess. The moment his dedication was in doubt, he could no longer claim the position of a respected *sevak*. Jugnu recovered from this fight, but a year later, when a severe attack of tuberculosis left him weakened and unable to attend to his duties, his position of authority in the temple was diminished for good.

Status classifications in the temple change with time and context. They are established through the communicative action of worshippers. How much did this one donate? How often does that person attend? How long has he been supporting the temple? How much devotion does she show? Does she get possessed? Has he been able to help people? These are only some of the questions that provoke comments and engage worshippers in discussions. Through gossip, devotees assess the quantity and quality of people's contributions, which in turn become an indication of their closeness to the deity and the basis for a judgement which classifies them and accords them a particular status and authority.[8]

With reference to the contextuality of status evaluation, the data from Bhopal differs from that of Appadurai and Breckenridge. Here the closeness to the goddess is not established through pre-established and fixed rights to contributions, but is rather an emergent quality that differs with the momentary social positioning of the individual actors. A varying group of *sevak*s, devotees and religious specialists must invariably re-establish their authority by convincing the ever-changing group of worshippers of the depth of their dedication and the amount of their work. If they have been successful, their activities are publicized and rewarded through praises and verbal propaganda, as well as through the gift of special *prasad* and the right to perform important services.

However, it is not only the goddess who bestows authority on her devotees; the devotees create the temple as a socio-religious place by securing the goddess's presence in the temple through their conducts of rituals. Respect and authority are not only the result of religious devotion, but are also the pre-condition for participation in a routine that secures the divine presence in the temple. Although temple routines usually follow an established tradition, their performance depends on ever-renewed acts of interpretation, which leave much room for contestation. Those who have earned respect are most influential in establishing what 'correct' behaviour and the 'necessary' performances are. Thus, there exists a mutual reinforcement between the socially evaluated status of the human servants and the ritually secured divine presence. Ritual performance transmits social status while social status becomes a pre-condition for the performance of ritual duties, which in turn secure divine presence, the basis for the evaluation of social status. In order to understand this relationship and see how the temple becomes alive in performance, the following sections investigate the negotiation of ritual activity at the centre of temple life.

THE TEMPLE AS RITUAL SPACE

For an overview of the many ritual activities observed in a temple, it is useful to distinguish between public and private rituals. The term private ritual refers to performances initiated or conducted by individuals to serve their personal interests. They are distinguished from the regular rituals performed by ritual specialists said to serve the whole world in general (Appadurai and Breckenridge 1976: 192-3; Diehl 1956: 153; Good 1987; Fuller 1992: 76, 1984a: 10, 1992: 62). I believe this

[7] *Arti*—the main ritual of the daily ritual routine, during which a camphor flame is waved in front of the deity—formed the sole exception, which whenever possible was performed by an employed Brahmin priest.

distinction between two different types of rituals to be useful, but I have reservations about the terminology, since rituals in both categories—whether they are performed occasionally by worshippers or regularly by ritual servants—serve individuals as well as the community.

Attending a temple regularly, an observer soon learns to distinguish between the ritual routine conducted every day in the same way by the temple servants, and the number of different rituals initiated by changing groups of worshippers. While the former follows an established pattern and does not allow for any deviations, the latter rituals are voluntary and change according to interest, day of performance and attending persons. Worshippers are free to conduct their individual *puja* as they wish.

Usually devotees follow a minimal ritual procedure encompassing the greeting of the goddess, the reception of *darshan* and the acceptance of *prasad*. Many worshippers also bring offerings—flowers, coconuts or sweets—which they present to the goddess, then to receive part of it back as *prasad*. People symbolically wash the goddess, circle oil-lamps or incense sticks in front of her in form of an *arti*, say private prayers, or recite *mantra*s (sacred formulas) sometimes in combination with particular body-movements—like bowing in front of the goddess, standing on one leg, or twisting their ears. At first sight it appears reasonable to call such rituals private, even though they are conducted in a public place, since they generate a communication solely between the particular worshipper and the deity. But the classificatory problem starts when devotees, before leaving, distribute their *prasad* among other worshippers, sharing with them the blessing they have received.

The performance of *katha*s (a group of people engages a priest to read a stipulated sacred text and preside over the performance of a *havan*) in the temple brings this classificatory ambiguity even more to the fore. In most cases a *katha* is organized by a (joint-) family, occasionally by a group of friends or business partners, in order to ask a favour from the goddess or thank her for having fulfilled a particular wish. The participants settle down together with the priest in front of the sanctuary and jointly perform the *katha*. However, in spite of this being a 'private' ritual, conducted and intended to benefit a clearly defined group, participation is not restricted. People do not hesitate to join if they so desire. Participation is actively encouraged when the

[8] Gluckman has referred to this function of gossip: 'gossip, and even scandal, have important positive virtues. Clearly they maintain the unity, morals and values of social groups. Beyond this, they enable these groups to control the competing cliques and aspiring individuals of which all groups are composed. And finally, they make possible the selection of leaders without embarrassment' (Gluckman 1963: 308).

organizers discover someone's interest. The 'private' ritual finally goes fully 'public' when at the end *prasad* is distributed to *all* the people in the temple. Through the reception of *prasad* everyone partakes in the blessings the performance has generated.

Let me add another example of a typical ritual activity conducted in a temple which escapes clear classification as either public or private. In both the Kali and the Durga temples there exists an informal group of worshippers (mostly women) who regularly meet to jointly revere the goddess by singing *bhajan*s. Such performances can hardly be described as either public or private, since as a congregational form of worship it is potentially open to everyone, but is privately organized and mostly attended by a fixed group of participants. Not part of the stipulated routine, it could also be categorised as private ritual. But once again, since this form of special devotion increases the attraction of the temple and the holiness of the site, it can also be said to be of service to the whole community.

A similar ambiguity exists in relation to the daily ritual routine organized by the temple as such. Some of the prescribed rituals, particularly *arti*, attract a number of worshippers who participate by observing the priests' activities and joining in the singing of the hymns. In accordance with the classification found in the literature, *arti* would range among the public rituals as it serves to secure the temple as a place of the divine. Seen from the perspective of each single participant, however, the ritual is also a private one, since participation in the performance is a voluntary act of personal devotion and brings particular blessings to those present. Taking all these arguments together, it should have become clear that the terms 'private' and 'public' are inadequate for a classification of temple rituals. Instead, I propose as an alternative to talk of *stipulated ritual*s of the daily ritual routine, and contrast them with the *voluntary ritual*s of (occasional) visitors, a terminology which also comes closer to the way devotees themselves perceive the rituals.

After this conceptual introduction, let me turn to a description of the problems emerging from the organization of the obligatory daily routine. The rituals of the daily routine are of particular relevance to the present study, as they create and secure the temple as sacred territory. By treating the deity like an honoured guest, they demonstrate the devotees' respect and reverence and thereby bind the divinity to the temple. In the literature it is emphasized that the performance of the daily sequence is not stipulated by any need of the deity. It is conducted because it serves as the only medium for humans to demonstrate their reverence for the divine powers. By treating deities with respect, people hope to attract their benevolent presence. Any omission in the daily ritual sequence is dangerous, because disrespect could anger the divinity and provoke a withdrawal of the benevolent power from the temple, or worse induce divine punishment (Fuller 1984a: 14-17, Mearns 1995: 191-2, Good 1987: 7-8).

In the temples of Bhopal, the ritual routine is not organized with reference to any authoritative text.[9] People instead take recourse to a general cultural repertoire in order to fix the daily sequence. Special importance is given to the washing, decorating and anointing of the deities, as well as to feeding them. In the majority of temples a ritual is performed in which incense is burnt in front of the deity. It is explained as a means to awaken the spirit of the deity in the statue, and can be conducted in form of a *havan* (where the incense is burned in an immobile censer) or as *dhup arti* (where the bowl with the burning incense is waved in front of the deity). The ritual climax in every temple is the performance of *arti*, a ritual during which a camphor flame is waved in front of the deity's image. It is considered to be an absolute necessity, even in small shrines.

This basic outline is found in many variations. Two case studies will show how these general principles are translated into practice through a performance that is negotiated between many different actors. In order to understand the social logic through which the ritual routine is established, further discussions on the internal hierarchy of 'temple-society' will be required.

NEGOTIATING RITUALS IN THE KALI TEMPLE

Studies of Indian temples convey the impression that daily rituals have to be performed by Brahmin priests, the only persons allowed inside the sanctuary (Mearns 1995: 188, Good 1987: 5, Fuller 1984a). While this observation holds true for the Durga Temple, the situation is different in the Kali Temple. Here all the prescribed rituals—with the general exception of *arti*—are performed by volunteers, who do not work as priests and are rarely members of a Brahmin caste.

It is not difficult to find an explanation for the low importance given to (priestly) Brahmins at the Kali Temple. At the time of its construction, the Khatiks wanted to provide their goddess a new home. With Chacha, someone from the Khatik caste itself was found who could provide the necessary service to the goddess. He performed the daily services of the goddess representatively for all other caste members, and was chosen to conduct the rituals in accordance with established caste traditions. This form of ritual self-reliance is not uncommon in the

[9] This is different in the temples of Tamil Nadu where the rituals are based on the *agamas*. There too, in spite of their textual basis, variations in performance appear, not least because most priests are ignorant of the actual content of the texts (Fuller 1982, 1984a, 1984b, Presler 1987).

caste system of India. There are many low caste communities who have since long relied on ritual servants from their own ranks for priestly services, since Brahmins were and often are reluctant to work among them (see for example Vidyarthi 1960: 211-13).

What is more surprising is that in spite of Chacha's permanent presence in the temple, a Brahmin was employed for the performance of *arti*. This is only becomes comprehensible if one considers the process of sanskritization that has taken place among Khatiks. The effort to rise in caste status is apparent in the renaming of the caste, in some cases by replacing the name Khatik with that of 360 Gautriya Kshatriya Samaj, thereby suggesting a martial origin. Many individual members have supported this interpretation by adding the Kshatriya title, 'Singh', to their names. There is also evidence of the reform of caste practices according to Brahmanical ideals, like the banning of blood sacrifices and the discouragement of drinking, gambling and meat eating (Maljoniya 1984). Viewed in this context, the employment of a Brahmin priest can be interpreted as a means to help the caste rise in status and to also make the temple attractive to people of high status and high caste origin. However, the employment of a Brahmin has not always been smooth, since a number of Khatiks are discontented with a 'Brahmanized' ritual performance that ignores or violates what they consider to constitute the established ways of worshipping Kali.[10]

Aside from the controversy over the performance of *arti*, all tasks in the temple are conducted by voluntary helpers. The day starts at 5 a.m., when the temple is opened and cleaned. The goddess is then woken up, bathed and anointed. At 6 a.m. *dhup arti* is performed. *Arti* follows at 7 a.m. At 11 a.m. the goddess is fed and then left to rest from 12 noon to 3 p.m., a time during which the shrines are closed and the deities hidden behind a curtain. In the afternoon, *dhup arti* takes place at 6 p.m., and *arti* at 8 p.m. At 11 p.m. the goddess receives her evening meal and is allowed to sleep. The temple is cleaned and the remaining offerings are thrown into the lake, the form of disposal considered correct for sacred items. In the absence of a central authority, the *sevak*s have apportioned the ritual duties among themselves. This is a complicated task since a regular observance of all rituals is absolutely necessary. In order to guarantee the regularity of the services, a fixed routine has developed with the same persons conducting the same rituals every day. Once a *sevak* has taken over a task he is personally responsible for its regularity as well as its correctness.

*Sevak*s are proud if the responsibility for a ritual has been entrusted to them. The regular performance of an important ritual draws a performer closer to the deity and grants him privileged access to the divine

[10] Historically Kali used to be associated with groups that existed at the margin of Hindu society, such as low castes, adivasis, or dacoits.

power, and thus high status and authority among the devotees of the goddess. Therefore competition over ritual performances is high and often leads to internal friction. Consider, for example, the difficult situation that develops when a person fails to show up in time for his duty. Anyone else in the temple, even if acquainted with the ritual, would be reluctant to take over, since this would mean upsetting the internal hierarchy. Later he could be accused of depriving the appointed *sevak* of his chance to offer his services to the goddess and thereby deny him access to the deity. Such an accusation can lead to major fights, which might even cause people to leave the temple for good.

Besides fights, there are a number of other incidents that force the restructuring of the ritual organization. A person might be removed from his office because he is accused of incorrect performance. People also voluntarily leave because they lose interest, get involved in other activities, marry and move away, or fall ill. Each time a ritual servant leaves, positions have to be recast. It is during these moments of crisis that status negotiations become most apparent, because it is then that people have to decide who is reliable enough to be entrusted with the important duty, and lengthy debates about the advantages and disadvantages of different posting arrangements ensue.

The frequent changes of personnel and the wide variety of participants in the completion of the daily ritual routine—there are learned Brahmins, low caste workers, unemployed youths, businessmen and school boys—has an effect on the performance of rituals. In the absence of any authoritative source or text with instructions concerning the ritual performance, people learn their task by imitation and fall back on a cultural repertoire accessible to them by recourse to family and caste traditions. In discussions with *sevak*s in the Kali Temple about the necessary elements of rituals, ambivalences in their attitude became apparent. All shared the belief that a ritual is a stipulated act that has to be performed exactly in accordance with the tradition. Yet in practice they showed a remarkably relaxed attitude, allowing for great variations. All *sevak*s in the Kali Temple, for instance, were convinced that for every ritual there are a number of prescribed *mantra*s. However, almost all of them have to omit these *mantra*s, because they have not memorized them.

Consider another case. Mohan is a highly respected *sevak* in charge of the evening *dhup arti* in the Kali Temple. One day he was in a desperate search for a substitute. When he could not find anyone acquainted with the ritual, he asked Vijay—the workman in the temple—to take over. But Vijay refused, feeling too incompetent to shoulder such a responsibility. Mohan in turn was not ready to take no for an answer and insisted, encouraging Vijay by playing down the need for any expertise. 'Come on, you will be able to do it, it just involves moving around the vessels a little bit like this and that', he said, while demonstrating with his hands what he meant.

Confronted by the need to justify the incongruence between stated ideal and actual performance, ritual servants argued that for people with less knowledge any approximation to a given ritual ideal was good enough. The only absolute necessity was that the actor centred his concentration on the divine mother. *Sevak*s further qualified their statement by saying that if one had specialist knowledge—which at least among *sevak*s of the Kali Temple is considered a luxury—that was laudable, but if not, one had to manage without. This opinion, which favours the right attitude over minuscule regulations, leans on a popular understanding of *bhakti*, a form of worship that gives a core value to the devotee's surrender to the deity, his 'emotional "participation" with God' (Davis 1995a: 39).[11]

This ambiguity, inherent in the attitude towards rituals, is captured by Humphrey and Laidlaw in the paradox that a person is simultaneously the author and not the author of a ritual act. Humphrey and Laidlaw understand a ritual as a non-intentional act that is external to the author in the sense that it is prescribed by tradition and considered to have taken place only if the prescription has been followed. Nevertheless, the actor is considered to be a 'conscious and thinking self', an agent responsible for his concrete performance, because every performance calls for the interpretation of the prescriptions (Humphrey and Laidlaw 1994: 106). Likewise, Parkin points at the variance visible in every performance: 'In our fieldwork we never expect nowadays to see a ritual repeated in precisely the same manner, however much some of our informants may insist on standardization' (Parkin 1992: 19).

In the absence of an authoritative text, performances are rendered openly and ambiguously. There is not only the need in every performance to interpret the given rules anew, but every enactment of the ritual contains a recreation of the canon of essential rules.[12] Yet, in spite of this potential openness of the ritual process, the freedom of performance is limited, since it is subjected to public control and governed by a cultural repertoire. People do not accept just any performance as correct. They judge what they see in accordance with their past experiences. And only those who can convince others of doing the 'right thing' are tolerated as ritual performers in the temple.[13] It is in this sense that ritual action is structured, structure not meaning a timeless transcendent entity but 'simply the recurrent actions, or agencies, of other people' (Wrong 1999: 5).

[11] See also Eck 1991; Lorenzen 1995; Pande 1982; Thiel-Horstmann 1983; Werner 1993.

[12] See also Parkin 1992: 18-20.

In the Kali temple the structuring of ritual action appears democratic in the sense that any male person is potentially eligible to perform a ritual and anyone in the temple is allowed to voice comments and criticism. Yet, not everyone can expect to have the same influence on decisions. I have discussed the internal hierarchy that ranks visitors and trustees. Priests, ascetics and trustees are formally in a position of power and are most likely to be able to dictate terms. Yet, their actions are not beyond criticism, as the following incident shows.

In February 1996, Bagware, the president of the Kali Temple Trust, removed Om Prakash from the post of temple priest because he felt that his performance of *arti* was not satisfactory and that the irregularity in his attendance could not be accepted any more. Bagware searched for a more orthodox priest. But when he engaged a new priest he had to realize that the public in the temple did not accept the chosen person. A large group of women complained that the newcomer had a meek voice and could not sing the *arti* properly. Others protested that the new priest conducted *arti* in a way that was inappropriate for Kali. As a result, Bagware was forced to cancel the new employment and bring back the old priest.

Bagware, as temple president and employer, was not able to impose his policy. Nor was the priest, normally the highest authority in the temple, able to enforce his ritual ideals against the will of the devotees. Instead, a process of negotiation was set in motion during which the style of ritual performance as well as the apportioning of authority was subjected to debate. While this incident did not weaken Bagware's position, it showed the limits of his influence and proved that authority is an emergent quality that has to be brought about and proved in and through social action. Only those who are able to carefully balance the different interests and opinions are able to gain power and be acknowledged as having power.

Consider Foucault's stand that power must be seen as a relational concept, which is fluid and crystallizes only in moments of interaction in which people are ranked and their position of power acknowledged (Foucault 1998: 94-7). Butler states in response that power is a *Name* (Butler 1997: 57). It is the acknowledgement of someone as being powerful in the social discourse that creates his power by informing the thinking and action of people. It is through such acts of 'naming' that power is given and taken from people in the temple—like Jugnu the night-watchman or Bagware the temple president. They have become powerful through their association with positions considered to be invested with power. Yet to retain their authority, they have to constantly prove their worthiness of these positions in concrete interactions. Losing a fight means an undermining of position, especially when the memory of the fight is kept alive. In extreme cases this can lead to the removal of a person from office or the devaluation of a position that no longer appears to carry an aura of power. The fluidity of power and the need to prove it in action is heightened in the case of the Kali Temple, where positions and offices are only vaguely defined. The intersection of various conflicting hierarchies—a former 'untouchable' as manager and owner, the priest as employee, a leading ascetic who is too debilitated to speak for himself—opens the floor for verbal contests based on many different ideals of correct social and ritual behaviour.

By way of comparison to this very open and fluid situation in the Kali Temple, I will now investigate the case of the Durga Temple, where rituals are organized much more strictly along ideals of orthodoxy, with Brahmin priests in control. They are employed full time and conduct all important rituals. Worshippers and *sevaks* are not allowed inside the sanctuary and have to follow the priests' instructions. Yet, even in this setting there is considerable room for negotiations.

RITUAL LIFE IN THE DURGA TEMPLE

In the Durga Temple, the ritual routine is attended to by two groups of employed priests. The main shrine is served by the head priest—an illiterate Brahmin who in spite of his lack of education enjoys great authority and is addressed with the respectful title 'Maharaj'. Since Maharaj is too feeble to attend to the temple during the full opening hours, he has ordered one of his sons and a nephew—whom he has called from a village to live with him—to help out. When, in 1996, the temple was extended and new side shrines added for Hanuman, Shiva/Parvati, and Sita/Ram, a further group of priests was employed to serve the additional deities. The new employees, a father with his two adult sons, are orthodox Brahmins from Ujjain who look back on a long family tradition of priesthood. They attend to the Durga temple taking weekly turns.

A day in the Durga Temple begins at 5 a.m., when the temple is opened and the deities are washed and decorated. A small *havan* is performed in the main shrine, followed by the performance of *arti* at 6 a.m., observed simultaneously by two priests, one attending to Durga, the other to the deities in the side shrines. *Arti* is again performed at 9 a.m. At 11 a.m. the goddess is fed with food especially prepared for her by the wife of the main priest, and then left to rest between noon and 5 p.m. When the temple is opened again at 5 p.m., another *havan* is performed in front of the Durga statue. The next ritual is *arti* at 8 p.m. A final *arti* takes place at 10.45 p.m. just before the temple is cleaned and closed for the night.

This basic routine was established by Maharaj, who initially was alone in charge of the temple. Even though he was not a professional priest but a sweet vendor, he had been selected as a priest for the Durga Temple directly after its construction. This choice was a continuation of an older tradition, according to which the honour of serving the goddess in the temporary Durga shrine at Somvara built earlier during the nine days of Navratri always rested with just the same sweet vendor. After the construction of the permanent temple he left his business to his adult sons and became priest. Employed by the Temple Committee, Maharaj has been in charge of the temple ever since, with the exception of a two-year period in December 1983 following a fight between him and some worshippers, which led the temple committee to remove him, but subsequently call him back after bad experiences with his successor.

During all these years, Maharaj kept strict control on the Durga shrine, not allowing anyone outside his own family to serve the goddess. He also regulated the entry to the main sanctuary, reserved for priests. Occasionally devotees are called inside for the performance of special rituals during festival times. Maharaj also keeps a watch on other duties, calling upon *sevak*s if he feels that the service system of the temple does not function adequately. When, in 1996, Maharaj and his family members were joined by the new priests employed for the side shrines, a competition started to develop over authority as well as the finances of the temple: Maharaj claimed supremacy in his function as head priest and the employees in the side shrines insisted on their claims of a higher authority, due to their knowledge of the scriptures and their long family tradition as priests.

The temple committee solved the financial dimension of this fight through the employment of a manager. He was instructed to direct all donations to the committee, leaving the priests only with the income they were able to generate through ritual services for individual worshippers. Likewise, an informal division of labour seems to have emerged with regard to the question of ritual authority. The traditional priests leave the organization and direction of everyday rituals to Maharaj, whom they nevertheless openly denounce as ignorant about ritual. In turn, the priests from the side shrines are left to organize the special rituals on festive occasions, during which Maharaj takes a back seat.

In spite of this clear distribution of tasks there is considerable room for status negotiations and ritual variation, which becomes clear when the personal histories of the performing Brahmins are compared. There is Maharaj, the illiterate sweet-shop-owner turned priest, who started his career in the temporary Durga shrine of the Navratri festival. His knowledge of rituals is rather limited, drawn from a general cultural repertoire. He confines himself to the performance of a particular form of *arti*, the distribution of *prasad*, and the blessing of worshippers.

Maharaj is supported by his son Niresh, who rather reluctantly took over duties in the temple because he was pressurised by the whole family to help his feeble father but wants to leave the temple as soon as his father dies. At the moment he sees to the morning duties from 6 a.m. to 12 noon. His disinterest in temple matters shows in his performance. He only comes to the temple during fixed working hours, when he performs the bare minimum of tasks. His ritual knowledge is restricted to the ability to perform the *havan* and the *arti*.

The story is quite different with Ramesh, the nephew of Maharaj, called from the village to help in the temple. He now takes care of the afternoon routine. He shows great interest in his occupation as a priest. Initially he knew little of his duties as priest, as he openly admits. He learned by imitating others, and slowly started to attach himself to a number of respected priests in the city whose acquaintance he made in the temple and who have accepted him as a student, now teaching him the numerous tasks of a priest. Although he is the youngest in the temple, Ramesh is more versatile in ritual matters than his relatives.

In contrast to the rather unorthodox life stories of the three priests of the main shrine, the employees of the side shrines have received a traditional education as priests and are well versed in Sanskrit and the sacred texts. The father has worked his whole life as a priest, and has not only instructed his sons in religious matters, but also provided them with a university education. Having had a choice, the brothers decided to remain priests, because such an occupation promised a higher income. The younger of the two brothers is particularly respected by worshippers due to his exceptional knowledge of the scriptures and astrology, while the elder is praised for his great interest in decorating the deities and shrines.

There is no one standard biography for priests, or a standard way of performing rituals. Everyone engages in temple matters in his own way, depending on his own history, interests and knowledge. While the elder brother at the side shrine spends most of his time decorating the deities, he pays little attention to other rituals, performing just the bare minimum. In turn his younger brother spends most of his time in the temple reciting texts and advising people in matters of astrology. His father hardly ever talks to the worshippers, and is fully dedicated to concentrating on the deities. Maharaj, sitting at the main shrine, woos his religious customers, and extols his religious insights and his ability to mediate divine blessings. This way he makes sure that he generates a lot of attention and money with his presence. In contrast, his son behaves as discreetly as possible, wishing to finish his work as fast as possible. Ramesh, on the other hand, uses all his contacts with other priests and often skips his duties when he is called for private rituals elsewhere. This is why, lately, another relative, Ramvishal, has been summoned from the village. He has not yet fully adjusted to the temple duties, so he performs as well as he can by copying the others.

Even among this small number of performers, all Brahmins, we find a great variation in the way the ritual duties are perceived and exercised. And just as in the Kali Temple, the participants and other priests make extensive comments. Through this process each group of priests lays claim to superiority. The priests at the side shrines give their support to every worshipper who finds fault with Maharaj. They in turn are opposed by those who praise Maharaja's dedication to the goddess, claiming that the criticism of the priests from the side shrines is motivated by their envy for the better position in the temple.

Besides the question of ritual correctness, the competition between the two groups of priests also centres on money. Each one is trying to outdo the other in terms of income, and in their accusations about corrupt practices. In the ongoing process of proving one's worth as a ritual performer, questions of ritual correctness and closeness to the goddess are placed in relation to the money earned. Can a person be truly religious if he aggressively asserts his demands for payment? Should a priest's monthly income be fixed in relation to his ritual knowledge or by reference to his position in the temple? Are donations made to the goddess added to the income of the priests, or should they be handed over to the temple committee? These are important questions that influence the way the priests' work is evaluated, since a hunger for money seems to stand in the way of real dedication. Greed can only be judged in comparative terms. This became clear during the period when Maharaja was removed from the temple in 1983 for his bad temper and avarice. After only a year, he was recalled because the committee members realised that the new priest had turned out even less reliable and more corrupt.

To sum up, the terms in which ritual performances are evaluated may vary, placing more or less emphasis on the dedication of the performer, their ritual correctness, or the legitimacy of the officiate. As a result we find that rituals are an open process. They are established as an effective action through the communicative activity of performers, participants, audience and employers, who establish both the legitimacy of the performer and his performance. Any such evaluation has its validity only for the moment, and can be called into question with every new performance. It is a risky enterprise that can fail when it falls short of convincing the audience of its efficacy (Schieffelin 1996).

Yet even the rejection of a ritual is a complex social process. Not every criticism leads to the dismissal of the performance or the performer. Opponents have to show their credentials just as much as performers do, so that rejection becomes just as much an act of persuasion as the performance. In the temple of Bhopal it is the performer who is in the more powerful position. Calling ritual performances into question can endanger the whole working of a temple. Thus it is a far-reaching act that will only gain sympathy and have consequences when the case is strong. Normally criticism is part of the everyday life of a temple. It accompanies almost every performance and serves visitors to position themselves in a social field made up of different factions, while having little consequence for the ritual performances, which continue undisturbed by the critical voices. Before actively intervening in the ritual process, most visitors would prefer to avoid the rituals or attend a different temple, where they feel a greater sense of belonging.

Yet not every visitor is concerned with the way rituals are performed. Indeed a great number of people attend for anything but religious reasons. This becomes clear when, during the performance of stipulated rituals, small groups of friends leave to go to a nearby tea stall, returning only after the performance has finished and the temple is once again empty and quiet.

SOCIAL CONDUCT IN THE DIVINE ABODE

Beyond its strictly religious functions, the temple serves many other purposes. It is a meeting ground, an economic enterprise and a service centre, especially for strangers in the city. Yet even where people make use of the temple space without engaging in devotional activities, they are well aware of the deities' presence. It is on purpose that they have chosen the divine *darbar* as a place to turn to, since spending time in a temple is considered a blessed activity, no matter what their motivation.

In the close proximity to the divine, human relations are transformed, producing a distinct social atmosphere that is freed of a number of otherwise strictly enforced taboos. Take for example the way strangers meet. Their contact lacks the suspicion so characteristic of the initial meetings of people who do not know each other. In the temple they readily enter into what could be said to be very personal conversation. It hardly takes them any time to open up and talk about their problems. There is no other place that could be thought more appropriate to present one's personal anxieties and worries than the divine hall of audience. When people open their hearts here they do so in hope of help, either directly by the goddess or via another devotee in lieu of the goddess. And indeed, there are many stories of miraculous

[13] Schieffelin emphasizes that a ritual is not only interactive but also invested with the risk of failure. He demonstrates this aspect of the discursive nature of a ritual through the description of a spirit séance, during which one of the performers was thrown out of the arena because people did not accept his performance as 'real' (Schieffelin 1996; see also Kendall 1996).

interventions by the deity, who healed, helped with personal problems, gave support during exams, and cured psychological disorders.

The temple is also a safe place for women. Here they can rest from their duties and escape the constrictions of their homes without facing accusations of neglecting their work or leading an immoral life. In turn, meetings between men in a temple are respected because it offers a healthy atmosphere for social interaction, devoid of alcohol consumption. Even the relationship between different sexes is more relaxed, since they are not seen from their erotic angle, but are interpreted as the meeting of two devotees, a fact gladly taken advantage of by teenage lovers who have no other chance to meet.

However, in spite of the potential freedom, life in a temple is not without its rules. Just like ritual, any other activity is closely watched and scrutinized through an ongoing public discourse that judges which behaviour is appropriate in the presence of the divine. There are a few generally accepted rules that are strictly implemented in practically every temple. Shoes have to be taken off, the drinking of alcohol and the eating of meat is prohibited,[14] entry in the sanctuary is only allowed for ritual specialists, and the polluting presence of women during their menses is forbidden. The list of such fixed rules is, however, short. Mostly regulations are the result instead of a process of negotiation in which the character of a particular temple is established in accordance with the image created for the residing deities. But the variety of visitors in any temple is great, and their ideas of appropriate conduct manifold, so that an agreement is not easily reached, and indeed most of the time the question of what is right or wrong behaviour remains unresolved:

Example 1

A voluntary worker gave a large quantity of best quality coconut as *prasad* to one of the regular worshippers, for which she was criticized by the night-watchman. It led to the following exchange:

Voluntary worker:	*But he is a good man!*
Night-watchman:	*Does that mean you can give him more and someone else less? Everyone should be treated equal!*
Voluntary worker:	*But I did not give less to anyone!*
Night-watchman:	*Still it is wrong!*

[14] Except for those temples in which alcohol and meat are offered in sacrifice and then consumed as *prasad*.

Example 2

It was the day after Navratri; the ashes from the *havan* were still warm. Two women packed some of the sacred ashes in order to take them home. This provoked the criticism of one of the respected *sevaks* who forbade them to take any of the ashes. Ignoring the order, the women wrapped up their packets quickly and said to no-one in particular: *There is nothing wrong in taking the ashes. We do that every year. We use the ashes for the havan at home whenever there are problems.* One of the permanent visitors to the temple from the Khatik caste replied angrily: *How dare you go to the ashes, even we as members of the temple are not allowed to take them. I should know. I have been here since ten to twelve years!* Little impressed, one of the women countered: *I am coming here for sixteen years!*

Both these examples show how tricky it is to come to a solution about correct behaviour where there are many different interests involved. In none of the cases was a final solution found or attempted. Everyone retained their own opinion, having good reasons to claim superiority over the other person. The case is different when there is a clear authority gap between people. In the Kali Temple, Chacha can give any order without being contradicted. Once someone dared to overstep this unwritten law, it led to a major crisis in the temple and to severe recriminations against the accused. In the Durga Temple, Maharaj holds the position of the main authority, strictly enforcing his ideas of correct religious conduct. Yet this does not curtail the freedom to negotiate in all cases, since often the religious authorities confine their intervention to cases that they feel are directly related to the honour of the deity.

Just as in the case of ritual performances, judgements on behaviour in the temple are open, inviting many to intervene, but rarely leading to a final conclusion. The question of correct behaviour is invested with great urgency, as no one wants to insult a divine actor. However, on turning to the domain of social action most rules of conduct appear to be vague enough to leave plenty of space for interpretation, so that almost any behaviour can be rendered appropriate if the reasoning is persuasive enough.

Fighting over correct conduct seems less a matter of strictly avoiding abusive behaviour, than a form of negotiating power relations. Claiming closeness to the goddess or religious knowledge invests people with the power to command and elevates them to a position of authority. Thereby even people who completely lack recognition outside the temple society—because they are beggars, of a low caste origin, or young women—may be invested with power in the limited space of the temple. Thus, in the presence of the divine, social relations are not only transformed because they are subject to different rules of interaction and valued in reference to the divine presence, but also because relations of dominance and subordination are evaluated in different terms, whereby the status outside the temple society only makes up part of the recognition a person receives.

CONCLUSION

I have argued in this chapter that the temple as a sacred place is set apart from its urban environment through the belief in the transformative powers of the deities.This has implications for interpersonal interaction. Efforts to organize the temple as a social space and a ritual domain involve complex negotiations in which the images of the divine reign supreme. Those who can claim the greatest closeness to the goddess wield maximum authority and are therefore most effective in influencing behaviour. Power in the temple is thus derived from divine authority which is borrowed by social actors and mirrored in the authority-structure that prevails in the temple.

True, the organization of temple life does not take place in isolation from its environment. The limits of negotiability of rules and status positions are set by a cultural repertoire that consists of transmitted, adjusted and re-interpreted traditions that define the domain of the religious and the role of different actors within this field. It is shaped through pre-conceived and constantly adjusted notions about the nature of divine actors and their interaction with and relations to human beings. It is only with reference to such shared conceptions that an actor can claim and establish the legitimacy of his position and his opinions.

In the case of a temple, reference to status as a Brahmin, the ability to act as a 'medium', and the display of special devotion and an ascetic lifestyle are particularly effective for gaining religious status. Parallel to this, ritual efficacy can be established through a performance that appears to follow orthodox rules or by presenting a convincing display of devotion. In this sense every ritual performance addressed two sets of audiences. It is meant to serve the deities and ensure their benevolent presence in the temple, and it is directed at the human world, in which the reality and validity of the ritual acts is established through a communicative process of believers. Thus, rather than being only symbolic, ritual is an effective action that secures the presence of the divine and ranks human beings by placing them in a field of shared communications.

Tambiah, quoting Austin, calls rituals performative in the sense that saying something is also doing something (Tambiah 1979: 119). The ritual communication evokes and effects divine presence and thereby transforms social reality. In the temple the life situation of worshippers is effectively changed, when they experience that their wishes have been fulfilled by the deity. The ritual also affects the ranking of people, which may vary social hierarchies relevant for social interactions outside the temple. A person considered a beggar in the economic world may well be an authority and respected *sevak* in a temple. Conversely, in a temple even the most influential of politicians is forced to show respect to the priest and bow before the goddess. In the temple all human relations are viewed with reference to the divine, however indirect. Being in the divine *darbar* has a special value, because it represents a form of worship and bestows divine blessings on all present.

In order to retain this transformative power of the place, the benevolent presence of the deity has to be ensured, through 'correct' ritual observance and the 'right' conduct showing respect for the deity. What this means can only be determined through social communications that connect performers and audiences, committee members and attending worshippers and integrated them into a field of shared activity. Through their assent and negotiated consensus the particular 'culture' of a temple is created and the relevant activities of believers established as 'correct' and 'effective'. However, the agreement is never final. There always remain ambiguities and differences of opinion forcing the re-negotiation of temple rules, thus supporting a process of constant change, however minor. This means that even though rituals have the aura of highly formalized and standardized acts that resist change, the actual practices show variation, especially when a great number of performers is involved (see also Rao 2000).

As a field for the re-framing of relations, the temple also intersects with many other institutions of the city and contributes to their shaping. The relation between the temple and the polity of the city was the theme of Chapter 2, where the way the temple supports the formation of trans-local communities has been discussed. The next chapter will take a closer look at individual politicians and the way they assert their political position by establishing and advertising their relationship to the temple and its deities.

CHAPTER 4

Temples, Leaders, and Religious Politics

The temple, besides being a place of daily worship, provides a central location for the celebration of religious festivals. On such days it attracts large number of devotees from all over the city who join the regular worshippers in a display of devotion. During such times the function of the temple as a 'stage' for political actors becomes particularly apparent. Young ambitious leaders appear alongside well-known politicians and members of the temple committee in highly visible places to preside over the religious activities, adding to the attraction and power of the celebrations and advertising their importance to the community.

Again the focus will be on the intersection between religious devotion and political activity with a discussion of the way representatives of power relate to the temple in their public activities. Since the involvement of leaders in the religious domain often triggers controversial debates about the legitimacy of the entry of party politics into the non-secular, the analysis of three religious events will be followed by an inquiry into the way the distinction between politics and religion is reflected in contemporary social discourses. This will bring to light the ambivalence at the basis of judgements on politico-religious activities, which on the one hand appear inseparable from each other because even leaders should be allowed to practice their religion, and because religious activities always include a display of power. Yet with the foundation of a secular nation state, on the other hand, the need to clearly segregate the political from the religious domain has become a widely accepted ideal.

Approaching the theme from the perspective of different social actors, this chapter will focus on the involvement of leaders in public religious activities and how their presence during religious performances is motivated, how it is justified and how different participants perceive it. From the analysis emerges a picture of the complex and often contradictory ways that issues with both a religious and a political dimension are separated or amalgamated.

THE STAGING OF SOCIAL RELATIONS DURING FESTIVALS

Navratri
Re-establishing Local Hierarchies

Navratri is among the most popular festivals celebrated at the Durga Temple. During the nine-day period, the temple is packed with people, with peak attendance being reached during the evening hours of the ninth day. At this time the fire sacrifice (*havan*) is observed, thus bringing the festival to an end. By choosing the early evening hours for the *havan*,[1] maximum public attention is guaranteed.

During the sacrifice, ordinary people are prohibited from entering the temple. The hall of divine audience is richly decorated and turned into an extended sanctuary, while a fire is set up on the street before the temple, separated by a barrier from the surrounding area from which the public watches the *havan*, performs individual *puja*, or takes *darshan*. As the temple boundaries have temporarily been extended. The whole crossing is turned into a religious site. The three sections of this temporarily re-defined religious territory also bear a political significance. The gaze of the audience is directed towards three different areas of socio-religious activity: (1) In front of the temple where the sacrifice is offered, (2) between the fire and the inner area of the temple, where the priests who lead the sacrifice are seated, and (3) inside the temple, where the organizers are busy ensuring that the various activities run smoothly.

The division of the foreground into three different 'stages' highlights three important social dimensions of the festival. First, there is the fire, the 'front stage', at which some twenty odd men offer the sacrifice. Those who volunteer to participate in this auspicious exercise are usually young or middle-aged men who are strongly motivated by their devotion to the goddess and/or their wish to be seen performing an important religious ritual before a large public. They are often recognized by the audience, for most of them have a certain prominence in the locality as businessmen, minor leaders, or regular visitors to the temple, which also gives them the authority to take a seat near the fire without being contested. The 'centre stage' hosts the temple priests alongside other religious authorities of the city, who jointly lead the sacrifice. They are given the most prominent place, where they display their

[1] This timing differs from that in most other temples, where the sacrifice is performed late at night or during the early morning hours, when most of the devotees have already left the temple.

expertise in religious matters, their central importance for the occasion, and their ranking according to their prominence in the city and their status as experts of Sanskritic rituals. Finally, there is the 'back stage', comprising the inner temple where the organizers are occupied with the smooth running of the festival. Their presence advertises the quality of the work done by the temple committee, which takes the credit for bringing about this grand and auspicious event.

Besides these main groups of actors, there are those who manage to make their way into the inner circle by asking the organizers for admission. Throughout the festival one can observe the ongoing negotiations on who may be permitted inside and who not. Many try, but only a small number of favoured persons actually manage to enter. First and foremost close acquaintances of the organizers will be called inside. They are given a particularly cordial welcome when their

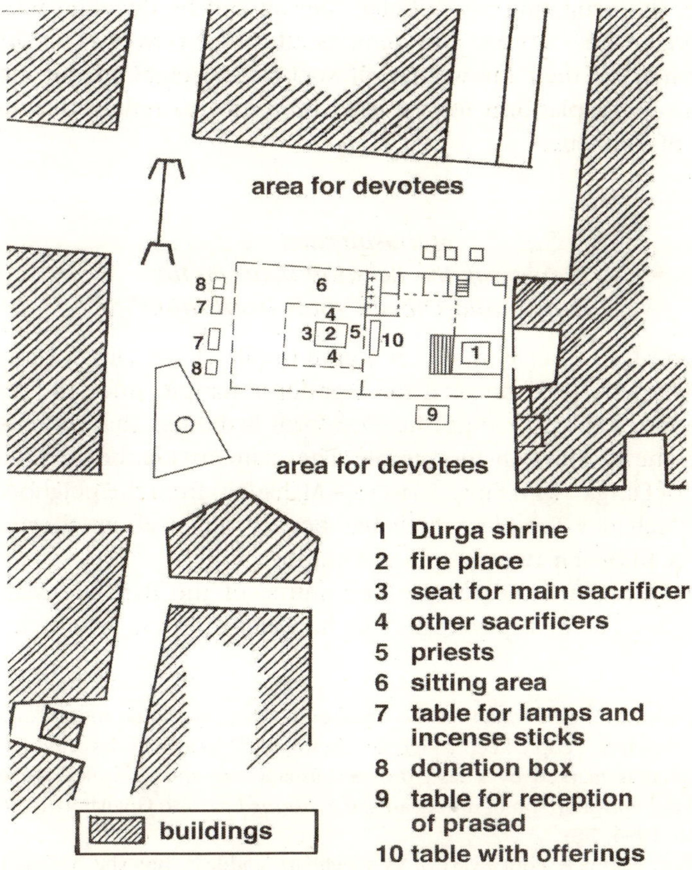

Setting at Pir Gate during the Navratri celebration

presence is likely to increase the prestige of those inside, as is the case with famous politicians, rich business men, well-wishers of the temple, or a foreign anthropologist. Second, worshippers with particularly pressing concerns are permitted inside, such as those who tell of a particular tragedy that requires divine attention. Finally, there is a small group of people who manage to force their way in by stubborn insistence.

The elaborate negotiations on who takes which position shows that the festival is concerned with more than the performance of a fire sacrifice. No doubt, the sacrifice is the main attraction, a transformative agent that loads time and territory with a religious meaning, thereby facilitating the realization of many different ambitions. People come together because attending a *havan* is an auspicious activity that simultaneously is entertaining. In this atmosphere, special favours can be requested, personal devotion displayed, and social relations renewed and advertised to the goddess, organizing committee, and wider urban audience. By facilitating a sacrificial offering and by deciding who sits where, organizers exercise and demonstrate their power. Their actions are informed by their knowledge of social hierarchies in the locality, and thus offer a platform for various authorities to renew their social position of eminence.

Mahashivratri
Renewing the Relation between the Temple and Other Urban Institutions

The second festival celebrated on a grand scale at the Durga Temple is Mahashivratri.[2] This is unusual for a goddess temple since the festival is in honour of Shiva. One justification for it is the fact that there is also a side shrine to Shiva in the temple. The main reason, however, is the marriage of Durga[3] with Shiva (Barevale Mahadev) from the neighbouring Barevale Mahadev Temple, which has been brought about through an agreement between two temple committees.

On Mahashivratri, the temple committee of the Barevale Mahadev Temple goes out in a procession in honour of Shiva, which through

[2] Mahashivratri is celebrated on the fourteenth day of the lunar month of Magha (January/February). People keep a vigil during the night before in devotion to Shiva. The day itself is marked by a fast, the performance of special rituals honouring Shiva, and the consumption of intoxicants, e.g. *bhang* (see also Gnanambal 1967: 19-20; Thomas 1984: 7-8).

[3] Durga is normally conceived of as a celibate goddess, but she has also been variously identified as the wife of Shiva, a tendency that seems to be on the increase (Kinsley 1986: 95; Masilamani-Meyer and Vogelsanger 1993: 113, 116).

the kinship that has been established between the two communities has taken on the additional meaning of a marriage procession (*barat*). After the knot between the deities has been tied, the reception of the bridegroom at Pir Gate every year is a must. It constitutes the annual renewal of the relationship between the two marriage parties. In fact, the reception of the Mahashivratri procession at Somvara now constitutes the climax of the celebration, since the Durga Temple has become the destination of the procession. A short description of the festivity at Somvara may bring to light the political and economic implications of this yearly celebration.

During the festival the Durga Temple is closed to the public by noon, when the committee members and their helpers give a final touch to the temple's decorations and make the required preparations for the feast. By afternoon, the statues of Durga and Shiva look resplendent in completely new attire. A red carpet is laid out in front of the temple leading to the prayer hall, the ground of which is completely covered with flowers, ready to receive the bridegroom. Cushions are provided inside the temple on the right, facing the Shiva shrine, for all those who accompany Barevale Mahadev in his marriage procession.

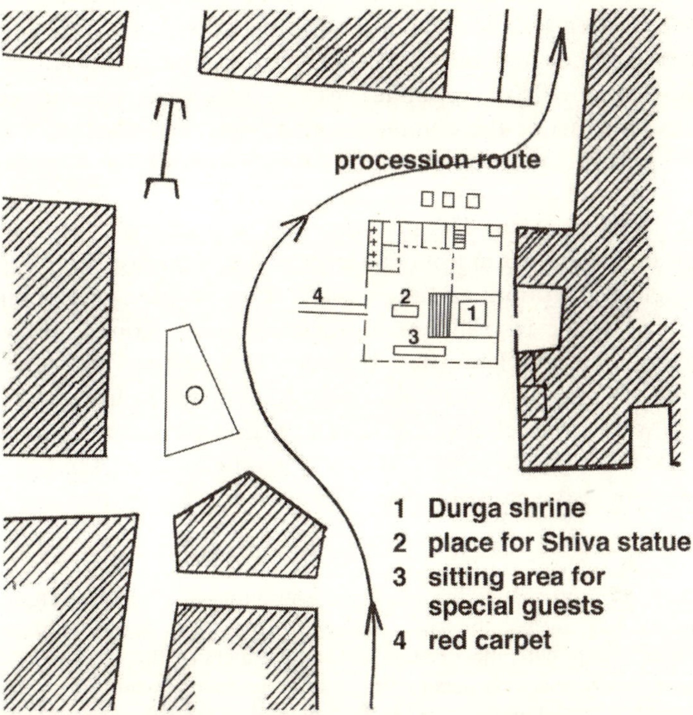

Mahashivratri procession route at Pir Gate

The number of helpers steadily increases while preparations are being made in the temple, including not only committee members but also young men from the neighbourhood, local dignitaries and businessmen. At about 4 p.m., they all stand prominently at the entrance of the temple to receive the guests. Meanwhile they take turns to announce the programme over a microphone and welcome the public on the occasion of Mahashivratri. Slowly the crossing, now blocked to cars, fills with people, while groups of dancing *hijras* (eunuchs) arrive to herald the procession. The excitement reaches its peak when finally the procession arrives. The statue of Barevale Mahadev enters the temple and is placed facing the goddess on the untouched flower carpet. The temple—which until then was almost empty—is suddenly thronging with people. All of the arriving VIPs receive a red vermilion sign (*tika*) on their forehead; they are greeted as honoured guests, are shown to their seats, and given *prasad*.

Meanwhile the members of the Durga Temple perform *puja* in front of the Barevale Mahadev statue, which is started by the temple priests and followed by the various committee members, and finally by others prominent in the temple. Then the ritual of *arti* (waving of a camphor flame) is performed in front of both deities. Again, the camphor flame is first waved by the priests, then by various committee members, and finally by other temple helpers and attendants. After these rituals the statue of Barevale Mahadev is again taken out, the guests leave, and the temple is opened to the public. Visitors than approach the shrines to perform *puja*, while the committee members, tired after the long hours of preparation and drunk from *bhang*—which is distributed on Mahashivratri as *prasad*—go home and sleep.

Like Navratri, Mahashivratri serves as a platform for local leaders when they can appear in front of a large public, advertise their importance and religious devotion, and re-establish their position of eminence. But more than other festivals, Mahashivratri is also concerned with the enactment of the relationship between this temple and other Hindu institutions in the city. Most obviously and conspicuously, the reception is a renewal of the relationship between the two temple committees as bride givers and bride receivers. This is significant since the two temples are the only large and important Hindu temples in the city centre.[4]

[4] This is about to change through the construction of a large Ram Temple at the heart of the old city. For the sake of this construction some leading businessmen have joined hands with the prominent Hindu leaders of the city, with the aim of creating a temple that will become the leading religious institution in the city. But there is still a lot of work left for the completion of the religious site, which, depending on finances, might take a few years. Only after the construction has finished and the temple has started to operate will it be possible to estimate how

Their respective committees consist of local businessmen, some of them from the leading business houses of the city. Through the marriage of Barevale Mahadev and Durga they have entered a relationship of mutual obligations that is typical of all marriages in India. It is a relationship of givers and takers that can never be dissolved and has also significance outside the festival period.

Dominated by members of the Agrawal caste who hold a large share of the city's jewellery trade, the Barevale Mahadev temple committee consists of some of the richest and most influential families in the city. For them the marriage means an extension of influence, for they are bride receivers and free to ask any favour from the bride givers. However, as a result they have also accepted new obligations; the receipt of a bride and the gifts accompanying her force them into obligatory reciprocity, in the classical Maussian sense. In this manner, the supporters of the Durga Temple, who are mostly smaller businessmen from the locality around Pir Gate crossing, have ensured themselves the patronage of business houses otherwise inaccessible to them. The yearly re-enactment of Shiva's marriage with Durga demonstrates the relationship of mutual dependence and creates the stage on which this relationship is celebrated and thus remembered, renewed and publicly announced.

There is a second important point to be noted in the set-up of the celebration. Since the Mahashivratri procession is the only one of its kind in the city, its organization is supported by the leading Hindu institutions in Bhopal, foremost amongst them the Hindu Festival Committee (Hindu Utsav Committee). This committee has some 300 members, among them most of the important Hindu leaders of the city. As a result of the help extended by this institution, its outstanding representatives are invited to join the Barevale Mahadev marriage procession. Although these leaders are invited as members of the Hindu Festival Committee, people are well aware of their functions as party leaders, parliamentarians, or as heads of Hindu nationalist organizations. Their prominence at the Temple during religious festivals creates an association between the Durga Temple and the political Hindu institutions. The things that are kept separate during the organization become mixed in the audience's reception of the event, when they make associations between the different fields of activities leaders are involved in. By affirming and renewing political and economic relationships through a religious celebration, Mahashivratri constitutes one of the major occasions on which the intersections of various fields of activity become visible.

---

the new religious place will change the power equations between the important religious institutions in Bhopal, especially in the old town.

Jagarans
The Staging of Leadership during Religious Celebrations

The word *jagaran* (literally: hold a vigil) refers to religious functions held at night, often in the form of collective singing.[5] In this section I intend to describe one specific form of *jagaran*, namely a performance of devotional songs by professional or semi-professional artists. While such *jagarans* can be organized anywhere and at any time, people usually prefer to stage them next to a temple on the occasion of a festival, which usually ensures them a particularly large audience. *Jagarans* are put on once or twice a year in all the larger temples of Bhopal. Yet, there is no other temple in the city that attracts so many of these overnight programmes as the Durga Temple.

Jagarans are usually organized by ambitious leaders who hope to increase their social prominence. In most cases, they are not members of the temple committee, but they will nevertheless integrate the representatives of the temple into their programme. In this way they establish a relationship of reciprocity, whereby a local leader increases the fame of the temple through a popular programme, also using the temple as a 'stage' to build up his constituency.

The *jagarans* follow a set pattern. During early evening the stage is prepared and decorated. This includes construction of a shrine, displaying pictures of the people who are to be commemorated, and hanging up banners announcing the various performers. From time to time loudspeaker announcements are made to advertise the program. It starts upon the arrival of the artists at around 10 p.m. with a *puja*, in front of the provisional shrine, first by the organisers and then by the artists. Then the special guests, seated at a highly visible place, are officially greeted. After that the committee members honour the artists, then each other, and finally those who helped with the preparations or those who simply stand out and can be spotted in the audience. They always made sure not to miss me, for instance, thus boosting their importance by demonstrating their 'foreign connection'. After these mutual honours, the performance of devotional songs begins. It lasts till the early morning.

For every programme a group of prominent guests is called to preside. Persons of high status are preferred. Usually prominent politicians are recruited for this purpose, in rare cases bureaucrats or religious leaders also. There is no certainty as to when exactly the guests will arrive, as they often delay their arrival in order to demonstrate their importance. Above all, the chief guest will make sure he comes

[5] For detailed descriptions of such vigils see Erndl 1993: 84-104; Thiel-Horstmann 1985.

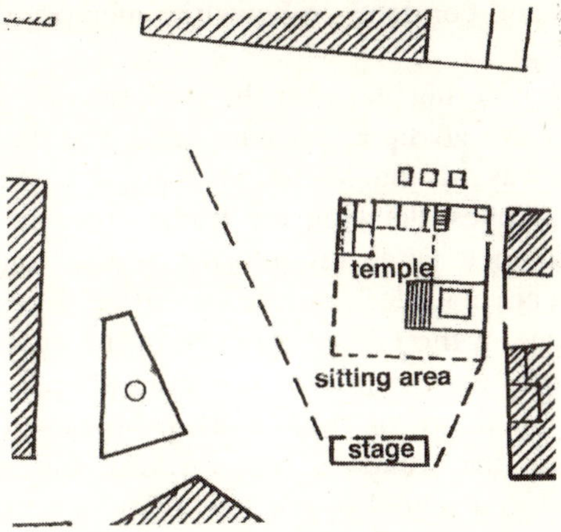

Setting at Pir Gate during a *jagaran*

last and leaves first. But no matter when an honoured guest arrives, he is instantly greeted and asked to perform a *puja* on the stage. After this he is invited to take a seat on the stage, though most leaders will not stay long. The duration of their stay is usually inversely proportional to their importance.

Jagarans are—just like the two other celebrations I have described—religious events that provide extensive room for the symbolic enactment of social relations. However, they are different from the occasions described above inasmuch as they are not supported by the temple committee, but instead offer people from outside a unique chance to use the temple as the backdrop for their own 'show'. By organizing a *jagaran* a person can popularize his name in the area without necessarily making a long-term commitment to the neighbourhood. He becomes known and accessible and simultaneously earns gratitude for providing people with a chance for devotion, an entertaining programme, and an occasion to meet their political re-presentatives. The organizers are further able to strengthen their connection to important politicians. The physical presence of important leaders serves to demonstrate the organizers' connection to them, and provides them with a chance to informally approach a politician in personal matters.

LEADERS AND THEIR AUDIENCE

To elucidate the enhancement of the personal and professional status of political leaders through their involvement in religious celebrations, I have presented three popular and also typical events. There are other occasions—like the welcoming of processions, the organization of public meals (*bhandara*) or invitations to devotional singing (*bhajans*)—that are used to make public statements about one's religiosity and social importance. This function is served only if the audience recognizes the persons involves and constantly renews the memory of their presence on stage.

And in fact, both during and after the performance, one finds people engaging in extensive gossip about who organized the event, who was present and who was missing. My inquiries about those involved always received patient replies, detailing the leaders present by their names, standing and influence. Often my informants also volunteered to take me to the respective leader's house or office. I realized that such detailed knowledge of the power network in the city and the position of individual leaders are essential to common people, who depend on leaders for solving many of their daily problems. Connections are always essential if one wants to rent a house, buy a plot, get one's children admitted to a school of good reputation, borrow money from a bank, access a government scheme, improve the water and electricity supply in their neighbourhood or find a job. In order to establish such connections and to know whom to approach for which task, people have to keep track of influential persons. By closely watching leaders during public performances they gain valuable information. Becoming oneself a member of a temple committee or a group that organizes a religious event helps establish connections.

The public display of personalities at the temple, therefore, serves both the public and the leaders, because it provides an occasion on which people see their leaders, talk about their achievements and bring up to date their knowledge about them. The leaders on the other hand increase their popularity and rise in importance with every successful performance—successful when seen from the angle of the audience. The temple is particularly suited to such types of activities, since religious programmes enjoy high prestige and popularity and thus draw large numbers of the urban public.

Interconnections between religion and politics are viewed with great suspicion when they pertain to the democratic institutions of the state. Many people feel that ideally religion should be free of power contests, although they also admit that religious organizations are in practice never free of competition, envy and tricks that people play on each other. There seems to be little hope for changing that. Yet, when religion enters state politics it threatens to destroy the secular setup of the political order. Yet, there is also opposition to the idea that India needs a secular state. In debates about an ideal political order for India opinions oscillate between constructing religion and politics as separate or overlapping domains.

Before entering into a more detailed debate about people's reflections on the legitimacy of religious politics, I would like to introduce the reader to another example of how religious devotion is a means to political advancement. It focuses on the inseparability of religious and political aspects in the life and bearing of some leaders. For this I will consider the role the temple played for the entry of two young men into politics.

RELIGION AS POLITICS IN THE CAREER OF LEADERS

Manish is a man of approximately 23 years who decided to become a leader some four years ago. Asked about how he started his career as a public person, he replied that he used to hang around the temple, where he got involved in the preparation of festivals. He felt encouraged by the public attention these occasions generated, started to take a prominent position addressing the public over the microphone, and thus slowly got used to taking a leading role. In the four years since, he has become a member of the BJP, attached himself to important leaders, and founded his own youth organization the Nav Yuvak Adhikar Manch (Forum for Young People's Rights) of which he is president and which he likes to portray as the youth wing of the BJP—which officially it is not.

He has retained Pir Gate as the centre of his political involvement, making himself known in the locality and keeping informed about ongoing events by paying regular visits to different shop owners, by resting for a chat at different tea shops, by holding informal meetings with members of his youth group, and by maintaining cordial relations with all those in power in the temple. This last aspect is of particular importance considering the influence the temple has on the power structure of the locality.

There are a number of people who have demonstrated that the Durga Temple can provide a good entry into politics. The president and the secretary of the temple committee were nominated in local elections as a result of their popularity in the area, which was based on the key role they played in realizing the temple. The son of the main temple priest even managed to get himself elected into the Municipal Co-operation thanks to the reputation his family has as brave fighters for the Hindu cause in general. At times Manish and his friends also discuss the benefits of a temple presidency for a political career. Everyone knows that being in charge of an influential temple gives you a lot of publicity. You are well known in the locality, and you can associate yourself with political heavyweights and make them do your work.

Even without any formal association, Manish leans heavily on the temple for publicity. He can hardly be seen in the temple on normal days, but he is there as soon as any important event takes place. There is no major festival in which he does not appear in the forefront. He also takes credit for the construction of the water tank adjoining the temple and he organizes his own *jagarans* and *bhandaras*. In order to use and retain the Durga Temple as a platform he maintains cordial relations with those who wield power in the locality, particularly the committee members, the priests, and the most important donors. Yet while Manish fosters his good relations at Pir Gate, he also makes sure to keep an appropriate distance from the temple authorities, because he wants to be remembered as an independent person and a political actor in his own right. By overstating his respect for others, people might either accuse him of hypocrisy or believe him to be nothing more than an errand boy (*chamcha*). It is the right balance that counts.

So far Manish is only a leader of minor stature, and there is still a long way for him to go. He will have to build relationships all over the city or even the state and prove that he is able to get things done. The temple is just a stepping-stone. But as such it has been important in providing the initial platform for him to start.

Shastri, a young unmarried Brahmin in his mid-thirties, started out in a quite different way. He was born in a farmer's family in a village, but left his parents to become a priest. He studied in different institutions and now has a command of Sanskrit, as well as knowledge of the Hindu scriptures and ritual procedures. On coming to Bhopal, Shastri worked in a number of temples. His last regular employment was in the Birla Temple—one of the major temples in Bhopal. But due to a dispute with the manager, he resigned in 1993. By that time he was already well established in Bhopal and could continue to work as a free-lance priest. In this function he also tried successfully to get employed for the major ritual events in the city. Such occasions offer publicity and direct access to influential politicians. As Shastri's political ambitions grew, he decided that only a relationship with the most powerful person in the city, the Chief Minister himself, would do. Whenever I asked people how it was possible for a relatively young and unimportant priest to approach the Chief Minister, they replied that no-one can refuse a priest. People assumed that he must have conducted a ritual in the Chief Minister's house, read from his hand, or made some predictions about his future, so that the politician was indebted to him.

Shastri's relationship to the Chief Minister bore fruit when he was nominated as a member of the Expert Committee for the Development and Upkeep of Temples in Madhya Pradesh (Dharmik Sthal Prabandhan Samiti, popularly known as the MP Temple Committee), formed by the Chief Minister in 1995. The committee works under the State Department for Religious Institutions and Endowments to make suggestions for the formulation of new legislation pertaining to the management of temples, to examine the payment and educational level of priests, and to work out a plan for the development and repair of (historical) religious institutions. Initially the committee was given a one-year term, since then regularly extended, and has an increasing number of members. So far, the committee has been unable to produce any results. But this hardly surprises anyone because such committees are popularly regarded as a means of patronage rather than a forum for serious work.

For Shastri, membership in the committee has proven to be highly useful. Through membership in it he could now tour the whole state at government expense, present himself as representative of a State Department, approach local authorities in this function, and extend patronage to temples all over. In this way he has built a body of followers which he hopes will ultimately get him nominated for state elections.[6]

Both cases demonstrate how an association with a temple is used by ambitious men to make it into politics. True, religious engagement is no guarantee of success, or a necessary precondition. Rhetorical skills, money, family background, titles, good relations, popularity, power in the party, all these are means for making progress in a political career, and usually only a combination will suffice. But an involvement in religious matters can be of great help in building up popularity, or to formulate it more radically, no leader who wants to scale the political hierarchy can completely ignore religious matters. Every day newspapers in India report on the appearance of politicians at public religious functions, or the involvement of a godman in party activities. According to a secular ideal this appears as an illegitimate crossover, a mixing of two domains which should be kept separate. However, there is a significant difference between the theoretical formulation of secularism and the judging of actual politico-religious activities that take place in the locality. While the former allows for easy dichotomies, the latter involves people in complicated judgements that have to deal with the inseparability of different aspects of social life in practice.

IDEALS OF SECULARISM

Independent India was designed as a secular state. The word 'secular' was added to the Constitution in 1976, when Indira Gandhi, in view of the increasing religious tension, had the term included in the Preamble (44th Amendment, 1976; Béteille 1994: 560). But the Constitution can only set the framework through which the relationship between politics and religion is defined. It cannot actually establish the details of this relationship. Secularism, Béteille (1994) has rightly pointed out, can have many meanings.

In one version, religion is seen as a private affair that should be completely divorced from politics. This formulation leans on a Western

[6] Because of his connection with the current Chief Minister, his involvement has been with the Congress Party. This will be a disadvantage if he is given the chance to contest elections in any one of the constituencies in or near Bhopal, in all of which the majority of voters tend towards the BJP. Furthermore, Shastri's patronage is usually connected to temples and extended to people associated with temples. Such people often, though not always, believe in the need of governmental support for the development of religion and religious institutions, and thus prefer the BJP.

understanding of the term, implying the separation of state and church. It is translated into the Indian context to mean a strict separation between religion and politics. This separation is to be accomplished through the increased secularization of society. Understood in this manner, secularization is said to be facilitated through education that will make religion a private matter or, in the Marxist version, lead to its extinction (Bhargava 1994, 1998; Chakrabarty, B. 1990; Desai 1984a, 1984b, Karna 1993; Nauriya 1989; Saberwal 1981; Shah 1981; Sheth 1991; Vanaik 1997; Verma 1985).

A second, competing notion is expressed by the formula *sarva dharma sambhava*.[7] It is used to communicate the need for a policy that treats all religions equally. People who support this idea are of the opinion that it is impossible in a country like India, with such a deeply religious population, to keep religion out of politics. Politics, they say, should in fact intervene in religious matters to arbitrate conflicts between different communities and to reform 'backward' religious practices. But it has to be assured that all religions are treated equally (Chakrabarty, B. 1990).

There is a third position, which gives secularism a substantially different meaning (Madan 1987; Nandy 1985). The idea is that religion understood as *dharma* (moral order, which is said to transcend any concrete religion like Hinduism, Islam, Christianity, etc.) should inform politics. Ashis Nandy (1985, 1990, 1993) is the most prominent representative of this position.[8] He argues that the modernization of Indian society begun under British influence destroyed religion as a way of life, 'a tradition which is definitionally non-monolithic and operationally plural' (Nandy 1990: 70). Religion, he says, has been reduced to a mere ideology, used as an identifier of groups, and manipulated by a rationalistic elite to pursue its political and economic interests. As such it is not only unsuited to politics, but dangerous, since it is religion as ideology that has brought communalism to India. What is needed in contemporary Indian politics is a re-establishment of a traditional religion of tolerance, which, according to Nandy's assessment, is still alive among the majority of people. Informed by religiously grounded forms of tolerance, a new society will emerge in which different rationalities and loyalties will find their place. Such loyalties would not have to be kept outside of politics, but instead should help stimulate a dialogue of opinions. In this dialogue the difference between religion and politics is dissolved. Politics is encompassed by religion (also Madan 1987, 1991, 1994, 1997; Miller 1987).

Each of these positions has received extensive criticism, of which

[7] Which means equal rights for all religions.

[8] See also Madan, 1987; Miller 1987.

one important angle is the question of their relation to actual life situations and their applicability in real politics. A major flaw in the first argument is that it fails to notice that it is impossible in everyday politics to fully divorce religious from political matters. A strong argument against the second is that it ignores the fact that the question of equal treatment is always one of perspective and that it is impossible to give everyone the feeling that they have indeed been treated fairly and justly. Any involvement of politics in religious matters is bound to catalyse the formation of identity groups based on religion and to increase the competition between them. The last argument finally works by simplifying dichotomies that pit the image of a 'good tradition' against 'bad modernity' and poses 'innocent people' against a power-hungry and selfish elite. It ignores the situatedness of social discourse, and underplays the complexity of power structures and the contextuality of terms like tradition and modernity or subaltern and elite (see Rao 2003).

These few remarks in no way exhaust the complex debate on secularism. And it would be against the intention of this book to engage in a detailed assessment of the various positions on secularism among Indian intellectuals. The aim throughout has been to look at actual social practices of strategic positioning in a field that revolves around religious issues related to temples. Yet even though in practice the commitment to religious concerns seems inseparable from social negotiations of power, social actors formulate ideals which conceive of a 'pure religion' that would be free of human selfishness. In this connection references are also made to the three positions quoted above. There is the hope that a separation of religion from politics, the equality of all religions, or a truly spiritual politics would lead to a just social order in which religion is liberated from its association with power contests.

Yet what appears so clear in a theoretical discussion becomes highly complex when it is applied to actual situations. Thus, it is not surprising to find that even those who theoretically distinguish politics from religion constantly re-adjust their opinion when it comes to the discussion of real-life incidents. In order to show the contextuality of the judgements about an appropriate place for religion in contemporary society, let me start examining the terms involved. The terms religion and politics were both used in two basically different ways by the people I talked with in Bhopal. Religion or the Hindi word *dharma*[9] was used to refer to religious praxis. In this case it meant specifically

[9] People use interchangeably either the English term 'religion' or the Hindi term *dharma*. For the meaning of *dharma* in the context of Hindu national politics see also Hellman (1996: 239-44).

the conduct of ritual, visiting temples, observation of festivals or even the construction of a temple. In a second sense, *dharma* had a more philosophical connotation and was used to refer to moral or cosmic order, duty or ethics. Politics (*rajniti*[10]) was used to describe the work of democratic institutions—in which case a translation with electoral politics or party politics seems adequate. Or, in a more general sense, the term politics (then mostly the English word was used) describes the negotiation of power positions, as they take place in all spheres of life. It is associated with intrigues, gossiping, politicking etc.

When asked directly about the relationship between politics and religion, most people would take this question to mean the involvement of democratic institutions in ritual practices and would opt for a clear separation. In Bhopal, the majority of elected leaders paid respect to this attitude, however superficially, by certain avoidance strategies. They did not mention their party affiliation on banners at religious festivals, and abstained from overtly political speeches at religious events. They were also careful when commenting on religious issues, remaining vague in public, while making their real opinions known through statements spread by their dependants.

Yet, where such tactics are employed, they are scarcely taken seriously. I have already mentioned that the presence of a particular leader at a religious event immediately triggers a lot of associations about his affiliation, network, influence and opinions, which become visible in more informal settings. The consequence is that party names are involved in almost every religious festival, even if such events are hardly ever organized explicitly by a political party. Consider, for example, the procession on Holi and Rangpanchmi in Bhopal in 1998. Both were organized by the Hindu Festival Committee, but people nevertheless remembered Holi as a Congress-sponsored event because Congress politicians headed its organization. In turn, Rangpanchmi appeared as an event of the opposition party, since it turned into a victory parade for the BJP, which had just won the national elections.

This apparent gap between the stated ideals of separation and the reality of intersections became frequent topics of debate. Different incident of religious politics were discussed in detail and politicians were denounced as using religion for their power games. Yet especially in more formal settings the gap could also be explained away by changing the perspective. The Chief Minister's decision to establish a committee for cow protection[11] was defended as a public hygiene

[10] People tend to use the Hindi term *rajniti* more often when referring to democratic institutions. When talking of politics as the negotiation of power positions, people tend to use the English word 'politics'.

[11] Cow protection has since the beginning of the twentieth century been a top priority for Hindu nationalists. Their aim has been to press for legislation that would

measure. The formation of the MP Temple Committee and the increased spending of government money on temples were explained as a means to protect historical monuments. When members of a BJP procession—which set out on the occasion of their party's electoral victory—perform *puja* at the Durga Temple, it was justified as a matter of private belief. After all, it was said, politicians also belong to a religion and one cannot forbid them from exercising their faith just because they are party members.

Given these realities, the question rises of how secularism as a separation of domains can be realised? When religion is understood as a moral order that lays down the conditions within which people act, it cannot be distinguished from politics. But how is one to demarcate religious opportunism from genuine religious belief? There seems to be no final solution to this question. It provides material for endless debate.

Would it be right for a non-party member to fight for a temple if it was wrong for a party member to do so? Or should one separate the two matters and say that a politician may work for the temple as a private person but not as a politician? But how could these two aspects be separated? These and similar situations where religious activities have consequences for the organization of social relations are the subject of repeated discussion. There are always many answers. Sometimes even one person can present quite contradictory statements, like one of my Khatik informants who complained in an interview that contemporary politics is 'dirty politics' because religious issues get dragged into it. In the same interview he later admitted that he saw no fault with a ruling party promoting Hinduism.

There is no way of resolving these contradictions. Judging the religious activities of leaders becomes a question of perspective. Public involvement in religious matters can be seen as an improper transgression of the border between two separate fields, performed out of self-interest or opportunism. However, it can also be judged as the fulfilment of a moral duty or an action rooted in personal belief. Similarly, abstaining from interference in religious controversies can be criticized as showing a lack of moral responsibility or may be praised as a demonstration of a 'true secular spirit'. Opponents and supporters of a leader are provided with a never-ending chain of arguments for or against their candidate all revolving around religion.

---

ban cow-slaughter, since the animal is sacred to Hindus. The theme surfaced again after the waning of the movement for a Ram Temple in Ayodhya, this time aggressively promoted by the VHP and other Hindu Nationalist organisations (for the history of the cow protection movement in India see: Freitag 1980, 1989: 148-74; Luett 1970; Pandey 1983, 1990; Yang 1980).

I conclude, therefore, that a majority of people involved in temple matters are ambiguous when it comes to the question of the right relationship between politics and religion. While they believe that a strict separation is desirable, they also know it is impossible. To judge a politician they take his religious affiliation into account. They notice whether he himself evinces faith or not, and may urge him to intervene in order to resolve controversies between religious communities or to support the interests of religious people. However, voters also know that religious issues are manipulated to serve vested interests. Religious engagement can be used to win status, money, or influence. But the fact that religious devotion brings worldly returns does not necessarily diminish its merit, nor does it *a priori* call the sincerity of a person's belief into question. What counts is the motivation. Through gossip, people permanently try to assess the sincerity of a leader's motivation, which in the end remains inaccessible and thus leads to constant reshuffling of opinions.

Leaders are caught in a paradox as Mines notes with reference to 'big men' in Tamil Nadu. On the one hand, they are expected to be altruistic in their engagement, motivated solely by the wish to serve the community. On the other hand, they can only be successful as leaders if they are good manipulators. 'Achieving simultaneously a reputation for both success and altruism is difficult because the two are seen as contradictory' (Mines 1996: 42; see also the discussion on leadership and the contextuality of caste-status in Indian cities by Holmstroem 1972). Translated into the context of my research in Bhopal, this reads as follows: leaders are expected to show their religious affiliation and to support religious activities through patronage. But if they do so, they are targeted as misusing religion for their power games.

The extent to which religious devotion and political careers can be intertwined can be demonstrated with reference to Bagware's life history. His entry into caste politics, facilitated by his educational success and hard work, also had its roots in a religious belief which prompted Bagware to view himself as elected by the Goddess Kali to take the lead in realising her divine will. After introducing Bagware as a leader in the first chapter, let me now caste light on the religious dimension of his engagement.

RELIGIOUS DEVOTION AND POLITICAL LEADERSHIP

Already as a young man Bagware was attracted to the idea of becoming a leader. But unlike some of his friends he did not choose a political career. He decided on the secure position of a state employee. He started as a clerk in the Department for Post and Telecommunication and has risen since to the position of an officer in the State Bank of India. His time-consuming job has not, however, curtailed his political ambitions. The list of organizations in which he has been active seems endless. They reach from caste organizations, to labour unions and a housing society.[12] Of all these activities, his engagement in the temple has always had a special importance to him. It provided for his entry into leadership responsibilities and is the most powerful post he holds till today. However, most of all, the presidency of the temple committee has given his life a new, religious, orientation.

In Chapter 2, I described how the temple became a vehicle for the young Bagware to reach a position of authority in his caste. His involvement in the temple was greatly appreciated because there were few in his caste educated enough for such a task. Yet his work was not merely altruistic, he also used his power and status to install himself in a leading position in the temple trust and the new caste society, which served as the basis for further political activities. As a temple president Bagware has a leading position in the caste and numbers among the city's dignitaries. This has been effectively demonstrated by the events surrounding the extension and legalization of the temple, as well as the green-flag incident where he negotiated with Muslim opponents. Both occasions catapulted Bagware onto the urban scene, where he demonstrated his ability to manipulate public opinion as well as to mobilise political and administrative support. The conflicts gave him a chance to display his skills as a leader who is strong enough to succeed in giving the people a voice, but also wise enough to lead as well as restrain people and prevent mischief and violence, showing his self-proclaimed potential as 'a voice of sanity'.

However, the temple also directed Bagware's life in a direction he himself did not foresee, and which he now considers to be the most decisive one. Bagware recalls that as a young man he had no interest in religious matters. This changed when in spontaneous enthusiasm he joined the temple project. During his efforts to help build the Kali

[12] A complete list of Bagware's organizational involvement includes: 360 Gautriya Kshatriya Navyuk Bundele Rajput Sangh; Student Welfare Society (Treasurer); Young Educated Person's Association (Joint Secretary, Joint General Secretary); All India Post and Telecommunication Administrative Officers Employee Union, Madhya Pradesh (Assistant Circle Secretary, President and Circle Secretary); Martyr Krishn Raj Singh Bagware Memorial Committee (Founder, General Secretary); National Martyr Memorial Trust (Founder Member, Secretary); 360 Gautriya Kshatriya Samaj (Founder Member, Chief Advisor); Kali Temple Trust (Founder Member, President); All India State Bank Group SC/ST Employees' Welfare Federation (Additional Secretary, General Secretary); Indian National State Bank Promotee Officers' Congress (President); Hindu Utsav Samiti (Member); Vijay Stambh Trust (Founder Member; President); Vijay Stambh Residents Welfare Committee (Chief Patron).

Temple he felt a special dedication and later a deep gratitude to the goddess, which lead to an alteration in the trajectory of his life-project (see also Koepping and Rao 2001, Rao 2002b). His first religious crisis goes back to the year when the temple had just been built.

Following the foundation of the Kali Temple, Bagware engaged in a search for religious guidance. On Guru Purnima[13] 1973, this search culminated in a sudden impulse to make the Goddess Kali herself his guru. However, as soon as he had completed the prescribed rituals, he started to be troubled by doubts as to whether he had taken the right decision. They intensified when he realized that the goddess had not revealed to him a *mantra*, even though this is the duty of a guru. Bagware feared that the goddess had rejected him or, worse, that she did not exist at all.

Help arrived from an unexpected quarter. Walking aimlessly around the city after the closing of the temple at around noon, Bagware suddenly found his former Sanskrit teacher, one of the renowned Brahmins of the city, sitting under a tree at the main crossing of the city centre. On hearing Bagware's story, he got very angry and scolded him for his actions towards the goddess, explaining to him that in the present Kali Yuga, deities can no longer be asked to serve as gurus for humans. But he then equipped him with a particular 'helping' *mantra* and advised him to meditate on it each night for three nights, and afterwards to sleep on the ground. If that did not lead to a personal *mantra* being revealed by the goddess, it would mean that she had rejected him.

Bagware did as he was told. For three days he prayed, meditated, doubted, harangued himself and the goddess, in short he went through a severe religious crisis. Nothing happened after his mediation on the first and second day. Finally, during the third night, the goddess revealed herself in a dream. She took him by the hand and flew through the sky, showed him the whole world, the heavens, and finally *parmatma*, the god himself. She also revealed to him his personal *mantra*. Bagware was overjoyed and overwhelmed. But then his 'rationalist' side resumed control and he started doubting the experience. To test its truth he began frantically to search for his personal *mantra* in the sacred books. But he could not find it. Again he approached his former teacher, who now scolded him for doubting the goddess instead of showing his gratitude for this display of divine grace. Bagware took the advice and has never since doubted the benevolent presence of the goddess in his life again. Today, he describes the change that took place as follows:

[13] It falls on the day of the full moon (*purnima*) in the lunar month Shravana (July/August).

Since then my life has changed [...] my whole interest was absorbed by the goddess, the temple and meditation. [Now all that seemed important was to] meditate, do my duties at home and work for the temple. [...] My mind and my soul (*atma*) underwent a change because of the temple [...] my route has changed. (my translation)

Today Bagware never misses his daily *puja* in the morning, and though busy, he takes time out for the study of religious books. For his engagement in the temple he compromises his career in the bank. But for Bagware a religious orientation means more than correct ritual observance, it is the complete surrender to the divine:

In my mind there is only one thing, when I wake up in the morning, when I sleep at night, [...] when I am awake talking. When I am talking to you, for example, my mind inside goes on. [...] It is not necessary to fully concentrate on the act of speaking [...] *'so ham ham so'*, within one breath a *mantra* can be said [in the mind]. [...] While I am talking, I can also say my *mantra*s. This is every person's *sadhana* (meditation). The work of *sadhana*. I am not a man of this time. (my translation)

Bagware also sees a relationship between the goddess and his career. Although he emphasizes that his achievements are a result of hard work, he qualifies this statement by saying that without the blessing of the goddess none of this would have been possible. He is also encouraged in his role as leader, which he is now able to understand as a vocation or religious duty. He finds confirmation for this interpretation in a published account about the miraculous appearance of Shiva in the house of his ancestors years back in Tikamgarh, through which, he says, his lineage was personally selected by Shiva to take an outstanding position in his service.

Shiva, the story goes, manifested himself in the form of a *lingam* (phallus representing Shiva) in the house of an old mother from his *gotra* in Tikamgarh. After his manifestation, Shiva ordered the king of the area to install someone from the *Bagavar*[14] *gotra* as priest in his new sanctuary. Initially the king resisted this order because he as well as the Brahmins of the kingdom found it inappropriate that people from a non-Brahmin caste (Khatik[15]) should be made priests. But when the Brahmins approached the house which, through the appearance of a *lingam*, had become a temple requiring ritual attention, the door miraculously closed. The door could not be opened again through any human effort. It only unlocked when someone from the *Bagavar gotra* was sent to perform the *puja*. In this way, Shiva forced the king to obey his order through which he wanted to give new status to the Khatiks (Bhadakariya 1958: 56-8).

[14] In colloquial writing this Hindi term is transcribed as *bagwar* or *bagware*.

[15] In this context Khatiks are presented as a Kshatriya caste, while in contemporary India, they are classified as a Scheduled Caste.

For Bagware this story clearly elevates his *gotra* to the special status of priestly servants of the divine. He believes that the call expressed in Shiva's manifestation is not only valid for Tikamgarh, or only for Shiva temples. Instead he believes that it was meant to promote all descendants of his *gotra* to a special status in the service of the divine. He personally has chosen Kali or—as one should rather put it with reference to Bagware's convictions—was taken by Kali into her service. He has complied with this call by taking on the responsibility for the construction and management of her temple in Bhopal.

Bagware gives further evidence for his religious calling. He explains that in a dream he learned of his last life in which he had been a hermit. Living in his lonely forest abode, he had been completely absorbed in meditation and almost reached liberation from the cycle for rebirth (*moksha*) but his life had been a few days too short to accomplish this. As a result of the merit accumulated in his life as a hermit, he has been destined in this life to become temple president.

To sum up, Bagware gives a multi-layered religious legitimization for his outstanding position. He ascribes his destiny to the blessing of the goddess, the vocation of his lineage and his merits, accumulated in the last as well as this life. Bagware sometimes also turns to a religious rhetoric when defending his actions as a leader.

> As a representative of Kali I have to act like her. I cannot allow people to constrain me. I cannot show any mercy to those who are against me. Kali also went wild, to the extent that she trampled on her husband. The situation in the temple is no different from that in the Mahabharata. There are Kauravas and Pandavas. I have to take the role of Krishna [by which he means the role of Krishna as mediator between warring interests]. (my translation)

Quoting from Hindu mythologies, Bagware discloses his idea of leadership. He sees himself in the role of a strict but wise patriarch who has to discipline his followers for their own good. Political manipulation, which he uses extensively to gain status and influence, becomes a means to bring about a just and peaceful order in which every subject is given a place in accordance with his abilities.

I met many other leaders who, like Bagware, saw their public commitment as an extension of their personal religious quest, as a vocation or a religious duty (*dharma*). Or they referred to religion as a necessary basis for human interactions, which guides people to become moral beings. Without such an orientation, they feared, society would fall apart.

This attitude is clearly demonstrated in the following statement of an MLA whom I asked about the appropriate relationship between religion and politics. 'Actually there is no relation between religion and politics but without religion no politics will be left. People have to fear something and there is only one thing they fear [...]'. The leader here refers to the common conviction that only the belief in a divine force that punishes will instil discipline in people. The promotion of religious belief—also by state representatives—thus becomes a necessary means for making society function.

Obviously this interpretation of the life history and self-portrayal of leaders as religiously inspired does not go uncontested. Often it is criticised as just one more strategy to manipulate relationships and gain power. I do not aim to resolve these contradictions, but wish rather to present the conflicting narratives, which lead to ever new controversies.

CONCLUSION

I started this chapter by showing the way in which the temple figures on the agenda of political actors. As a place for stating their importance, the sacred site allows leaders to enhance their popularity and enables them to show their religious devotion and their willingness to extend patronage. Since the temple is an important urban institution drawing the attention of a considerable urban population, it is a useful source for the promotion of a political career.

The attention politicians give to religious institutions triggers controversies about the appropriate place for religion in a modern democracy. In debates about an appropriate place for religion three positions are commonly encountered. Some people call for a strict separation between domains, others argue for the just intervention of the state in religious matters, and again others champion a state that is informed by a religious ethic. But everyday practice does not allow for any such clear-cut positioning since religious and political identities are not easily distinguished. Independent of a politician's self-presentation and personal beliefs, they are always seen also as a member of a particular religious community and are confronted with religious demands of believers. Acting in the name of the divine can be projected as a religious duty (*dharma*), but also be seen as a measure for popularity in the social domain and the success in politics.

The prevailing ambiguity makes religious negotiations susceptible to the manipulation of voters' sentiments in a democratic political set-up. To judge the motivation behind a politician's activities thus becomes an important part of assessing different contributions to the religious sphere. It opens the stage for extensive gossip in which opinions vary greatly and often change according to context. The line between genuine religious engagement and egoistic manipulation of religious events is constantly shifted. It remains vague and flexible because every public activity includes many actors who contribute various value judgements.

However, the assessments are not arbitrary. They are embedded in a historical discourse that is shaped through the available narrative structures. In the contemporary political context in India—that is also influenced through the pronounced activities of Hindu nationalist and their discriminatory rhetoric—accusations of 'communal behaviour' are triggered by almost every public religious activity of leaders. There always remains the suspicion that a politician who openly involves in temple matters is the supporter of a Hindu nationalist agenda and promotes religious interests of Hindus at the expense of religious minorities. Such accusations are often justified because politicians are themselves aware of the structure of the political discourse, in which the stance on religious issues also makes for a major divide between different parties. Open response to a religious demand or acceptance of an invitation to a religious programme, is used to make a public statement in the religio-political field. Those who are suspicious about loading democratic politics with religious issues, but do not want to lose out on their popularizing effect, usually find indirect ways of extending support for religious organizations and institutions.

Often local people see no other way of realizing their religious demands but to ask for political patronage. Thereby they submit part of their power of definition to a more influential agent. This can have a major impact on the movement. What started as a local engagement for a temple can then be subsumed under the agenda of a particular party and can trigger a controversy that may even culminate in Hindu-Muslim riots. Such developments may come as a surprise, or they may be anticipated and planned, and they may be noticed or remain unacknowledged. As a movement increases in scale, more and more politicians use the event to popularize themselves and openly disclose their sympathy for one or the other position. This kind of political absorption does not necessarily form a proper representation of those who started a movement, nor do the interpretations that emerge during the course of events present a complex picture that takes into account the numerous activities and beliefs that make a movement successful and acceptable. But in the political arena the reduction of complexity and the streamlining of opinions into a few persuasive positions is part of the strategy to gain a clear position and convince people of its rationality.

CHAPTER 5

The State and the Locality

While the involvement of politicians in religious matters is generally characterized by great visibility, they are not the only state representatives who are concerned with religious matters. Since temples are subjected to a number of regulatory measures by the legislative bodies, city administrators and state bureaucrats become entangled in the extensive power-struggles that often surround the construction and management of public temples.This chapter concerns the way in which state policies become relevant to temple matters, how they are implemented, and how they influence the urban religious landscape. It will also show the various strategies used to resist state orders and the ideologies that go into shaping the various positions in the conflicts over temples.

The ensuing discussion about notions of tradition and modernity shows how these categories become relevant to the way people frame religious activities, and how they are instrumental in formulating ideals about the appropriate place for religion in a modern nation state. This serves as a point of departure for the deconstruction of dichotomies of tradition and modernity as well as elite and subaltern in Chapter 6, since these oppositional distinctions are unsuitable for mapping the complex power-struggles that characterize contemporary conflicts over religion in urban India.

Before embarking on a detailed analysis of case studies that will demonstrate contemporary negotiations on temple matters between representatives of state and temple, a short summary will introduce the reader to the central themes that shaped the colonial involvement with temples and draw a picture of the current legal situation in Madhya Pradesh.

TEMPLES AS LEGAL INSTITUTIONS

Temple management became a topic of considerable debate once the British had established their colonial order in the subcontinent. In pre-colonial India the state involvement with temples was an integral part of the public order in those areas where Hindu kings acted as the chief servant of the principal deity, and built and managed the major temples in their territory.[1] Although the British claimed to continue this age-old practice of state patronage (Kennedy 1974: 269), they substantially changed the state-temple relation when they took over the position of protector of the temples.

The role of protector had been exercised by the king in his function as main donor to the temple, which bestowed on him the honourable task of managing the temple finances and arbitrating in temple disputes. The British and later the state governments of independent India stood, however, outside the distributional system of the temple. No longer dedicated to revering the temple deity, they did not function as donors and thus construed their task as the managers of endowments in the 'secular' sense of keeping track of the flow of money and gifts that went through the temples (Appadurai 1981a; Appadurai and Breckenridge 1976: 207).

However, British policy on temples was not totally consistent. Above all, Christian missionaries objected to the colonial Government's involvement in 'pagan' institutions. In 1942 a new directive was passed by the British parliament, probably under the pressure of missionary societies, which led to the withdrawal of the Government of India from its engagement in temple affairs,[2] leaving their management in the hands of local communities[3] (Kennedy 1974: 271; Baker 1975: 85; Singh and Batra 1995: 77). But in spite of this official withdrawal, the British never fully gave up their supervision of the temples. They retained indirect control, particularly through the courts, the last resort for conflicting parties to resolve disputes over temple matters (Kennedy 1974: 275, Presler 1987: 15-21).

At Independence, the regulation of religious institutions fell into the hands of the state governments, with each of them responding differently to the task. Tamil Nadu, for example, is known for the strict control it keeps on temples through a central institution that supervises the management of all larger temples (Fuller 1984; Kennedy 1974; Presler 1978). Andhra Pradesh and Orissa too opted for a high degree of state influence. In Madhya Pradesh, however, the government's concern with temples remains marginal. There are only three temples[4]—together

[1] For reflections on the involvement of kings with temple matters see Appadurai 1981a; Davis 1995b; Dirks 1976, 1987; Eschmann et al. 1978; Kulke 1974; Roesel 1980: XVII–XXIII, 18-28; Spencer 1969.

[2] Thereafter, twelve attempts were made to revise the act (Kennedy 1974: 273).

[3] This was an invention, since it left the power over temples in the hand of local leaders, who had never before been in charge of temple management (Kennedy 1974: 273, 273).

[4] Mahakaleshwar Temple in Ujjain (Madhya Pradesh Shri Mahakaleshwar Vidhan, 1953, reprinted in Sethi 1996: 109-23); Salkanpur Devi Temple in Salkanpur (Salkanpur Devi Mandir Adhiniyam, 1956); Sharda Devi Temple in Maihyar (The Sharda Devi Temple does not have its own act but is governed in accordance with the regulations established during the Muslim rule).

they form the major pilgrimage sites in the state—that are directly state controlled.[5] The management of all other public temples is left in the hands of local committees, which at times register as a public trust.[6] In that case the Collector[7] as the Registrar of all public trusts, controls the finances and can start an inquiry in case of suspected irregularities (Goyal 1996: 3). However, this does not guarantee effective control of all public temples, since there is no legal provision that can enforce registration.[8] In an official statement of the Collectorate of Bhopal, this reads as follows:

> A temple is not required to be registered under any law. However, considering public interest government may acquire management of any temple forming a trust, under the provision of Trust Act or may adopt any special act for the purpose. (Written statement prepared by the Collectorate Bhopal, April 1997, English original)

The Durga Temple committee took advantage of the uncertainty of the legal situation and registered the temple not as a public trust but as a society. In that way they could avoid major state intervention. There are also countless other temples in the state that are not registered at all and therefore completely escape state control.

The only temples that are financially supported by the state are 'historical temples'. The state is said to have inherited from its predecessors, the princely states, the duty to protect religious institutions. This is interpreted to mean that all religious institutions founded before Independence are eligible to state support, even today.[9] In 1998, a budget of ten million rupees was issued by the government for the upkeep and repair of 'historical temples'. The yearly budgeted money is distributed through the Department for Religious Institutions and

[5] Sites of historical importance are under the authority of the central government and subject to a management by the ASI (Archaeological Survey of India). The Shiva Temple in Bhojpur is a case in point.

[6] This is possible under the Madhya Pradesh Public Trust Act, 1951 (reprinted in Sethi 1996).

[7] He is allowed to appoint someone to take over this task. But the person should not be below the rank of a sub-divisional officer and should not be the Additional Collector (Singh and Batra 1995: 82-3).

[8] 'If the temple has not been declared as a public trust, and registered [...] under the Act, then clearly the Registrar has no jurisdiction to entertain any application under section 26 of the Act' (Sethi 1996: 14, see also the examples cited on page 66 and 86).

[9] In Bhopal there are no 'government temples', since in former Bhopal State none of the temples enjoyed government protection. Hence, the new state did not inherit the upkeep of Hindu religious sites. Thus, strictly speaking, none of the temples in Bhopal would be eligible to receive state grants. However, older temples profit from government grants. If they were not supported, this would result in an unequal treatment of different religions, as mosques are subsidized in accordance with laws pertaining to pre-independent Bhopal.

Endowments to the local state authorities (Collector and Commissioner) who decide which temples are in most need.[10] But even the allocation of state funds does not guarantee effective control. This was expressed by one of the officers in the Ministry for Religious Institutions and Endowments who, in a laconic statement, compared his work with that of a post officer. Thereby he expressed his frustration at the fact that the ministry's powers were limited to the distribution and delivery of money according to a pre-determined scheme.

Many high-level bureaucrats regret their lack of power to intervene in matters of temple management. Many share the opinion of the retired state officials Singh and Batra who wrote that temples have become 'breeding grounds for corruption and mismanagement' (Singh and Batra 1995: 77). Only strict bureaucratic supervision, many state officials feel, would guarantee the management of temples and endowments in a way that would safeguard public interest and end malpractice and irregularities. They look with envy towards Tamil Nadu, where the state has taken over the management of all major temples and believe that Madhya Pradesh should follow this example and pass legislation to standardize temple management and give the state greater powers to intervene (see for example Singh and Batra 1995: 86-8).

In 1983/84 an effort was made to this effect when the then Chief Minister Arjun Singh installed a commission of renowned politicians, administrators and public persons to work on a proposal for new legislation for religious institutions. But due to the premature dissolution of parliament following the assassination of Indira Gandhi, the commission was unable to complete the task. With the establishment of the Madhya Pradesh Temple Committee[11] in 1995, the current Chief Minister Digvijay Singh has made a renewed attempt to work towards greater state control over temples. Many observers are, however, sceptical about the sincerity of his efforts, claiming that the committee has not been called to do any effective work, but just to offer patronage to

[10] The money for religious institutions is sanctioned by the Minister in charge and distributed through the Department for Religious Trust and Endowment to the local authorities (Commissioner and Collector) who have the right to grant the money to particular temples. A special committee, including bureaucrats and persons of public importance, has been formed by the Commissioner for the distribution of temple funds in Bhopal, Raisen and Sehore (the neighbouring districts). The money may only be given to temples which are registered as public trusts and are said to be older than fifty years. The latter criterion is vague, since there exists no list for Bhopal which give a clue as to whether a particular temple has been in existence in pre-independent India or not. Determining the age of a temple is subject to guess work. At times, the foundation date is deliberately manipulated in order to qualify for government grants.

[11] For details on the Madhya Pradesh Temple Committee refer to Chapter 4.

supporters of the Congress government and to satisfy voters who call for greater state involvement in religious matters.

A discussion with members of the MP Temple Committee shows that the question of state interference in temples is not easily solved. The formulation of new legislation on temple management involves tackling the problem of the appropriate relationship between the state and religious institutions. Is it correct for the state as a secular institution to get involved in religious matters, and if so, under which circumstances and with what justification? The official answer to this question is that the state has no intention to get involved with religious matters. It is only concerned with the secular aspects of the temple. But how can life in a temple be separated into a secular and a non-secular part, and where should the line be drawn? These are highly controversial questions. Presler (1978) has demonstrated this with reference to two cases from Tamil Nadu that led to conflicts between the state and temple priests over the question of the limits of state interference. In both cases the conflict was resolved by a court decision based on an interpretation of Sanskrit texts.

In the first case, the state tried to end the hereditary rights to priesthood and opened this office to all castes by a state ordinance. The priests rejected this innovation as they saw the sanctity of the temple endangered. The court sided with their argument, saying that the state does not have the right to deviate from the established traditions when passing laws pertaining to the nomination of priests. But the priests were not fully satisfied with the judgement because the court also stated that the need to follow the tradition does not deny the state the right to formulate policies on priests. Priests are ordinary temple servants, the judgement went, since they are accountable to the trustees. The nomination of priests is thus a secular matter and therefore within the authority of the state (Presler 1978).

In the second case, the government stipulated that the language of the rituals be changed from Sanskrit to Tamil. The decision was justified by the minister concerned with the words, 'no language was unknown to God and it was wrong to say that God could only follow Sanskrit'.[12] But the court rejected this argument and placed a stay order until the matter could be reviewed, on the basis that the question of ritual language was a religious concern over which the state had no authority (Presler 1978, 1987: 114-18).

Both cases demonstrate that there is no easy way of distinguishing religious from secular matters. In Bhopal the situation is somewhat easier since there is no intimate relation between the state government and the temple. The main concern of state representatives relates to

[12] *The Hindu*, Madras, 21 October 1970 (Presler 1978: 116).

the financial management of the temples. They feel that priests take advantage of the faith, or, as some have it, the credulity of people, in order to lead a comfortable life. They wish to eliminate such corruption through bureaucratic control. Singh and Batra thus recommend that the Public Trust Act should be amended in such a way that the 'registration of religious/charitable institutions should be made compulsory' (Batra and Singh 1995: 87).

CONTAINING CORRUPTION

Far from being solely a concern of bureaucratic control, the question of how the income of a temple should be used, and how it has been used, appears to be a dominant theme both in talks about the temple as well as during interactions within a temple. The problem of corruption is almost an obsession with people with a commitment to a temple. There are state officials who believe that many trustees manage temple funds badly, trustees who accuse their employees of diverting temple income for personal gain, priests who express their frustrations with low salaries and miserly worshippers, beggars who are said to steal the temple's wealth, and worshippers who complain about corrupt trustees, greedy priests and selfish *sevak*s.

Derrett observes that this heightened interest in the ways money is channelled through temples in contemporary society is the result of a shift in the notion of donation, especially among members of the educated middle class. In traditional settings, Derrett argues, donations were gifts to the deity, through which a devotee could accumulate merit, a purpose that is fulfilled as soon as the donation has been accepted by the priest, the mediator between the worshipper and the deity. Whatever happens to the donation thereafter is irrelevant.

Today many people cannot relate to this disinterest in the use of donations. They feel that the temple's income is not meant for the personal gain of the priests but should serve the public. Hence, they demand strict controls on the way temple funds are used (Derrett 1966: 317-22). Following Appadurai, it can be surmised that the desire to control the finances of a temple has its roots in a changed understanding of the institution 'temple'. By establishing the temple as a public trust, the British changed the idea of ownership. While in a traditional set-up the deity was considered the owner of the donations, once the temples became public trusts, wealth was transferred to a group of trustees who were supposed to use it for the benefit of others (Appadurai 1981a: 173).

This new understanding of the temple as an institution for the redistribution of wealth for the public good is coupled with a transformation of the idea of priesthood. Priests are not supposed to simply live off the deity, but are expected to be educated and prestigious members of society able to offer spiritual guidance and consolation to devotees (Derrett 1966: 322). Following this line of argument, corruption charges against priests are not only a way of expressing concern about vanishing temple funds, but also a means of expressing doubts about whether temple employees are actually worth the money they receive, understood now as a payment for their services and not donations received due to the grace of the deity. Often complaints about the corrupt practices of priests are combined with calls for a standardized priestly education, which should qualify the religious personnel for their important task and impart to them a sense of morality, so that they are able and willing to distinguish between payments offered for their services and donations made to the public trust.

With the same logic that connects higher education to greater morality, people forward the argument that trustees should be selected from the educated strata, as only those persons will be able to account for the money they manage, or, to extend the argument even further, that supervision of temples by the modern bureaucratic institutions is needed to guarantee correct use of temple funds. However, there is also resistance to this view from those who question the motives and competence of a secular state to govern the affairs of a temple. Devotees know from their own experience that state officials are no less tempted to divert funds for their personal satisfaction. Many people are even of the opinion that leaving the temple in the hands of the bureaucracy will only increase the level of corruption, as it adds to the number of people who want to earn from the temple. Those critical of state intervention hope to find a solution to corruption through leaving the temple in the control of religiously-minded people who are expected to be dedicated to the deity and her causes, and not succumb to the temptation of diverting money for personal projects.

The problem of fund management, however, is not confined to finding the right agent to exercise control. Opinions are also divided on the way the donations should be used. Does the money belong to the goddess, to the employees, or to the trustees? Should they be used for the payment of services, for social and educational projects, or should they simply be accumulated in the name of the deity? Certainly most people would agree that, first and foremost, ritual services have to be ensured and temple upkeep guaranteed. Excess money should then be used for educational and social activities. Yet the details of each individual case are tricky. Consider, for example, the confrontation between Bagware and the priest of the Kali Temple over the collections during the ritual of *arti*. While the priest claims this money to be part of his income, which he receives as a special donation for his ritual services, Bagware sees the money as part of the donations made to the goddess, which should be part of the earnings of the trust. Since there is no general rule nor any agency that could resolve the dispute, the disagreement continues to simmer, each side trying to corner the money whenever possible, but accusing the other of corruption or theft.

This case demonstrates Pavarala's (1996) conception that corruption is a contested terrain, used by persons according to their social status to strengthen their own power-base while at the same time discrediting other status groups. The task of a social scientist therefore is not so much to identify corruption but to follow the 'politics of definition' that sanctions some transactions as necessary and moral while discrediting others as immoral or illegal. What Pavarala notes in relation to various elite groups and their way of judging transactions that take place in the domains of politics and bureaucracy is even more valid in the case of temples, a social terrain that is much less pervaded by legal definitions. The laws pertaining to public trusts provide only very general rules for the use of funds, and there are many ways of escaping even these elementary regulations.

While the answer of some people to the openness of the situation is to call for stricter laws, there are others who believe that the multiplicity of traditions does not allow for a uniform law as it could not do justice to the various established practices. As a member in the MP Temple Committee observed, 'Any effort to unify temple management results in local resistance, since for priests and worshippers such regulations represent an intervention into their religious prerogatives and traditions.' The argument goes that questions of what corruption is and how it is to be controlled have to be answered locally, since only people in the temple know the relevant traditions. Any effort to unify procedures would represent an inappropriate interference in religious matters.

This call for decentralization does not, however, resolve the problem of corruption. It redirects it to the locality, acknowledging the need to re-negotiate its meaning in every case anew. Thus, corruption proves to be a rather diffuse concept, as also expressed by a senior bureaucrat interviewed by Pavarala:

> The term 'corruption' is used rather loosely. There is no accepted definition. There is no drawing the line. Each person has his own definition. The line one draws will be a little higher when it is someone else. As time is going by, the meaning of corruption is also changing. Corruption is basically deviation from a code of conduct laid down in any walk of life. (Pavarala 1996: 53)

The meaning of corruption, a contested category, changes with context. It remains underdetermined as judgements over moral conduct can differ greatly according to people's strategic position in a social situation. Conflicts involve questions of what is right or wrong, of who should define rules of conduct, and who should be called to arbitrate disputes. So far Madhya Pradesh has opted for a minimum of state interference, leaving disputes to be solved in the locality or by the court of law.

The situation is totally different when it comes to questions of urban planning. Wherever new temples are built, the state claims the right to determine their locality and size. Yet the right to manage public land exists only in theory. In practice, most temples are built without state permission, which often leads to extensive power-struggles between local activists and state agencies, especially when a temple is situated in a densely populated area. Even where laws exist, the situation remains ambiguous due to the various interpretations given by strategically situated actors.

ILLEGAL TEMPLES AND THE COMPETITION OVER URBAN TERRITORY

The legal situation concerning the construction of temples on public land seems clear. They may only be built on government land when official permission has been granted. If state approval has not been obtained, the temple is considered illegal and may be destroyed. However, this law does not prevent people from erecting new shrines and temples all over the city without informing the authorities. The Kali and the Durga Temple are cases in point. That most temples are constructed without permission was confirmed by everyone in the city, including the authorities of the town planning office, who laughed when I asked them to grant me access to the permit records.

Asking one of the Hindu leaders why people did not build temples legally, his answer was simple and to the point: 'The thing about legal and illegal is that they do not give permission in advance. How can one then build a temple legally? All the temples were constructed as a response to the needs of people!' This statement reflects the popular attitude that people have a right to worship their deities and if they are not provided appropriate space for their devotional activities, it is up to them to change things. It also confirms the stereotypical perception of the state as an institution that is insensitive to the 'religious needs' of people, as forwarded by many believers and made popular through the polemic of Hindu nationalist propaganda.

No doubt a hostile attitude exists among many highly-placed officials towards what they call the 'mushrooming of temples', and they are outspoken about their disgust with being unable to enforce a law. It appears impossible to prevent the construction of illegal temples, and once they are built, their destruction always bears the risk of a public uproar, or even lead to violent clashes between different social groups. The opinion voiced by a leading police officer is repeated in similar fashion by many other highly-placed state officials.

> This [Kali Temple] is an illegal construction, a typical case of land-grabbing. People do this to get power and earn money. This is not the right type of temple [...] 99% of the temples are constructed illegally [...]. The people don't build houses but temples because they know that in this case no one can do anything against it and they can simultaneously earn money with it. Behind the shrine they can build their house in peace. All this happens because people are uneducated.

In this statement the temple does not figure as a religious institution but rather as an economic enterprise aimed to support the living of priests and trustees. There are at least two reasons for administrators to oppose such illegal enterprises. First, they stand in the way of systematic city planning. Normally built at crowded places, illegal temples frustrate the administration's efforts to ensure unobstructed mobility. Secondly, new temples can upset the social balance in a locality. This danger is particularly endemic in neighbourhoods with residents of different religious affiliation. Even a small shrine may then lead to the mobilisation of large crowds in support of or opposition to the religious building. Such movements can easily turn violent, and tend to create a feeling of uneasiness among the agents of law and order.

Secretly, many decision makers hope that a new temple will be discovered the same night it is constructed so that it can be destroyed before it has come to the notice of a larger public. Such strategic thinking does not necessarily imply a general opposition to temples, but rather frustration at the impossibility of controlling their number and location. It is contrasted by a vision in which citizens obey the law and construct temples in accordance with the regulations of the state. The police officer continued:

> In order to build a legal temple, one turns to the authorities of the city, the Collector or Commission, and asks him for the assignment of land for this purpose. If the site is considered reasonable for a temple, church or mosque, the government can decide to allot the land for this purpose [...] In every plan for a new colony a place for a school and a place for worship is included. The land is marked in the development plan. Any registered society may then apply for the construction of a temple on that site.

Here the state is interpreted as the only legitimate authority. Its agencies decide where and when a temple is built, how many temples are needed, and who should be entitled to their erection, namely only those religious groups that are registered as societies according to state law.

However, while it is easy to find bureaucrats who openly state that only the intervention of the state can rationalize religious matters, the portrayal of *the* bureaucracy as a unified whole hardly conforms to the experiences of everyday interactions. There is great variation in the opinions of state employees about the need to promote religious concerns and the correct way to do it, and also a significant difference between the formulation of an ideal order and the practical constraints involved in the decision-making process.

The fact that not all state employees conform to the ideal of secularism, in the sense of keeping strict neutrality in religious matters and doing equal justice to all religious groups, was already demonstrated in the case of the Kali Temple, built with indirect support from the staff of the local police station adjoining the temple. Not only did those in charge ignore Muslim protests, the head of the police station is even said to have instructed the Khatiks on the best tactics for constructing an illegal temple.

In the case of the Durga Temple the situation was more complex. When the Collector was requested to ignore the construction of a temple on Pir Gate, he reacted sharply, making clear that he could not be bribed into ignoring such a project. However, in spite of his determination not to side with the Hindus, the destruction of the temple left the Collector facing many ambiguities. There were the policemen who begged him not to order them to destroy the shrine, because the vengeance of the goddess would come down on them. Doubts about the right reaction intensified when the possibility of imposing a curfew to prevent further mobilization of Hindus was discussed. Could the wish of people to freely practise their religion—a basic right according to the Constitution—really justify such severe interference in individual rights? In this case the Collector decided for the implementation of a curfew, because he saw human life in danger. But with every new illegal temple the question of right measures has to be faced anew. Destroying a temple means preventing people from realizing what they consider their religious duty. As a senior bureaucrat put it, 'the removing of temples is a very sensitive issue, because human feelings are involved. One has to weigh between irrational feelings and public interest.'

After a stampede in the famous Mahakaleshwar Temple, a pilgrimage site in Ujjain, the local Collector decided in favour of the religious feelings of the people. After the tragedy, a rumour circulated in the city that interpreted the stampede in terms of divine intervention. The tragedy was thought to be a sign of Shiva's anger, aroused by the decaying of the silver *yantra* (mystical diagram) in the sanctuary. On learning about this rumour, the Collector immediately sent people in search of an artist who could restore the *yantra*. He then called for donations, himself contributing the first kilogram of silver, and encouraged all the other officials to follow suit. Of course, the restoration of the *yantra* did not remain the only measure. The Collector also had new fences erected and security stepped up. But the repair of the *yantra* was of particular importance because it functioned to restore confidence that the problem had really been solved.

These examples show the constraints of administrative intervention. The odds have to be weighed in each case, because the interests of many people are involved. The people who plan a temple recognize this potential openness of the situation, and take advantage of the power to negotiate that it grants. Activists carefully investigate the opinions of various decision makers and keep track of the internal power struggles in the state. In this way they can estimate the chances of opposition to their project and make plans in case things go wrong.

Yet even though the construction of a temple is usually planned carefully, believers rarely perceive it solely in terms of human actions, but rather as the implementation of a divine will.

Anyone who has researched religion in India will have come across narrations of divine self-manifestations (*svayambhu*), for they are part of a standard repertoire of believers (see Davis 1995: 629-30). A great number of stories about temples start with the observation that the statue (normally a stone) miraculously appeared from the ground and invited the construction of a temple. Also Bagware, who claims the status of a Western-educated, rational citizen, cited such an event when telling the religious history of his clan.

A *mata* [old lady] of the Bagware clan of the 360 Gautriya Kshatriya Vansh of Tikamgarh [...] was grinding grain in a mortar at her house. [...] While she was grinding, blood started appearing in the mortar. At the sight of the blood the *mata* got frightened. She took the remaining grain from the *kunda*, put it on the ground, covered the mortar with the *kunda* and left the house. She told the event to the women and men of the neighbourhood. Hearing the news, people reached her house. When they uncovered the mortar they saw the blood emerging from the mortar and found that a small *pindi* had appeared with a little [...] wound from which blood streamed. [...] Daily the *mata* poured *ghi* on the wound for it to heal. The wound closed and the *pindi* started to grow day by day.
When this news reached the reigning Raja Tikamgarh, he came to see the place. When he saw that in her house Shri Mahadevji personally had manifested himself he told the *mata* and her family that he would have a temple constructed at this place in which she and her family could reside. (Bhadakariya 1958: 56 8)

It is easy to find other such stories, making similar claims about almost every temple. When discussing self-manifestations, people seldom wonder whether such things really happen, but discuss where and when they took place. The closer a person is involved in the construction of a temple, the less the chances of his taking recourse to explanations of a miraculous manifestation. It is therefore not surprising that many middle-class people lament that modern temples do not have the same aura, since only historical temples have their origin in divine manifestations. New temples, they say, are erected by humans in order to show off. Thus, while stories of *svayambhu* find wide acceptance, their plausibility increases with growing temporal and spatial distance, as is normal with processes of mythical legitimization.

Such stories of divine intervention pose a challenge to the law enforcement agencies. People maintain the right to worship and defend a temple as legitimate, even when in official terms it is illegal. For many believers the question of temple construction does not fall into the competence of the state, since divine manifestations cannot be controlled by a secular institution. This is not to imply that people ignore the claims of the state to sole authority over its territory, or do not understand them. But they may at times place divine authority above that of the state.

To avoid misunderstanding, tales of the miraculous appearance of deities are not the only explanation worshippers give as reasons for the construction of temples. And even if they are given, they seldom stand uncontested. I have already mentioned that their plausibility decreases when people have detailed knowledge of the historical developments. Depending on the standing in the struggle, a person may also point towards the efforts of a neighbourhood, the laudable engagement of a leader, or the courage of a community to defend its religious needs *vis-à-vis* the state or other religious groups. There are also more negative explanations that give the reasons for temple constructions: economic gain, people's continued adherence to 'superstitions' or the effort of fundamentalist forces to strengthen their base.

It would be misleading to try to distinguish 'true' from 'false' explanations. Every explanation has to be taken seriously as a particular strategic way of strengthening one's own claim. Instead of searching for 'a true story' I found it more promising to extract various standardized ways of narrating the story of temples, which through their constant application and reiteration shape and direct people's perceptions and memories. Depending on their standpoint in a concrete situation, people may prefer one or other culturally available explanation, sometimes also breaking with established clichés. Thus I found myself in the situation of listening to a Muslim lady defending the construction of Hindu temples on the grounds that Hindu deities manifest themselves. I also encountered a leading police officer, who is known for his secular attitude, defending illegal temples because they provide employment to innumerable uneducated people.

With shifting contexts, positions may change. This is particularly evident in the case of leaders and politicians who, in order to be able to negotiate in disputes over temples, have to be willing to take the differing views seriously. On the one hand they have to be willing to listen to the grievances of local people who feel that they are unable to do justice to their deity, but on the other they must relate to the demands of officials to retain control on public land. They will try to find a solution that demonstrates their ability to reach a compromise.

Given that the construction—and destruction—of temples is defended in terms of different narrative strategies, prominently those that emphasize the right of the state to control public land, the need to consider the religious feelings of people, the willingness of divine actors to become manifest, the wish of leaders to make their presence felt, and the interest of people to improve their economic situation, let me now investigate strategic actions that are used to gain ground in the struggle over the use of public land for religious purposes.

RESISTING STATE POWER THROUGH ILLEGAL TEMPLE CONSTRUCTIONS

State intervention is often anticipated by activists, why they are usually well prepared to confront it. In the case of the Kali Temple, destruction never occurred, but remained a threat that was defused by political intervention. The case of the Durga Temple was more dramatic, but even here the state finally withdrew its claim to sovereignty over the territory at Pir Gate and allowed the re-construction of the temple.

Let me now consider a third case where construction, destruction and re-construction were carried out for years on end, with no side gaining the edge over the other. I am referring to the Nilkantheshwar Mahadev Temple situated next to the busy crossing of MP Nagar in New Bhopal. The temple originated when, twelve years ago, an old ascetic settled down at the place and started collecting money to slowly build up a temple of his own. The temple grew fast and soon extended onto the street.There appeared to be no end to the ambitions of the ascetic and his followers. Besides a number of shrines with images of various deities, the temple also consisted of a living room for the ascetic, a water tank, and a number of shops for devotional objects and consumer goods.

In spring 1997, the state intervened for the first time and destroyed parts of the temple. But the local activists, recon-structed the destroyed parts, and further extended the temple. Again the state intervened a year later, destroying the same parts a second time. But even though devotees, *sevak*s and the ascetic were outraged, they did not get discouraged. They had newspaper articles published on the issue, set up a *dharna*, sent a protest note to the Collector, and mobilized support to reconstruct the ruins.

A detailed look at the confrontation will disclose the different strategies employed by the state and the devotees. The Collector was aware that he could not get away with the destruction of a temple. In order to make his legal point, he turned to destroying only the 'secular parts' of the temple, which in this case meant the ascetic's quarters, the only room without a statue. When reconstructing this part, the local temple supporters not only enlarged the rooms and increased their number, but also decorated the outside walls with depiction of deities in order to give them a devotional meaning and thereby discourage destruction. But this did not impress the city authorities. Again they went ahead with their action, demonstrating their power by destroying all buildings not containing statues one night before a political function on Ambedkar's birthday was to be held on the crossing. In this way they could be sure that their determination to implement the law communicated to a larger urban public. The last statement I heard before leaving Bhopal in 1998 was that the devotees would of course reconstruct the broken parts again, but this time they would install statutes in all rooms.

Here we find the typical opposition between secular and religious aspects of a temple, also mentioned earlier in the struggles over temple issues in Tamil Nadu. The defence of the destruction with reference to the secular nature of the building is telling insofar as it makes an indirect reference to the popular perception that the state has no authority to intervene in religious matters. Knowing well that the supporters of a temple will not accept a legal argument when it comes to religious buildings, the administration touched only the 'secular' parts of the construction, hoping that this would increase the legitimacy of the intervention also among believers.

A retired IAS officer from Madhya Pradesh and a determined fighter against illegal temples takes up a similar theme in one of his favourite stories:

> Once I had a case where a man had constructed an illegal restaurant. On top of it he had erected a temple, hoping that this way no one could take measures against the restaurant. But I had the restaurant destroyed. When objections were raised by all kinds of leaders I argued that: 'see, I won't touch the temple. I am just destroying its foundation. If the temple is holy it will remain there floating in the air.' But of course it did not. It came down together with the structure.

Destroying the building here was justified by the fact that only the secular part was taken down. However, such courses of action are unlikely to impress believers, since the fact that a deity chooses not to intervene in a particular case does not disprove its existence or its ability to act, even against the laws of nature.

The supporters of a temple can strengthen their case against state intervention through strategic actions. Local actors know that their ability to negotiate with the state agencies on equal terms ultimately depends on support from eminent personages. The selection of the trustees is often a strategy for securing the support of 'heavy-weights'. Important people from public life are made trustees, because their presence is expected to facilitate the unobstructed realization of a temple and help in times of a crisis. That such a strategy can be successful is illustrated by Bagware's narration of the 'green-flag-incident', where his status as a bank manager helped him to save the temple.

> Yes, the temple benefits from the fact that I am office-bearer in the State Bank. [...] At that time when the court case about the green flag was on, when the incident was reported to the ADM [Additional District Magistrate], the ADM knew that I was the president [...]. He said: 'You have to give 10.000 Rs otherwise you will be sent to jail.' What did I do then? Do you know? [...] I replied 'I am S.N.S. Bagware, the Branch Manger of MLA Rest House Branch [...] you please go ahead and [...] send me to jail.' [...] I did not present myself as chairman of the temple. [...] I played my reputation as Branch Manager of the State Bank of India. In turn the officer said: 'Please [...] do not give any money. Everyone will be left free.' How often did I cash in on that?!

Bagware here acts on the assumption that a state officer would be more impressed by his status as bank manager than by his function as temple president. This perception that decision makers are little inclined to listen to temple presidents who have no direct means of putting pressure on administrative procedures is confirmed by a former Chief Secretary. He explains that a temple president may be able to win ground in the world of electoral politics, which depends on popular support, but often fails to impress bureaucrats, except of course when they themselves support religious projects or fear the political influence a person is expected to mobilize.

The construction of the Durga Temple at Pir Gate was successful because the committee had all the Hindu leaders on its side and could claim political support from the highest ranks. The 'green-flag-incident' is another example. The Muslims residing next to the Kali Temple had already experienced that their protests against the temple had little success without prominent support. When taking up their protests again years later, they mobilized a member of the Youth Congress from the locality, who was able to convince a respected Muslim leader of the city to fight their case.

In all cases we find that a combination of two strategies is used. Initially, people act on the territory, ignoring state laws and hoping that no one will interfere. This is a reasonable expectation, since the public administration prefers to only intervene in cases where public order is seen to be in grave danger. In cases where state agencies oppose the temple, devotees turn to the public and to eminent personalities, preferably politicians, in order to increase their power of negotiation.

The various activities of ignorance and activism are secondly defended or opposed by using the different narratives quoted above, in which the tale of a particular temple and the struggle for or against it is embedded. Temples are destroyed on the basis that they are seen as purely economic enterprises or strategic actions in a political game, or because they are believed to stand in the way of rational city planning and endanger communal peace. Their construction and re-construction, seen as legitimate even while qualified as illegal, is done on the basis that they give expression to people's needs and wishes and remain outside of the influence of the state. These highly standardized reflections often include arguments about tradition and modernity and place the temple in an ideological discourse of authenticity and progress.

TEMPLE CONSTRUCTION AND THE RHETORIC OF TRADITION AND MODERNITY

A common reflex of those who oppose the construction of illegal temples, and who are disturbed by the social conflicts that arise from religious causes, is to call for more education. Illiteracy is made responsible for the enthusiasm with which people fight for their religious demands. For some it is the persistence of tradition within a modern environment that is responsible for people's inability to appreciate the merits of a modern, rational life. Another version forwards 'incomplete' or 'uneven' modernization as a reason for the disturbance of urban peace. It has uprooted people from the 'natural wisdom' of tradition without yet filling the gap with new, modern ideas and ideals. In a polemic argument, the majority of Indian people are declared to have become prone to the seductive power of religious propaganda by political forces. With further education they will give up 'irrational beliefs' and 'superstitions'. Only then will they realise their 'real' interests and become immune to the leaders' efforts to mobilise them in the name of religion (Chakrabarty 1990; Chandra 1984, 1991).

What escapes the attention of this argument is the possibility that the insistence on religious rights may not be due to innocence or ignorance, but could also be an act of resistance to a legal situation perceived as inadequate. In that case, it is conceivable that further education would make people even more rebellious, leading to other forms of social unrest. Such a perception goes against the notion of modernity, which sees in Western rationality the solution to all social problems.

For those who project modernity as the solution to religious conflicts, modernity is depicted as the establishment of the Law of Reason, brought about by an unbiased state as the agent of transformation. Religion, where it is not the private affair of individuals, is then subsumed under the authority of a state, which will manage its affairs presumably to the satisfaction of all. Modernity here becomes a totalizing project that does not tolerate anything outside its own realm. Its supporters are suspicious of any alternative claim to truth. Science is seen to have the monopoly on filling the moral and social space.[13] 'The process of alleged scientific reasoning—alleged scientific moral reasoning and social optimisation—is reluctant, even opposed, to admitting other modes of consciousness or other world orientations into any space it already occupies, for it imperialistically expands to fill all the spaces available' (Tambiah 1990: 151).

The naive trust in modernity is criticised by a set of intellectuals who hail tradition as the place of tolerance and peace, an argument that was introduced in the last chapter as an anti-secular attitude. Those who oppose modernity in general—and not only certain aspects of it—hold it responsible for the increase in social tension. The only solution to the violence of modernity is a re-establishment of tradition in a *post*-modern society that will overcome the totalitarian project of modernity, and help tradition to develop its full potential in a society that has deliberately opted for its re-implementation (Nandy 1984, 1987a, 1987b, 1988).

Both these conceptions of modernity, as the solution of, or the reason for, social tension, are far from adequate descriptions of the everyday reality of religious discourse. No doubt, religious practices and beliefs are informed by a cultural repertoire that is believed to be rooted in tradition. However, these traditions have not remained unchanged. Through the praxis and reflections of people they are constantly re-worked and re-adjusted to the new conditions. In their everyday practices, people are unconcerned about the question of whether modernity as a theoretical concept has a place for religion or not. Their worry is a practical one, of finding adequate ways to translate their religious tradition into an urban reality they conceive of as modern.

An example from the Mahakaleshwar Temple in Ujjain may help to illustrate this point. In order to increase the attractiveness of this pilgrimage site, a television screen was installed in the entrance hall of the famous temple, which constantly transmitted pictures from the sanctuary. The initiative for this innovation had come from the newly posted Collector, a young man who, *ex officio*, was president of the temple trust. Together with other important trustees, he shared the opinion that the television would instil discipline in the devotees and increase their satisfaction, since their attention would be diverted during the long waiting hours by experiencing a continued *darshan* on screen. However, there was also opposition to the project. Older priests voiced their objections, saying that the importance of the sacred object was diminished through its constant availability on screen. Another argument

[13] See as an example for such an attitude, Jain 1990.

they made was that people started entering the sanctuary for the wrong reasons, not out of religious devotion, but in order to appear on television. What struck me in this case was not so much that the opinions lay so far apart, but rather that everyone from the worshipper to the ticket-seller, from the official to the priest, had an opinion on this matter and defended it with full vigour in a rhetoric that saw modernization either as a way of improving or of polluting tradition. It was obvious that the issue was not only controversial but also highly emotional, involving a community in a discourse on how much innovation a religious tradition could endure when adapting to new conditions of life.

There are other examples, where modernity appears not as an agent of change but rather as a means to explain the 'hidden logic' of traditions. Take for example the basil plant (*tulsi*). People point to the fact that *tulsi* is a herb that helps to cure numerous diseases, as science is now able to prove. Keeping this plant and worshipping it is seen as an ancient way of cultivating this knowledge and pointing towards the plant's importance and powers. By a similar logic, prayers and ritual attendance are rationalized as gymnastics that keep the human body fit, the ritual bath in the morning appears to be a measure for physical hygiene, and the ceremonial application of sandalwood paste to the forehead as a means for cooling the brain. Religion, a Khatik summed up in line with this type of reasoning, 'is made for health, and every religion is made to match the requirements of a particular society. *Dharma* are rules made for well-being'.

Here we do not find the classical opposition between tradition and modernity, but rather the opinion that in order to understand and save the intrinsic value of tradition, it has to be translated into the modern world in the right way. Here modern is not a theoretical concept or an ideal condition, but means rather the order that dominates the new urban life style. It is characterized by participation in formal education, technical innovations, new social freedom, the structuring of life through fixed working schedules, the weakening of family-ties, and so on. Whether positive or negative, these conditions are generally accepted as the given circumstances in which the negotiations of everyday life take place. People may then applaud or regret the changes in religion, which they believe are the result of the changed living-conditions. They complain that there is less time to go to the temple, that the youngsters do not care for the religious traditions of their parents, and that life has become too money-oriented. But there are also opposite opinions. There are remarks that nowadays devotees donate more money for religious purposes, that festivals are now celebrated with greater vigour, and that temples have become bigger and more beautiful.

According to this reasoning, tradition is not the 'Other' of modernity, but a valuable resource inherited from the past and relevant today, even if in new and changed ways. This is not to say that people know of all the ways in which traditions are actually readjusted or even invented. It is rather to emphasize that people can draw on a general awareness that tells them that traditions undergo changes. It is at moments like the installation of the television in the Mahakaleshwar Temple that it is brought to their attention.

It thus appears that India has reached a condition of post-modernity in which various rationalities exist alongside each other. People get involved in extensive power struggles, in which everyone insists on a right to his worldview in a pluralistic democracy. In this context the authentication of religious traditions takes place with reference to the memory of the old, as well as by acknowledging the efforts of the young to translate transmitted knowledge and practices and adjust them to the modern life-style.

To value tradition usually also means to accept the plurality of it. Most people show a great awareness of the existence of many different traditions, and are generally convinced that everyone has to be true to his own inherited knowledge. However, this attitude, which allows for the parallel existence of many different traditions, should not be confused with tolerance, as is the case in the writings of people like Nandy (1990) or Miller (1987).[14] Often the non-interference with other people's ways is an effect of social distance. Conflicts do not arise as long as people do not come in conflict with other traditions. Yet where interests overlap, even the occurrence of violence cannot be excluded. This has become clear in many studies of Hindu-Muslims riots, where the competition over religious time and space that occurred when important festivals of the respective communities fell on the same day also triggered violence in areas less known for religious competition. The argument about 'tolerant traditional masses' fails to consider the contextuality of acceptance.

Any religious action can be seen either as a genuine realisation of a person's duty or as a corrupt practice. Ambiguity also prevails when people judge politicians' involvement in religious issues, which may be classified as true devotion or as selfish manipulation. People often join the movement of a politician in order to realise their own agenda. They are not blind to the politicians' self-interests, they know of 'dirty politics', but they simultaneously acknowledge that the leaders' goals may coincide with theirs, and that even leaders are at times able or

[14] Mio (1999) criticized Nandy on the same point with his material from a Sufi Saint's Mausoleum in Rajasthan, showing that the joint ritual observances of Hindus and Muslims at a shrine classified as Muslim do not necessarily imply religious tolerance or harmony.

willing to help subordinates. Any help, of course, is based on a relationship of reciprocity.

The argument that declares people to be unable to judge their own situation in a changing environment should itself be seen as part of the power-struggle in which different persons and groups are fighting for supremacy. In this context, the rhetoric of 'uneducated masses' and 'incomplete modernization' is used to raise one's own status *vis-à-vis* an imagined 'Other'. Who is considered educated and who uneducated is determined by context. Learned priests and trustees demand the education of temple priests; Bagware wishes to help his caste fellows 'grow up'; men talk of the need to educate women and well-off temple worshippers wish to put an end to begging. The belief in the superiority of the educated also surfaces in the form of an internalized self-accusation. An excellent example is given by Fuller, who demonstrates that the priests in Tamil Nadu have largely internalized the critique of their profession, as un-educated and corrupt (Fuller 1982, 1984a).

The world as modern appears to remain a colourful place. In the everyday interactions of a religious discourse, modernity does not mean an ideal that is to be reached, a possible final condition in which reason has come of age, but is a process through which urban reality is created, in which scientific thinking has its place next to the belief in divine intervention. Rationality is acknowledged to help organize many aspects of life in a more efficient way, but beyond this there are many questions that remain open. A general acknowledgement of the reality of actors of various kinds and the legitimacy of their interventions does not, however, result in an attitude of 'anything goes'. Through constant negotiation people struggle to establish the right place for traditions and beliefs in contemporary society. The arguments forwarded in debates can be extremely intolerant, dismissing others as 'irrational' or 'manipulated', but there are also other times when people see no objection to the parallel existence of different perceptions.

CONCLUSION

Negotiations over temple matters have proved to be a complex power-game, in which various actors bring to bear their viewpoint. Constructing or managing a temple can be seen as an emancipatory project as well as a way of strengthening authoritarian social structures. It can be fought in agreement with or against the directive of state institutions that takes responsibility for the regulation of religious affairs. For some people, corruption and illegal temple construction call for state intervention. The strict implementation of law, the unification of religious practices, and the accountability of financial transactions are considered corner stones of a policy that aims at reducing the misuse of religious institutions. Others query the motives of a secular state intervening in religious matters and they prefer to see devoted individuals in charge of temples.

While most conflicts over temples remain local affairs, they nevertheless have an impact on the overall social structure. Through acts of protest alternative views are made public. They force negotiations in which the various images of an ideal order confront each other. The conflicts between them are only resolved momentarily and in the context of a concrete setting. They surface again and again as the concepts that inform the different positions appear irreconcilable.

The central concern of many of these conflicts is the common wish of many different actors to establish a fitting place for religion in contemporary society. More seems to be at stake than the questions arising out of a particular case of temple construction or management. What is being negotiated is the turn modernity will take and the place it will give to religion. Embedded in a narrative structure of progress, temple matters are framed as backward practices that belong to the past, or are defended as important traditions that will help shape a human modernity respecting cultural diversity.

Yet it would be overstating the point if all religious activities are portrayed as being monitored by a reflexive process that rationalizes the activities even while they are carried out. Every human activity is always a combination of habitual practices and reflexive processes. The reader may also be reminded of Bourdieu's formulation that praxis belongs to different order of things that can never fully be encompassed by reflection. Whatever efforts in planning are made, they can never suffice to contain all the uncertainties with which social practices are invested, since human actors lack knowledge of the effects their actions will have as well as an overview over all the other activities and thoughts carried out at the same time (Bourdieu 1987: 158-9, 165). Nevertheless, reflection as an interpretative process of giving meaning to events is an important part of social practices. Through reflections the uncertainties of the future are addressed, meaning is adjusted as events unravel, and memory is shaped through the re-appropriation of events during later recollections.

I would thus like to emphasize once more that the religious discourse is shaped through *both performances as contextual practices and their re-appropriation in a socially shared reflexive process*. Describing the way that state power is resisted by the presence of temples and the activities involved in this, does not mean that every or even most illegal temples were planned as conscious acts of resistance. Often their construction is the result of a spontaneous impulse, part of a personal life planning, of a political project, or the result of a particular local constellation. The decision to construct a temple may initially be little concerned with official positions on the matter or larger political power struggles. Yet as a temple starts to take shape and comes to the attention of more and more people, it is made sense of in many conflicting ways, and thereby becomes a platform on which religious questions are negotiated and a means through which power relations are realized.

I treated temple constructions as social processes the outcome of which is determined by the way events enter the consciousness of different actors during ongoing communicative actions. Emphasising the contingency of social events and the constant need to re-adjust strategies, activities and perceptions, I described the activities of temple management and temple construction as dynamic processes that can neither be neither fully planned nor fully determined by any one group or person. Success means the ability to imprint one's own point of view on a movement as it takes shape, by convincingly presenting one's own perception as an adequate, or even the only adequate, description of reality. Thus, power rests with those who have the capacity to shape the imagination, as Zygmunt Baumann notes (Baumann: 1992).

CHAPTER 6

Formulating Religious Alternatives

Explaining religious practices with reference to a dichotomy of tradition and modernity is neither new nor original. There exists a long tradition within the social sciences in which religion has been conceptualized as belonging to the domain of tradition. However, social practices show that even where religion is constructed as part of tradition, actors constantly struggle to find ways to adjusted inherited knowledge to the modern world. I will therefore start my discussion by further investigating the debate on tradition and modernity in order to show how it becomes relevant for the formulation of an ideal social order among believers, but also to point at the limits of a discourse that categorizes social practices in terms of opposites.

Along with the distinction between tradition and modernity, the opposition between subaltern and elite will be confronted. In view of the complex power games we have seen, it seems inappropriate to clearly distinguish between two different social domains. While summing up the findings of the study, the contextuality of sub- and superordination will be discussed and the terms subaltern and elite rendered contextual. Various groups will be seen as powerful agents who contribute to urban discourse of religion. The existence of conflicting ideologies is imprinted on the territory of the city through the presence of temples that counter the claims of a democratic nation-state to sovereignty. Resisting the subsumption of their projects under the labels of 'irrational' and 'illegal', believers fight for a place for their deities in the city, a fight that is always both religious as well as political.

CONCEPTUALIZING MODERNITY AND TRADITION

For the fathers of sociology and anthropology, modernity created a new condition—clearly distinguished from tradition—in which social life would be based on rational principles. Max Weber believed that modernity would lead to an ever-increasing routinization of life, using the metaphor of the 'iron cage' to describe the future condition of the social world. Durkheim, more optimistic, hoped that the discovery of laws of social existence would lead to the realisation of a more just and moral society.

For better or worse, modernity has not brought the fulfilment of these expectations, and certainly has not created uniform conditions, as exemplified by the search of the founding fathers of the social sciences for a clear-cut division or nomenclature based on some preconceived notion as to what is modern or pre-modern. Until the late 1960s anthropologists characterized the new nation states that failed to conform to their ideal of modernity as 'pre-modern', 'modernizing' or 'unevenly modernized'. They were seen as lacking a rational organisation that was made responsible for the various internal conflicts. The hope was that with further modernization conflict would disappear (see for example Geertz 1963, Dumont 1970; Singer 1972).

More recently, however, doubts have surfaced in the scientific community, as the problems of the new nation-states did not diminish with further modernization—which is normally taken to mean an increase in rational control over nature and society, although the most recent critics would query the very notion of scientific rationality as the only meaningful way of explaining the world.[1] A number of recent studies have shown that many of the conflicts earlier believed to be rooted in tradition, such as (violent) conflicts between religious communities or ethnic groups, are not so much a legacy of pre-colonial history but a result of changes set in motion by colonial intervention, the very same forces that wanted to instil rationality into the social order of all other societies.

Thus, the construction of trans-local religious communities and the consolidation of caste are placed at the onset of modernity. As the British tried to make sense of a foreign cultural environment and to fit the complex social reality of India to the needs of a unified administrative system, people were categorized according to caste, language and religion. The process of classification resulted in new perceptions of Indian society, which was nevertheless constructed as inherent in the social order of the colony. This effort to make a foreign people administratable and achieve clarity saw the emergence of the trans-local element, which was to become a force of change that had repercussions on modern Indian reality and discourses. Local variations were ignored and people were grouped into trans-local communities. Along with the construction of these ideological and administrative

[1] Habermas has challenged the view of a single rationality seeing all forms of communication as intrinsically rational. However, he makes a further differentiation by basing his theory on an evolutionary model, according to which a higher form of rationality (explicit rationality) develops in the form of self-reflexive reasoning (Habermas 1981; see also the critical appraisal of Habermas's work on rationality from an anthropological perspective by Linkenbach 1986).

constructions, society changed, since people realised the potential of the new perception for their own power struggles. New technology for communication and faster means of transport worked into the hands of a process through which trans-local communities as ideological constructs emerged in the consciousness of people and became guides for actions (see Anderson 1992).[2]

Such new insights into the dynamics of colonial intervention have made scholars doubtful about the dichotomy between tradition and modernity. Rudolph and Rudolph (1967) were among the first to criticise this dichotomy. They underlined the modernity of a number of traditions and the persistence of traditions within the context of modernity (refer also to Borden 1989; Comaroff and Comaroff 1992: 4-6). As a result of the increasing dissolution of a clear opposition between tradition and modernity, anthropologists no longer talk of different degrees of modernization. Modernization is no longer defined with reference to one particular idea of modernity. With the realization that the contemporary world is not only characterized by an increasing uniformity but simultaneously by a process of diversification, anthropologists have taken to defining modernity rather loosely as a condition identified with nationalism, capitalism and the powerful role of the state.[3] Ivy gives a good example of this for Japan, identifying in her definition of modernity not only the basic features but also pointing towards the importance which colonialism had for its spread.

> What I mean by modern—as if one could simply define it—indicates not only the urban energies, capitalist structures of life, and mechanical and electrical forms of reproduction [...] It indicates the problems of the nation-state and its correlation with a capitalist colonialism that ensured Japan would be pulled into a global geopolitical matrix from the mid-nineteenth century on. (Ivy 1995: 5)

Understood in these terms, modernity has indeed taken root everywhere in the world. The new world order has fundamentally changed the conditions of life everywhere, though not in a uniform way. It has set a global frame of reference in which social discourses take place. Nor does this viewpoint allow modernity to be perceived any longer as the opposite of tradition, for it does not constitute the other side of 'the great divide' (van de Veer 1994: 12). On the contrary, the adjustment of tradition is an essential part of the discourses about modernity (see, for example, Chatterjee 1997). It finds expression in

[2] This process is described for the problem of caste by B. Cohen 1968; Dirks 1989a, 1989b; Rudolph and Rudolph 1960, 1967. The question of trans-local religious communities is discussed by Dalmia and Stietencron 1995; Das 1990a; Freitag 1989; Ludden 1996; Pandey 1990; Sarkar and Butalia 1995; Weiss et al. 1996.

[3] For the discussion on modernity, globalization, and the effects on culture see: Alam 1999; Appadurai 1990a, 1990b, 1996; Bird et al. 1993; Eade 1997; Featherstone 1990; G. Kapur 1991; D. Miller 1995; Robertson 1992; Strathern 1995.

fierce battles over the desirable role of tradition in contemporary life. There is the belief that modernity has to be made human by the inclusion of tradition or conversely the conviction that modernity can only reveal its benefits once it is cleansed of the 'old' ways of thinking.[4] In both cases tradition is identified with the past. But the past is not simply preserved in traditions. It is appropriated by the present. Traditions do not remain unchanged. They are re-worked, adjusted or even invented (Hobsbawm and Ranger 1983).[5] At times, this also comes to the attention of the actors themselves, as I have shown in the last chapter.

In order to bring out the conscious appropriation of tradition in contemporary life, Alam (1994, 1999) distinguishes between two different meanings of tradition. Tradition, he says, is available to people as an unquestioned, taken for granted, every-day form of knowledge. In this way 'tradition is directly accessible to people as a moral economy, a meaning system, a repository resource—both social and personal—a psychological support mechanism, and so on' (Alam 1994: 24). It is what Comaroffs call the hegemonial power of culture (Comaroff and Comaroff 1992). With the rupture brought about by modernity, Alam continues, tradition has lost its self-validating quality and has become subject to debates by people who believe that they stand outside tradition. It is re-worked, invented and re-created through the intellectual dialogue that tries to re-establish an imaginary 'true' past. This conclusion should not be mistaken to mean that tradition remained unchanged before the 'great rupture', but that the dialogue through which it was negotiated and changed used to be of a basically different nature. The process of interpretation and re-interpretation of tradition in pre-modern India, Alam claims, took part within the realm of tradition. It 'has been an internal component of the symbolic system in India' (Alam 1994: 24), In modernity, in turn, tradition is negotiated from an outside point of view, from a standpoint that has broken with tradition and now re-appropriates it intellectually (Alam 1994: 23-6).

This notion shows close affinities to Giddens, who states that modernity is characterized by reflexivity. In a modern condition, tradition can no longer lay claim to authority on the basis of simply representing things the way they used to be. Tradition continues to play a role in the 'post-traditional' society only when it can be justified from the reflected point of view of modernity. We thus deal with a

[4] Interesting in this context is Augé's remark that we should not only pay attention to the way people try to integrate the modern and the traditional, but also ask about the motivations and—I would further add—the perceptions that lie behind the wish to create such an integration (Augé 1998: 92).

[5] Consider for example the interesting article by Narayan (1993) in which he demonstrates how religion is constantly re-adjusted to the social environment by the adaptation of religious stories to current circumstances.

completely different meaning of tradition today. Tradition no longer represents a 'formulaic truth', but is 'justified tradition'. It comes 'in sham clothing and receives its identity only from the reflexivity of the modern' (Giddens 1990: 38, 1994).

Without wishing to blur the differences between the theories of these two scholars, I see them based on similar assumptions, since both try to make a clear distinction between tradition and modernity, not on the basis of modernity replacing tradition but by maintaining that tradition is of a fundamentally different nature within the context of modernity. Here the ambivalences of concrete actions are reduced in favour of a clean cut between a traditional and a modern time. Both theories are unable to deal with the fact that even in contemporary society, social life as self-evident is still influential in guiding people's action (see Comaroff and Comaroff 1992: 6-7). Even when people engage in reflection they do so from a particular standpoint, a standpoint that takes certain assumptions for granted. That means that the hegemonic force of the 'taken-for-granted-life' can be applied to both normal social action as well as reflective thought about social action. While both theories seem to miss this basic point, Giddens hints at this fact. He writes that if modernity is reflexive then nothing is sacred, which means that even this basic principle that 'nothing is sacred' cannot be exempt from scrutiny (Giddens 1994: 88). But this comment remains no more than an aside, and does not trigger reflections on this self-evident presumption that Giddens himself takes for granted.

By the same token tradition also exists in the form of a reflexive quality, tradition that is reformed and re-appropriated from an 'outside' point of view, as Alam and Giddens have described it. The distanced view on tradition is just as much part of people's lives as the self-evident presupposition. Thus, while I believe that the distinction between taken-for-granted and reflexive life is highly valuable as an analytical tool, I do not follow the assumption that these two approaches to living existed in historical succession. At least for modern society we can claim that they both exist side by side. It depends on a person's standpoint within a society whether traditions have a taken-for-granted quality or are reflected on from an outside point of view. It is an equation that changes with time and context.

The data in this study have shown that people rework traditions simultaneously from the inside and the outside. On one hand there are the negotiations in the temple that are only concerned with the correct way to worship which often constitute an effort in adjusting traditional knowledge to contemporary situations. Their sole aim is to 'get it right', not to defend religious practice against an onslaught of Rationality. However, these contestations take place within a society in which religious traditions are also looked at from the outside and where questions arise as to which beliefs should be continued and which are to be regarded as outdated. Believers in divine agency interact with scepticals who try to convince them of the irrelevance of their practices. Worshippers may ignore critical remarks concerning their religious orientation, or they may feel challenged to come up with elaborate explanations that rationalise traditions and defend their worth in terms of an inner logic that no longer remains obscure to an enlightened citizen.

In this sense modernity and tradition have to be thought of together. They do not constitute diametrical oppositions, since forms of modernity are constructed with reference to traditions, as self-evident knowledge and reflexive awareness. Similarly, much of the shaping and re-working of tradition in contemporary society takes place with a critical distance to a time when many traditions were not defined and singled out as traditions, since they constituted part of the taken-for-granted knowledge. This concern with tradition makes sense only from a standpoint that is defined as modern, and constructed in opposition to the world of tradition. The obsession with traditions and the belief in their historical reality as well as their authenticity appears to be part of the implicit knowledge that constitutes the modern condition and remains unreflected in most settings.

Thus, while the usefulness of the dichotomy of tradition and modernity is questioned here, I also acknowledge that this antithesis constitutes an important device that serves people to make sense of their world and map their position in a plural society. The religious discourse is no exception. Here standpoints are explicitly marked by establishing the relevance of traditions for the development of contemporary society. Therefore, the rhetoric of tradition will play an important role in the next section, which characterizes various standpoints on religion, which have so far remained implicit in my work.

THE MEANING OF RELIGION

As a point of departure for the discussions on the various meanings given to religion and ways of establishing the importance of tradition, I would like to start with a review of the three positions found in the debate on the politics of religion in contemporary India. The first view is an evolutionist perspective, which conceives of society as progressing towards modernity and secularization. India is believed to be 'underdeveloped', not only in economic terms but also in 'mentality'. Education is needed to popularize a 'rational world view'. It is thought to lead to a decline of religion, conceived of as a remnant of the pre-modern past. Here religion and science come as antagonistic and irreconcilable standpoints, whereby the latter is seen to supplant the former (Chandra 1984; Nauriya 1989; Shakir 1984; refer also the discussions of communalism by Dumont 1970; Geertz 1963; Saberwal 1981; Tyabji 1994).

Simultaneously there is a counterargument which, instead of adhering to an ideal of modernisation, clothes the need for development in terms of tradition. Most visible among those who call for the recovery of religious traditions are the political forces that fight for the establishment of a Hindu nation. They wish to re-establish a political condition that is said to have existed in the past, where harmony existed among men and between humans and deities. This model counters the ideal of a secular nation, since religion (here as Hinduism) is seen as an essential part of the national culture, which cannot be separated from the latter without destroying the very fabric of the nation (as primary sources see for example Golwalkar 1945, Savarkar 1949, for secondary sources are Graham 1990; Hellmann 1996; Jaffrelot 1996; Weiner 1978).

Both of these conceptions, that of a secular and that of a Hindu nation, are criticized by a third standpoint that opts for a strengthening of the plurality of traditions (Kothari 1988; Madan 1997; Miller, Donald 1987; Nandy 1990; Nandy et al. 1997; Thapar 1985, 1991, Thapar et al. 1977; Sarkar 1993). These critics do not accept the idea that modernity is superior to tradition. In fact some of them fully reject modernity as being intrinsically violent and oppressive (Alvares 1992; Nandy 1988). But they also oppose the political vision of the Hindu nationalists who declare their construct of Indian tradition to be the only 'authentic' one. They attack both hegemonic projects—that of modernity as well as that which comes in the name of tradition—for their 'false' understanding of Indian tradition. Instead, they see as the core of Indian tradition its plurality and tolerance. Religion is said to be dangerous when it is harnessed to an ideology. Yet it is considered beneficial when exercised in its 'traditional', tolerant form, because then it lends itself to guiding people's actions without allowing itself to be misused in political power struggles.

Given the religious practices that have been described in this work, any attempt to intellectually capture the discourse of religion by reference to these three positions must fall short of its aim. No doubt these views mark important positions in the altercations over religion, and capture various ideals which are projected onto the future and which stand for the hope to improve social relations through the transformation of political systems. But they all see religion as a social system and neglect the idea of divine agency, so central to the belief of many people.

The belief in divine agency and the orientation of believers towards their deities invites the opposition of those, who value religion solely as a means of instilling values in people. It has its roots in the very beginnings of the sociology of religion. Durkheim is famous for his theory that the essence of all religions is their ability to hold society together. He writes in the introduction to his *Elementary Forms of Religious Life* in 1915:

> The general conclusion of the book which the reader has before him is that religion is something eminently social. Religious representations are collective representations which express collective realities; the rites are a manner of acting which take rise in the midst of the assembled groups and which are destined to excite, maintain or recreate certain mental states in these groups. (Durkheim 1979: 10)

This attitude explains religion in terms other than what is expressed by believers themselves, and therefore leads to a devaluation of the opinions of the actors. It does appear in Durkheim's writing that people's religious beliefs are right because they intuitively serve the aim of social unity. Believers themselves are seen to miss this point as a result of their literal understanding of religious myths and rituals, and their resulting inability to understand religious representations in a purely metaphorical sense.

> But from the fact that a 'religious experience', if we choose to call it this, does exist and that it has a certain foundation—and, by the way, is there any experience which has none?—it does not follow that the reality which is its foundation conforms objectively to the idea which believers have of it. The very fact that the fashion in which it has been conceived has varied infinitely in different times is enough to prove that none of these conceptions express it adequately. (Durkheim 1971: 417)

Talal Asad (1983) criticizes this trans-cultural and ahistoric way of defining religion. He addresses his critique to Geertz, who like Durkheim argues for a view of religion as a functional system. Geertz sees religions as systems of symbols, which 'formulate a basic congruence between a particular style of life and a specific [...] metaphysic, and in so doing sustain each with the borrowed authority of the other' (Geertz 1966: 4). Asad opposes a generalizing theory of this kind by arguing for a re-historization of the study of religion that pays attention to the particularities of every religion. 'There cannot be a definition of religion which is universally viable because and to the extent that the effects of these processes are historically produced, reproduced and transformed' (Asad 1983: 238).

In my study I have followed Asad's demand for a contextual study of religion, although diverging from his proposed emphasis on the question of how power creates religion (Asad 1983: 252). My aim has been to show the power-constellations that exist within a religious setting and how they are established and re-affirmed through the constituting practices of a wide range of actors. Therefore my analysis of the discourse of religion starts out from what people themselves think and say about religion.

Three positions have become distinguishable as a result of the religious practices and reflections I collected in the temples of Bhopal. First and foremost there is a large group of believers for whom religion is essentially concerned with communication between human and divine beings. This position considers the ways deities are present in this world and provides ways to access them. The temple as the divine abode in this world is seen as a place that grants privileged access to the deities, who are directly present in the form of divine images.

In a second meaning religion is used to describe forms of ethics, morality or duty. As a guideline to the realization of an ideal social condition it is considered to be the glue that holds society together. How this happens is explained in two different ways. Some say that people stay on the road of moral conduct solely because they fear the intervention of divine powers. The confrontation with a deity (in the temple) inculcates values in devotees and reminds them of their duties. The other explanation is 'secular', close to what Durkheim says about religion. It interprets the temple and the deity as a symbol of and for the community. It is the place around which the community can be organized and which gives identity to the group and meaning to life.

Finally, religion is understood as a route to spiritual progress. It is a philosophy that teaches the nature of things and a technique that helps to attain mental peace. The temple serves as a possible place for this purpose, because it is said to help focus the mind and offers room for religious instruction. But the temple can also be an obstacle, such as when it is characterized as a noisy place focused on money-making, which as a result of commercialization has lost its quality as spiritual centre.

All these three meanings of religion are expressed and realized with reference to a particular view of tradition. Religion is seen as an application of traditional knowledge to concrete situations, visible in the worship of deities as well as in practices intended to heal and liberate the self and society. Here agency is not attributed to the actor but to tradition, which is said to inform social practices. Dealing with the imaginary agent of tradition triggers disputes since tradition as an ideal is constructed in various ways, and its application demands an act of adjustment. In an effort 'to get it right', people welcome such negotiations, because they recognize that knowledge is dispersed and that pooling it as well as exchanging experiences will help them to conform to an ideal of which they often have only a vague picture.

There is also a theoretical way of viewing traditions based on assessing their value within the social order. Such an 'outside' point of view considers the functionality of tradition for the organisation of social life, as happens when religion is hailed as a way of ensuring a healthy society or peace of mind. Here arguments are only partly concerned with the correct way of implementing traditions, and concentrate rather on which traditions are supportive of contemporary society.

These ways of relating to religion and tradition are not necessarily mutually exclusive. Yet, there remains a basic conflict, a dividing line that separates those who generally count on the possibility of non-human intervention and those who reject the idea of deities as agents. The fast growing number of temples in urban India seems to indicate that the belief in divinities is nowhere on the decline. This runs counter to the common expectation that with modernity religion is bound to disintegrate. Thus, my next task will be to analyse how people make sense of devotion to the divine in contemporary societies defined as modern, and how they integrate their beliefs into a dominant discourse that cherishes 'scientific thinking'.

HOW TO PROVE DEITIES?

The conviction that Western scientific thinking offers the only rational approach to the world has fostered doubts about the possibility of divine intervention. There are a number of people who are convinced that modernity has no place for beliefs in non-human agents, and who see religion as empty ritualism, the 'opium of the masses', or as disruptive ideology. Yet most people I met in Bhopal had the distinct but vague feeling that 'there is something', which implies that there exists a power greater than that of humans. Most impressive in this respect was the way belief in non-human agency manifested itself during the 'milk miracle' of 1995. Life came to a standstill in India on the day people were convinced they could genuinely see statues of Ganesh drinking the milk he was offered. Millions of Hindus rushed to the temples in order to see whether the god would also accept their offering (see Vidal 1996: 5). Such a belief in the reality of the divine forces and their ability to act in this world is demonstrated in a less spectacular way by the narration of occurrences of divine self-manifestation, the belief in possession, the stories of miraculous healing, and by the accounts of revelations.

Yet even when the existence of divine forces is proclaimed, many ambiguities and uncertainties are present. Why do the deities not always help when they are approached? Is it because they also have their own moods, or because they were not approached in the correct way, or maybe even because they do not exist or do not care? These doubts surface when things go contrary to expectations and destroy the hopes of the believers. It appears easy to believe in a miracle that has taken place many years ago or in a far away place, but what about here and now? These were also the questions that occupied Bagware's mind when he had made the goddess Kali his personal guru and was unsure whether she had accepted him as her disciple or whether she even existed.

Questions about the reality of the divine also result from the participation in different meaning systems that exist parallel to each other. This is the case when people simultaneously operate in the context of scientific reasoning when embarking on a search for religious experiences. The two contexts demand the application of different rules. They lead to different constructions of reality for which they claim superiority over all others. How is one to explain a miracle that overcame laws of nature? And how to verify a revelation in terms of the scientific demand for proofs?

But we have to be cautious, for otherwise we may assume these conceptual queries are also applicable to the realm of praxis. A sick person may well turn to a hospital first, but if the doctor is unable to help he can still consult a medium or pray directly to a deity for a cure. There are many such cases. The search for a lost son may be done with the help of the police, but simultaneously the deity can also be addressed. If medical treatment is unable to help a barren woman she can still turn to the goddess. People apply different forms of reasoning in different situations. These do not come in conflict with each other, since every context calls upon only one particular meaning system. Praxis is selective, for it does not bring all manner of different concepts to mind, but only specific ones that are relevant to the concrete situation. It is in this sense that Bourdieu characterizes the realm of praxis as 'closed'. Specific connotations are called up in relation to the praxis in which they are applied (Bourdieu 1987: 158-9, 165). In view of a lack of systematic reflection that characterizes people's ways of acting, Richards calls social practices *performative skills*. He distinguishes them from *reflexive knowledge* because people's ability to perform is not connected to their ability to explain what they do and how they do it (Richards 1993).

But the dilemma of different explanatory frameworks comes to light as soon as people start to reflect on their different ways of acting. People might try out different things just to be on the safe side, leaving the question of whether they really believe in the power of the act momentarily open. But when they want to explain what happened, they have to decide on the one or the other of the available frameworks in order to integrate the event into a consistent narrative order. Such decisions are important strategic devices that will inform future behaviour and guide people's decisions in conflict situations, where strategies of 'as well as' do not work. The temple study has offered examples of situations in which people are entangled in fights over correct interpretations of a situation. When the sudden appearance of a statue creates a controversy, people are forced to take sides and find words in which to defend their engagement. These are not only conflicts between individual people, but confrontations of discourses. The belief in divine agency is contradicted by a discourse that denies the possibility of non-human agency. As an answer, believers have found ways to make sense of the existence of divinities in a language borrowed from science.

One clue is given by Bagware's narration of his religious search that followed the day he made the goddess Kali his guru. He remembered that it was thanks to the goddess herself that he did not lose his faith during this time. He tested her by setting her the task of revealing a *mantra* to him. When she fulfilled his wish he *knew* that she existed. From then on his religious devotion was for him no longer a question of faith but a *proven fact*. Many devotees narrate similar experiences in situations where they approached a deity on account of ambiguities and pressing problems in their daily lives. If the deity complies with the devotees' wishes, it is taken as a 'proof' of their existence.

Seen in this light the 'milk miracle' appears in a totally new light. The day Ganesh drank milk worshippers were offered a unique chance to *see* the god act. Here *belief* was turned into *knowledge*. It is interesting to note that after the miracle, people never asked me whether I believed what happened. They wanted to know whether I had *seen* the miracle. For many, the occurrences were not a question of belief, it was a nation-wide or even world-wide 'experiment' that proved the existence of divine powers (also Vidal 1996, Csordas 1996).

However, the metaphor of experiment is problematic. For believers intervention can demonstrate the existence of deities, but abstaining from intervention cannot disprove the existence of non-human forces. Deities are conceived of as having agency, since they have a choice. They may intervene and help out, thereby also offering the devotees a chance to actually experience divine protection. But they can also abstain from revealing themselves, breaking the expectations and hope of their devotees. Doubts about the possibility of containing deities through experimentation are also raised with reference to the reliability of sensual experience. After the 'milk miracle' sceptics raised the point that seeing was not enough: it did not prove anything because the important thing was not what was *seen* but how the occurrence could be *explained*. What happened could also be the result of a specific constellation in the natural environment or a trick that deluded the senses.

Yet these doubts did not perturb devotees who see no incompatibility between having religious experiences and their esteem for scientific thought. Rather they borrowed metaphors from the language of science to explain religious phenomena.

Another conceptual parallel was drawn with experiences at school, by calling religious devotion a skill, a mental ability to read the signs of the divine world in the here and now. Bagware illustrated this with a picture of Kali. When I asked him whether the goddess was really in this picture, he replied that this is a question of approach. It is the same, he continued, as with a written text. Those who are able to read the signs can grasp its meaning, those who cannot decode them throw the paper away because the signs do not convey any meaning to them. Only believers, he said, can grasp the meaning of a devotional picture. To be religious means to have acquired a certain kind of 'literacy', this implies that people who cannot decipher the religious meaning are 'blind' to a particular knowledge. The ability to communicate with the divine is measured with reference to a perception that gives education and literacy primary importance. Just as school teaches children to read texts and to understand nature, religious praxis teaches people to understand the divine world.

Arguments that foster a conceptual integration of religious experiences with a discourse dominated by scientific rationality are at odds with the opinion that in the modern world, religion has its place in a sphere outside or complementary to science. It is a view well established in the social sciences, as two examples may show. Bell (1977) argues that only religion is able to answer the predicament of the human condition and elaborates that with modernity a process of secularization[6] (differentiation of institutions) and profanization (dis-enchantment) was set into motion. It is characterized by the development of a radical individualism, the replacement of religion through expressive arts, the 'decline of belief in Heaven and Hell, and the rise in the fear of nothingness, or the void, in the realm beyond life, the coming to consciousness, in short, of nihilism' (Bell 1977: 430). It is this deficiency of modernity, which leaves human beings without an answer to the specific problems of suffering and death—which gives nourishment to the 'new religions'. In close agreement with Weber's thesis, religion is seen as 'a set of coherent answers to the core existential questions that confront every human group' (Bell 1977: 429).

[6] For Bell secularization is not a process of vanishing religion but rather a transformation religion undergoes in modern society. For a recent contribution to the debate on the term secularism and its meaning see Laermans et al. 1998.

Koepping's (1998) article on the place of religion in the contemporary world points towards another way in which religion is established in a domain left void by science. Koepping follows Max Weber's distinction between instrumental rationality (*Zweckrationalitaet*) and value-rationality (*Wertrationalitaet*). He explains that science has established itself in the domain of means-end rationality. It dominates in the field of technology but it does not provide any guidance for human action. 'Scientific rationality as instrumental rationality can only supply the means, it cannot define the ends: because the ends of human aspirations should not and cannot be determined or governed by this form of rationality' (Koepping 1998: 96). This gap left open by science is filled by religion, becoming a guide for human relations as it constitutes the domain for creating values.

Both these theories help to comprehend the standpoint of non-believers, who value religion for the effect it has on human beings. At the same time, the theories stand in contrast to the efforts of some believers, who try to accommodate their religious convictions within the modern world by making sense of them in terms of scientific reasoning, and not by seeing them as irrational, non-rational or metaphorical. Instead, the existence of the divine appears to be a well-accounted phenomenon that is in line with a scientific understanding of the world.

Independent of the way the meaning of religion and religious experiences is established in theory, the problems of the praxis remain unsolved. Even accepting the assumption that the existence of non-human agents can be experienced, people have to address the dilemma of interpretation anew in every single situation, because the acknowledgement of the compatibility of different explanations does not relieve human agents from the need to select the 'correct' explanation in any given situation. If a stone appears from out of the ground, it could be a divine self-manifestation, or equally an outcome of erosion. The 'milk-miracle' may be of divine origin or the illustration of a specific law of nature. A case of possession may be real, a fake performance, or a pathological condition. There are no absolute guidelines for deciding what is what, but people do have their own criteria for deciding (see Schieffelin 1996).

To sum up, while religion is commonly defined as existing outside the domain of science, efforts are also made to explain experiences with divine agents by applying concepts of 'experiment' or 'skill'. Such efforts help to reconstruct religious knowledge in a way that makes it consistent with discourses of modernity, also observed where believers justify religious traditions as following a 'hidden logic'. This effort of integration of different discourses exists parallel to other ways of conceptualizing religion. At times the world of religion can also be posited as being in opposition to the dominant discourse of science and the nation state. In fact, in many parts of this thesis the temple has been interpreted as a social world that through its orientation to the divine offers an alternative formulation of the social order.

RESISTING STATE POWER THROUGH RELIGIOUS PRACTICES

I have presented the temple as an institution that participates in various discourses. Emphasis has been given to the temple as a caste and community organisation, as a ritual institution, and as a political stage. On comparing these different perspectives, a paradox emerges: while the temple appears to be integrated into the urban power struggles in numerous ways, it also exists as a separate domain where human relations—when they are oriented towards the divine—are governed according to principles differing from those in the 'secular' world.

The temple as a unique place is characterized by its sacredness. It constitutes the territory of divine authority, which is reflected by direction given to human action and the way social relations are organized. It is more than simply an opening to supernatural forces that secures the connection between the world and the divine—as Eliade puts it (Eliade 1991: 27). The temple is divine territory. It is the deity's place in the world. From this it follows that authority in the temple is indirect authority, derived from the supreme power and validated through a relationship characterized by devotion and benevolence.

In the political institutions of a secular democracy, divine authority lacks any legitimacy. It is meaningful only via the influence of those voters who select politicians on the strength of their interest in religious issues. Within the context of the modern urban city, the temple suggests an alternative way of perceiving the world and the social relations in it, and as such is a place for resistance in the widest sense of the term. However, to acknowledge the independence of the temple as an institution and the challenges it poses to other ideologies is not to deny its integration in a communicative system in which various ideologies are juxtaposed, mixed and partly integrated. I have shown the influence that the rhetoric of science has exerted on religious conceptions in the last section. Even more apparent, and focused on in numerous studies, is the interconnection between religious conceptions and political ideologies in the Hindu nationalist project. As an alternative to the secular ideals of the Congress and the Left Wing, the Hindu nationalists have emerged as a powerful political force. Their ideas of a religiously informed polity find expression in political speeches and electoral campaigns built on a religious rhetoric, in political campaigns for the realization of temples, in the stylization of Hindu kings and saints as national heroes, the commitment to religiously informed codes of conduct and a hostile attitude towards religious minorities. Here a particular vision of Hinduism is fostered that also informs the way people in the temple imagine the divine and realise the sacred in their actions and thoughts.

The views propagated in the mass media when tackling religious issues also participate in the definition of an imagined 'Hindu culture'. Notable in this context is the showing of serials and feature films that appeal to the popular taste for religious subjects. By creating images of the divine, they influence ideas of how deities are, how they act, how they relate to the world, and how they should be approached. Deities are fashioned and popularized, religious beliefs and morals are concretized, and diverse versions of mythological subjects fused and unified (see for more details: Dalmia-Luederitz 1991; Malinar 1995; Thapar 1985, 1989b).

The organization of temple life is not independent of such trends. In Bhopal this is particularly evident in the history of the Durga and even more so the Ram Temple,[7] which are supported by the prophets of a strong unified Hinduism and informed by an ideology that strives for a unified, Brahmanic and aggressive Hinduism. There are also other trends, as shown by the history of the Kali Temple. It stands almost as an antidote to a project of unified Hinduism. Its internal organization realizes ideals of equality that have been brought by democracy. So far the religious life in the Kali Temple has resisted appropriation by any one group, such as leading politicians, Hindu nationalists, Brahmin priests or even trustees. It is shaped through the interaction of a changing group of worshippers from very different backgrounds. They all bring to bear their knowledge, which covers a broad spectrum because here people of different castes, classes, gender, status and educational background all interact.

Characterizing the temple as a space for resistance thus does not mean situating it in opposition to or outside of current discourses. Following Foucault (1980), I contend that any discourse is constrained by the regime of truth supported by a given society. The temple offers an alternative because it lies at the confluence of *different* discourses. It acknowledges the divine and interprets its will, often also at variance to the will of political actors, especially where otherwise marginal people are invested with the power to speak. As one place where meaning emerges through the contextual activity of people, the temple itself becomes part of the urban discourse of religion. As such it is not a unified whole, that counters other discourses, but rather a variously

[7] There has been a great increase in Ram Temple constructions in India since the movement for a temple in Ayodhya started.

interpreted space, the realization of the imaginary of many different actors, who juxtapose and integrate the available streams of thoughts in many different ways.

I have introduced in this book Bagware, Shastri, as well as Manish, as persons who mediate the religious and the political domain, and who all have their own ways of connecting religion with politics. Their life histories showed that when viewed from a different standpoint, discourses that are at times construed as in contemporary India separate, and which in concrete practice also seem to contrast with one another, can also define a common field. In the life of leaders, certain domains become indistinguishable. They overlap because authority in the field of religion may support authority in competition for political positions. Here the discourse of the temple becomes integrated and indistinguishable from the struggle for status and meaning in the field of state politics.

This discussion, which highlights the contribution of many different people to the defining and re-defining of the religious sphere and its significance for the urban discourses, calls into question the dichotomy between the dominant and the subaltern. If the temple is a place where people from diverse backgrounds join the negotiation for meaning, then it blurs the dichotomy between those who have power and those over whom power is exercised. Instead of an opposition between dominant and subaltern we find that people are related in complex relationships of shifting positions. This is not to say that everyone has the same chance to contribute. But any analysis has to take into consideration, that power relations are paradoxical in the sene that they are always potentially open, undetermined while at the same time they are defined and crystallised in positions and status.

VISUALIZING POWER RELATIONS

I concur with Foucault's view that power as such is neither bad nor good, but a reality of life. To support this proposition does not mean to accept every concrete form of domination as unavoidable or even necessary or just. (Foucault [(1981] himself is very clear on this point, stating that even if power is all-encompassing this should not lead to our acceptance of any form of control we experience as unjust.) It is rather to assert that the fight against a particular form of power is in itself an exercise of power, and leads to the establishment of (different forms of) power relations. Consequently the avoidance of any *a priori* judgements on power (including resistance) and its manifestations is not aimed at discouraging social movements, but rather at encouraging an analysis that considers the different ways of exercising power and the rationales used to justify them.

A variety of attitudes towards the exercise of power are to be found in the social discourse. Forms of domination may be accepted as legitimate, benevolent or necessary, or rejected as illegitimate, malevolent, unjust or violent. In most cases it is assumed that the truth lies somewhere in between, so that social relations are simultaneously characterized by coercion and resistance as well as persuasion and collaboration, as Guha notes (Guha 1989: 229-32, see also Luedtke 1991). In the present case the dichotomy introduced by Blau is transcended. Blau distinguishes between power as a brutal and illegitimate force and authority as an accepted and therefore legitimate form of domination. He underplays the complexity of power relations and their judgement, which, from different viewpoints and to different degrees, may appear simultaneously as legitimate and illegitimate (Blau 1964: 130). Foucault points at the complex network of relations at the heart of any power relations:

'One sees why the analysis of power relations within a society cannot be reduced to the study of a series of institutions, not even to the study of all those institutions which would merit the name 'political'. Power relations are rooted in the system of social networks. This is not to say, however, that there is a primary and fundamental principle of power which dominates society down to the smallest detail; but, taking as point of departure the possibility of action upon the action of others.., multiple forms of individual disparity, of objectives, of the given application of power over ourselves or others, of, in varying degrees, partial or universal institutionalization, or more or less deliberate organization, one can define different forms of power. The forms and the specific situations of the government of men by one another in a given society are multiple; they are superimposed, they cross, impose their own limits, sometimes cancel one another out, sometimes reinforce one another. (Foucault 1983: 224)

I have introduced Bagware as a caste leader, and a man with great influence among Khatiks. His leadership does not, however, go uncontested. People may often obey him, but they also voice their opposition and have even tried to demolish his dominance. His survival as a leader is due to his skilful manipulation of relationships and of the disagreements in the assessments of his contribution that are made by caste members. Shifting alliances with caste members in and outside Bhopal, relatives, and traditional authorities, have so far secured his position in the caste. He holds onto his position through a carefully weighted use of different strategies: strictly enforcing his will at one time and co-opting his caste fellows through compromises and concessions at other times. His power depends on a legal document that makes him president of the Kali Temple Trust and chief advisor of the caste organization, and on the consent of the people who re-admitted him into the caste, realizing that instead of opposing him, it would serve them better to co-opt Bagware for *their projects* by asking for his patronage.

Bagware's ability to extend patronage again depends on access to powerful leaders and important urban institutions. The temple presidency and his command over Khatiks in Bhopal form part of his power-base, which gives him access to leading politicians. Yet there are also contexts in which these offices carry no status or even a negative image, and where he presents himself rather as an officer in a state institution. Furthermore, there is his background as the member of a scheduled caste, which again gives him an ambivalent status. On the one hand it weakens his position *vis-à-vis* people of high caste origin, who dominate some of the political sub-groups. On the other hand he uses his status as Khatik leader to demand representation in the name of membership in a Scheduled Caste.

Finally, there is Bagware as a religious person. As temple president and on the strength of his personal religious experiences he also lays claim to authority in religious questions. He imposes his ideals of ritual correctness through his selection of temple employees, by directly intervening in ritual procedures, and by enforcing certain forms of behaviour in the temple. But also in this field he is not uncontested. Not all temple visitors or ritual servants comply with his orders. At times they even openly oppose Bagware, as in the case of the rejected temple priest.

Simultaneously placed in different spheres of influence, Bagware is neither completely powerless nor all powerful. He holds certain strategic positions in a complex network of power relations. To realize the potential of these positions he carefully weighs the use of coercion and co-option, knowing well that the responses to his impositions are potentially open, which makes action dangerous and their outcome only partly predictable. It is in view of this complexity in the power relations that a clear-cut dichotomy of dominant and subordinate must be called into question. It is far from my intention to reject these terms as analytical tools. However, I believe that a further qualification is needed to assess their strength and weaknesses.

WHOSE POWER?

Ranajit Guha introduced the term 'subaltern' in the first volume of *Subaltern Studies* in accordance with the *Concise Oxford Dictionary* to mean 'of inferior rank'. He goes on to explain that 'subaltern groups are always subject to the activity of ruling groups, even when they rebel and rise up' (Guha 1982: vii). This formulation stands in a certain disparity to his characterization of the subaltern project. It is the declared aim of the Subaltern Study Group to recover the voice of the subaltern in history by paying attention to their world views, which are said to have been autonomous—even if not completely sealed off—from elite discourse. It is the search for popular perceptions informed by tradition, which are said to be fundamentally different from elite perceptions shaped by the views of the colonial intruders (Guha 1982: 1-8).

Following the development of *Subaltern Studies*, one finds that this contradiction between an independent subaltern space and subalterns as always subjected to domination is later resolved by acknowledging a number of different perceptions that mutually influence each other. Gyanendra Prakash sees this change setting in with Volume III (Guha 1984):

> Of course, the tension between the recovery of the subaltern as a subject outside the elite discourse and the analysis of subalternity as an effect of discursive systems was present from the very beginning. It also continues to characterise Subaltern Studies scholarship today. [...] Recent volumes, however, pay greater attention to developing the emergence of subalternity as a discursive effect without abandoning the notion of the subaltern as a subject and agent. This perspective, amplified since Subaltern Studies III, identifies subalternity as a position of critique, as a recalcitrant difference that arises not outside but inside elite discourses to exert pressures on forces and forms that subordinate it. (Prakash 1994: 1480-1)

It is thus only consistent that Guha in his introduction to Volume IX no longer talks of a subaltern domain (1982: 4) or subalternity in the singular (1982: 5), but speaks of 'small voices' and 'myriad voices' of history[8] (Guha 1996). The use of the terms in the plural suggests that there is no simple dichotomy in social reality between one superior and one subordinate group. Instead, we are confronted by shifting hierarchies that connect people and groups by complex and changing relations of subordination and super-ordination. Re-writing history in the sense of the Subaltern Studies project means not only recovering a particular group, but bringing to light the many different perspectives and many different ways of expression.[9]

Following up Guha's suggestion, I discovered that the majority of believers in Bhopal, in spite of being aware of their structural

[8] It is surprising that Guha titles his contribution 'The Small *Voice* of History' (Guha 1996: 1, my emphasis), using voice in the singular instead of in the plural.

[9] Guha gives a concrete example for the multiplicity of voices of resistance. He reviews a feminist critique by Kannabiran and Lalitha (1990) on Sundarayya's (1972) study on the Telangana People's Struggle for independence in the years 1946-51. Sundarayya's study was started with the aim of recovering agency for the subaltern by reading their struggle against the Nizam of Hyderabad as an expression of their independent goals. But by reading this struggle as a unified group's aspiration, the author negates the diversity of this struggle in which many different groups with a number of diverse motives were involved. Sundarayya, is criticized by Kannabiran and Lalitha for recovering the subalterns' voice only from a male perspective (Guha 1996: 7-8).

subordination, nevertheless perceived themselves as agents who are invested with powers to create and partly realise their own agenda, knowing well that the dominance of the powerful depends on their consent, which they can refuse. Resistance as a means of exercising power has surfaced where people entered into negotiations with politicians, administrators and Muslims to realize a temple project. It was visible where Khatiks refused to change traditional forms of caste organization. It was expressed by worshippers who did not follow the priest, or visible where trustees and devotees followed different agendas concerning the organization of temple life.

While bargaining for the realization of a concrete project, people use different strategies of persuasion, trying to conduct the argument in the language of the relevant discourse. In the case of a temple construction, devotees often chose to talk of the religious needs of the people when trying to convince a leader to help, about the miraculous intervention of a non-human agency to mobilize the support of believers, and of the granted right to freedom of religion when confronted with the administration. In the ritual context people talked of traditions, divine instruction, popular opinions, long term experiences or their religious status as a means for influencing behaviour. People carefully weigh the arguments, anticipating possible responses, which are no less standardized or strategically placed.

Yet, sometimes, none of the strategic lines of argument help. What if a politician promised to help but then forgot the matter? How can the members of the Khatik caste defend themselves against an all-domineering Bagware? How are they to act when believers find themselves disqualified as 'superstitious'? If negotiations fail, there always remains the option of imposing one's will through direct action. The construction of an illegal temple represents such a case. Here Hindus force their will by creating facts overnight. Another example given in this book was the groups of Muslims who forced the Kali Temple Trust into negotiation by planting a green flag inside the temple compound. There is also the example of Bagware, who was forced to reconsider his politics when some of his caste fellows rifled the temple funds and placed their locks on the donation boxes. Also beggars use this strategy when they are chased away from their place at the entrance of the temple. After waiting for a while, they simply return, knowing full well that all that can happen is that they will be chased away again. The list of such acts of dissidence is endless.

The reactions of those in power to such incidents are ignoring them, condemnation, and severe punishment. However, no-one is surprised about the occurrences of dissidence because acts of defiance are part of an expected, even if not always accepted, behaviour. Furthermore, since they represent a common practice it would be far from accurate to describe them as blind activism. They are better characterized as the taking of a calculated risk, because people carefully weigh the potential gains and losses of such actions.

Forcing one's opinion through action is not only a strategy used by people in subordinate positions. Those who hold positions of power use the same strategies to establish their dominance over subversive activities. Take, for example, the police interference at Pir Gate or the destruction of the temple at the Board Office crossing. These actions are different in the sense that they are sanctioned by law, although that does not necessarily increase their acceptance. By the same token, illegal actions are not necessarily considered immoral. People justify them as their last resort to prevent injustice and re-establish what they consider to be their rights.

I would summarize the two forms of resistance, negotiations and activism, in the following way. On the one hand, people use negotiations to defend their projects as rational, just and legitimate. The other option is to reject a dialogue and re-establish oneself as a powerful agent by creating a new reality through protest, violence or avoidance. But even in extreme cases when action deteriorates into riots, such activities always seem to lead to the re-establishment of the dialogue, albeit a dialogue in which the power equations have changed. Memories of misery, violence and heroism alter people's perceptions and as a result a new power balance emerges; this is not to imply that the new equation is any more just, since it is most likely to suppress other, alternative voices.[10] Here we return to the statement made at the onset of this discussion about power, where I quoted Foucault, saying that power is all-pervasive because it establishes as well as breaks its own rules (Augé 1998: 71).

With these observations in mind, let me return to the dichotomy of the elite and the subalterns. All the quoted examples show that there is a difference between the structural opposition marked by position and the actual situation in the concrete practice of negotiation. The image of society as split into two opposite entities underscores the complexity and flexibility of power relations. It also does not meet with the self-perception of the structurally subordinated, who do not perceive of themselves as fully determined by the elite, otherwise they would hardly take to pressing their opinions via negotiations and actions. The terms elite and subaltern can only be analytically useful if they are rendered contextual.

First, most people experience both the power to dominate and the need to subordinate themselves. Since each person has a whole range

[10] See for this matter also the literature on the re-establishing of normality after a riot: Das 1990b, Pandey 1991b

of social identities he finds himself in shifting positions of sub- or super-ordination. Secondly, every setting produces its own rules of authority. An ascribed status may give authority in the one setting but be fully negligible in another. Thirdly, domination and subordination are relational terms, which characterize a practice that is potentially open, allowing for the transgression of established rules. Such transgressions have the potential of rendering structurally subordinated people momentarily powerful, or may even trigger the reorganisation of power-structures.

I do not intend to argue for a concept of free-floating power relations. Ascribed status as well as access to legitimate force can carry persons far in realizing their intentions. Yet the exercise of power is never independent of actual relationships in which various people bring their influence to bear and make their presence felt. Thus, instead of proclaiming the opposition between powerful and powerless along established hierarchies and pre-conceived notions of society, analysis at the local level can show various ways of inter-connecting that cause effective action.

CONCLUSION

There are various ways of relating to religion, and opinion is divided on the reality of non-human agents. It puts into opposition those who accept and wish for the intervention of deities in this world to those who place the human at the centre of all actions. Believers in deities use the temple as a place to produce and cultivate their worldview, which at times opposes the claim of the state to sovereignty. Experiencing divine agency, they fight for a place for their deities in this world. Their struggle takes place within the political arena—where believers act as representatives of the divine. They manifest vested interests and are part of the struggle for power and dominance. In the process of development any religious movement can be appropriated by different social forces and invested with their aims and used to realize their agendas.

This conclusion, which sees disagreement, dissidence and protest as part of the normal negotiations of power relations, stands in direct opposition to Blau's (1964) sociology in which resistance is the exception, the result of a break-down of the system. Following Mauss's (1969) idea of exchange and reciprocity, Blau portrays power relations as a system of exchange in which ideally an equilibrium exists between the dominant and the subordinate, in which both contribute to and profit from their relationships. His social theory, which emphasises harmony over conflict, simplifies social processes by ignoring the multiplicity of views held by different actors at any given moment.

I have adopted an approach that draws its conclusions from the analysis of a number of social situations, thus following a contemporary notion of structure understood not as a transcendent abstraction, but as an attribute of social life that emerges during its realization, which can never be seen as fixed. Hence, my emphasis was on context and negotiation, which, however, does not mean to negate continuity. To come to grips with the complexity of life, I have grouped opinions together, showing that they are informed by certain recurring narrative structures which shape perceptions and structure conflicts. Assent and consent was shown to be concentrated in action and performance leading to the focus on social processes which resulted in structural formulations and re-formulations.

As a result also the understanding of the term modernity is rendered contextual. As an emergent social process, modernity is not the final establishment of an ideal condition. It appears rather as a contextual concept of actors who, in their effort to create a modern world, or to come to terms with what they understand to be the modern world, invent it through their diverse and often conflicting practices. What comes to our attention in this local analysis is that practices and notions of modernity differ according to the position of people in the social discourse. There is no general answer to the question of what modernity is, or the problem of where religion or, more generally, tradition should find its place within the modern world. The problem rather defines a contested terrain in which many rationalities appear to exist side by side.

CHAPTER 7

Conclusions: Situating the Divine

In their efforts to create a home for their deities in close proximity to themselves, people in temples get entangled in negotiations of power which at times also question established relationships. In this sense the temple is a place of both religion and politics. Here social practices resist a simple categorization as either political or religious. But in spite of being blurred in practice, the terms still carry weight in people's reflections on the structure of the social world. They use the terminology of religion and politics as tools to distinguish between 'good' and 'honest' devotion, and the questionable 'manipulation' of religion for other purposes. These efforts to make distinctions are means to enable persons to judge concrete performances and thereby find a position from which they can fight for their ideals regarding the organization of human relations as well as relations to the divine.

I disclosed Bagware's controversial position. I introduced him as a person who is praised for his engagement for the community. At the same time his opponents accused him of misusing the temple for his ambitions as a leader. Knowing this ambiguity of his stance, Bagware himself takes an intermediary position and claims his actions to be divinely sanctioned (Chapters 2 and 4). He differentiates between devotional activities and political power struggles when discussing caste-activities, but blurs the distinction when it comes to his own activities, which he sees even in their political dimension to be sanctioned by the goddess and a result of his personal *karma*.

A similar approach could be found among those who fight for the unification of the Hindu community and its representation in the urban space (Chapters 2 and 4). There can be no doubt that the organization of Hindus in the public sphere may be and often is a political statement, as could be seen with reference to the history of the Durga Temple. People often approach the goddess, build her temples and celebrate her festivals explicitly for worldly reasons. They expect help in their domestic lives, they want to be seen as devoted believers in public, or wish to advertise the good work done by a leader or a community. Sometimes the motivation is also to provoke members of other religious communities. However, approaching the goddess is also a deeply religious act. Believers are attracted to the temple in their search for communication with non-human agents. Seen from this angle, the temple is not only a symbol for community or its organizational centre, but also its religious core and the realization of the believers' religious aspirations.

The ambivalence between worldly and other-worldly orientations also surfaced during the observation of the everyday activities of the temple (Chapter 3). Beggars, for example, are seen as a nuisance to a temple because they distract attention from the holy centre. Yet to chase them away would mean preventing humans in their search for closeness to the divine. Conceptual ambivalence also exists in the ritual domain: should there be an insistence on ritual orthodoxy, offering the goddess the best one can provide, or should one have to accept every ritual performance as legitimate as long as the actor is truly devoted to the goddess? The conflicts over ritual correctness have implications for social relationships and status positions which are in the process of undergoing re-definition amid urban living conditions.

Situating the divine and judging people's relation to the deities are intertwined with efforts to come to terms with modernity. Modernity is identified with industrialization and social changes set in motion by Western influences, and most clearly identified with the spread of literacy and school education, the functioning of a national bureaucracy, and the existence of a democratic nation state. However, there is great disagreement about how best to shape modernity and how to understand the role of traditions in this context (Chapter 5). With reference to temples, this question finds expression in people's efforts to come to terms with secularism. It is also present in controversies over the power the state bureaucracy should have over temples and the organization of urban space. It is negotiated when people organize temple life in accordance with the living conditions of their environment, and it comes to the fore when people define what it means to be a Hindu and engage in organizing their religious community.

In these conflicts the temple, as a place of divine manifestation, stands in opposition to a materialistic view of modernity that wants to overcome belief in non-human agency. It eludes an ideology that gives absolute power to the state and facilitates an alternative imagination of reality (Chapter 6). Yet while providing a space for opposition, the temple does not exist independently of dominant discourses or well-established narratives prevalent in society. The conceptions of the divine and people's approaches to temples are influenced by, and used to support, established classifications, such as that between religion and politics, Hindus and Muslims, or educated and uneducated. Temple politics also builds on the popular idea that construes India as a cultural entity in opposition to others, such as Pakistan, 'the West', or the 'Arabic World' (see Schiffauer 1997b). Ideas of the divine are also influenced by Brahmanic ideals of religiosity, supporting a well-established (discriminatory) caste system (see Ilaiah 1996).

However, even while people are influenced by these standard narratives they are not determined by them. Every new situation demands the application of concepts that are adjusted and re-shaped in the process. The ability of a temple to function as a place for alternative models of reality is an outcome of its situatedness at the intersection of a number of discourses among which the belief in divine agency reigns supreme. The ideas of politics, religion, modernity, tradition, democracy, law and order or the social good take on different meanings when seen in relation to the will of divine actors. Here distinct although never fully independent claims are made for the organization of the social.

Consequently the temple has to be seen both as a place for confirmation and resistance, for the deconstruction and the sanctioning of pre-conceived notions of reality, or as Moore formulated it: in every event 'prefabricated totalizing ideologies are both fragmentarily adopted and intermittently resisted' (Moore 1987: 735). This double function of events is a result of the multiplicity of meaning every message carries, which allows for the simultaneous presence of contradictory interpretations. Anthony Cohen (1985: 15) made this point in reference to the inner dynamic of community organization, in which members share symbols but not necessarily their meaning. Their solidarity is precisely a result of the multivalencey of symbols that allows for conflicting interpretations and the adjustability of their meaning according to context (see also Kertzer 1988).

The temple as a place that is situated at the intersection of a number of different controversies and discourses prevailing in contemporary urban life in India comes into existence only through the act of placing the temple at the focus of the analysis. By organizing this analysis around the temple, I have done more than show how the temple as place is created. I have myself created a temple narrative by demonstrating how I see it related to questions of identity, the establishment of relationships, and the construction of history (Augé 1997: 52). By interacting with people in Bhopal's temples and by interpreting their actions, I constructed a community of believers and a discourse of the temple.

However, in spite of my constructional work, I claim to represent urban reality in Bhopal when talking of a discourse of religion (and politics) surrounding the temples, because I abstracted it from my observations of and involvement with real people. I follow a notion of discourse as proposed by Foucault, according to which discourses are not only produced through linguistic acts but also through habitual actions as non-intentional forms of communication (Foucault 1972, see also Abu-Ludghod and Lutz 1990: 7-10, Veyne 1992). Many activities remained without comment. Not all people offered verbal reflections on the meaning of their acts and the reality of the temple. They nevertheless participate in the construction of the temple as an urban institution by integrating concrete temples and shrines into their area of activities thereby offering their understanding of the places in a non-verbal way.

In my description I have tried to avoid privileging any one particular view, and to concentrate rather on the description of various power struggles and the way they are influenced by and influential on perceptions, standard narratives and structural constraints. This resulted in a blurring of history and myth, as two ways of narrating the history of a concrete place. Rumsey has pointed at the overlapping of these categories with reference to the interpretation of landscape through Australian Aborigines. He asserts that the sacred landscape acts as 'the main locus for memory, and all associated discursive elaboration of it as exegesis, by which stories are [...] *retrieved from* the country' (Rumsey 1994: 127, emphasis in the original). These stories, he goes on, cannot be classified as either mythic or historical, they rather represent both, mixing freely the different forms of comprehending and constructing social life by preserving it in the landscape.

My interpretation of the temple has been similar. Throughout the work I have abstained from distinguishing between 'real' and 'false' stories. I have engaged instead in an exercise to extract the contexts and efforts involved in ordering and understanding. In the end, there is no *one* tale about the temple. There is a multiplicity of stories which are inspired by the physical presence of temples. In this sense they are retrieved temples, as built environment and imagery. However, there is no way to extract a true core.

Breaking up the story into many single narratives does not always result in clarity; it also means making a mess of it, as Guha once said (1996: 12). Dissecting the temple, I have established it as a place of both resistance and overpowering, where coercion and persuasion as well as co-option and resistance have their place. While I claim that the temple is a place for resistance, I do not hold that it is always a place of emancipation. Again I follow Foucault, who insisted that protest is not innocent, and does not make a rebel's voice more sane or in any way closer to truth. Listing to voices of dissidence does not mean that one has to agree or sympathise with them, but it is nevertheless useful and important, if only because 'they have against them so much which is set up to silence them' (Foucault 1981: 8).

Once we have reached a point where we understand the complexity of social constellations, it becomes impossible to make clear distinctions or offer unambiguous value judgements. In this sense our situation is no different from people in Bhopal who make every effort to distinguish (good) religion from (bad) politics, well aware that they often fail and that their decision requires frequent re-adjustment. I see this as a warning against all-too simple solutions that denigrate any voice not in congruence with a particular idea as illegitimate, irrational or insane. Rather than judging the rationality of a particular perspective, I have tried to demonstrate the way different perceptions are connected with the organisation of relations, the interpretation of the divine, and the perception of the social order. My critique thus does not lie in denouncing any one specific set of opinions as false or illegitimate, but in showing their contextuality and relativity (see also Béteille 1992). This procedure has been informed by my conviction that finding one's own stance should not start with a condemnation of other opinions, but rather be informed by an effort to understand the other, as conceived in the mind of the observer.

Glossary

Akshay Tritiya	The third day in the month of Vaisakha (April/May), which has become the traditional day for the arrangement of mass marriages.
arti	Central temple ritual during which a camphor flame is waved in front of the deity.
barat	Marriage procession.
barhkul	A hereditary office holder within the caste, who functioned together with the *patel* as caste headman of the Khatiks in Bhopal.
bhandara	Public distribution of specially prepared *prasad* through a donator.
bhajan	Devotional song, hymn.
bhakti	A form of worship that gives a core value to the devotee's surrender to the deity.
darbar	Hall of audience.
darshan	Beholding of the deity. Through the visual interaction between the deity and the devotee divine substance is believed to be transmitted to the devotee.
darshanarthi	Worshipper.
dharna	Sit-down strike.
dhup arti	Temple ritual during which a container with incense is waved in front of the deity.
Ganesh Chaturthi	A festival which takes place on the fourth day of the lunar month Bhadrapad (August/September). Prior to this day provisional shrines with clay images of Ganesh are set up everywhere in the city and special rituals are offered to the deity. On the day of Ganesh Chaturthi the clay images are taken in processions to a water resource.
ghi	Clarified butter.
gotra	Endogamous group or lineage; for male persons the *gotra* consists of all relatives of the last seven generations, women count five generations back.
hariyali amavas	A festival which is celebrated by Khatiks in Bhopal on the new moon day of the lunar month of Shravana (July/August). On this day all male Khatiks assemble to offer an animal sacrifice to the goddess Kali.

havan	Fire sacrifice.
hijra	Eunuch.
Holi	Holi is a festival celebrated on the full moon day of the month Phalgun (February/March). On this day all people meet as equals, throwing colours at each other and hugging each other.
IAS	Indian Administrative Service.
jagaran	Religious functions, often in form of collective singing, which last a whole night.
katha	Here specifically referring to a ritual called by a group of people who engage a priest who reads a stipulated sacred text and preside over the performance of a *havan*.
karma	Destination as a result of merit accumulation.
Kasai	Muslim caste, traditionally engaged in the meat trade.
Khatik	A Scheduled Caste found throughout north India. The traditional occupation of Khatiks is the business with fruit, vegetables and (goat) meat.
kunda	A large shallow earthen bowl for grinding.
lagan	Bundle with offerings and horoscope needed in a Hindu-marriage ceremony.
lingam	Phallus representing Shiva.
Mahashivratri	A festival is celebrated on the fourteenth day in the lunar month of Magha (January/February). People keep a vigil during the night before in devotion to Shiva. The day itself is marked by a fast, the performance of special rituals honouring Shiva and the consumption of intoxicants (e.g. *bhang*).
mantra	Sacred formula.
mata	Mother, address for an elder lady or the goddess.
Navratri	Navratri is a festival of special goddess worship celebrated twice a year once during the first nine days of the lunar month Asvin (September/October) the second time exactly half a year later during the first nine days of the lunar month Caitra (March/April).
panchayat	Here the term in used only in the sense of caste-*panchayat*. According to the tradition in the Khatik caste the *panchayat* encompasses all male members of the caste group in a specific locality.
patel	A hereditary office holder within the caste, who functioned together with the *barhkul* as caste headman of the Khatiks in Bhopal.
pindi	See *lingam*.

puja	Individual worship.
prasad	Divine leavings.
Ramlila	A festival celebrated all over north India during the Dashara holiday, usually starting in late September (lunar month Ashvin) and lasting for several days of even weeks. On this occasion the *Ramayana* is enacted in plays and processions.
Rangpanchmi	A festival similar to Holi celebrated five days after Holi, on the fifth day of the dark half of the month of Phalgun, on which people regardless of their status mix freely and throw colours at each other.
rishi	Sage.
sadhana	Meditation.
sadhu	Ascetic, hermit.
sampraday	Religious group or movement, also referred to as sect (without any negative connotation).
sanyasi	Ascetics.
sevak	Voluntary servant in the temple.
svayambhu	Divine self manifestation.
tulsi	Basilica plant.
varna	Caste, referring to the four castes mentioned in the Sanskrit literature: Brahmin, Kshatriya, Vaisha and Shudra.
yantra	Mystical diagram.

Bibliography

Abu-Lughod, Lila and Catherine A. Lutz. 1990. Introduction. Emotion, Discourse, and the Politics of Everyday Life. In: Catherine A. Lutz and Lila Abu-Lughod (eds.): *Language and the Politics of Emotion*. Cambridge: Cambridge University Press.

Abu-Lughod, Lila. 1991. Writing against Culture. In: R.G. Fox (ed.): *Recapturing Anthropology*. Santa Fe, New Mexico: School of American Research Press.

AIDWA, CWDS, MDS, NFIW 1995: Report of the Women's Delegation to Bhopal, Ahmedabad and Surat. In:Tanika Sarkar and Urvashi Butalia (eds.): *Women and the Hindu Right*. Delhi: Women for Kali.

Alam, Javeed. 1994. Tradition in India under Interpretative Stress. Interrogating its Claims. *Thesis Eleven* 39, 19-38.

______ 1999. *India. Living with Modernity*. Delhi: Oxford University Press.

Alvares, Claude. 1992. *Science, Development and Violence*. Delhi: Oxford University Press.

Anderson, Benedict 1992 [1983]. *Imagined Communities. Reflection on the Origin and Spread of Nationalism.* London: Verso.

Appadurai, Arjun. 1981a. *Worship and Conflict under Colonial Rule. A South Indian Case.* Cambridge: Cambridge University Press.

______ 1981b. The Past as the Sacred Resource. *Man* 16, 201-19.

______ 1990a. Disjuncture and Difference in the Global Cultural Economy. In: *Public Culture* 2, 1-24.

______ 1990b. Global Ethnoscapes. Notes and Queries for a Transnational Anthropology. In: R.G. Fox (ed.): *Recapturing Anthropology*. Santa Fe: School of American Research Press.

______ 1996. *Modernity at Large. Cultural Dimension of Globalization*. Delhi: Oxford University Press.

Appadurai, Arjun and C.A. Breckenridge. 1976. The South Indian Temple: Authority, Honour and Redistribution. *Contribution to Indian Sociology* 10, 187-211.

Asad, Talal 1983. Anthropological Conceptions of Religion. Reflections on Geertz. *Man* 18, 237-59.

Ashfaq Ali, Syed. 1987. *Bhopal—Past and Present*. Bhopal.

______ 1990. *A Guide to Bhopal*. Bhopal.

Augé, Marc. 1997 [French org. 1992]. *Non-Places. Introduction to an Anthropology of Supermodernity*. London: Verso.

______ 1998 [French org. 1994]. *A Sense for the Other. The Timeliness and Relevance of Anthropology*. Stanford: Stanford University Press.

Ayrookuzhiel, A.M.A. 1995. The Religious Factor in Dalit Liberation. Some Reflections. In: Bhagwan Das and James Massey (eds.): *Dalit Solidarity*. Delhi: ISPCK.

Babb, Lawrence A. 1975. *The Divine Hierarchy: Popular Hinduism in Central India*. New York: Columbia University Press.

——— 1981. Glancing: Visual Interaction in Hinduism. *Journal of Anthropological Research* 37, 387-401.

——— 1987. *Redemptive Encounters. Three Modern Styles of the Hindu Tradition*. Delhi: Oxford University Press.

Bagware, Shiv Narayan Singh. 1996. *Shri 360 Gautriya Kshatriya Samaj, Madhya Pradesh, Bhopal.* Bhopal: no publisher.

Baig, M.R.A. 1970. Enlightened Communalism. *Seminar* 125, 12-14.

Bailey, F.G. 1996. Cultural Performances, Authenticity, and Second Nature. In: David Parkin, Lionel Caplan and Humphrey Fisher (eds.): *The Politics of Cultural Performance*. Oxford: Berghahn Books.

Baker, Christopher J. 1975. Temples and Political Development. In: C.J. Baker and D.A. Washbrook (eds.): *South India. Political Institutions and Political Change.* Delhi: Macmillan.

Banerjee, Sumanta. 1991. Hindutva—Ideology and Social Psychology. In: *Economic and Political Weekly* 26, 97-101.

Banu, Zenab. 1989. *Politics of Communalism*. Bombay: Popular Prakashan.

Barnouw, Victor. 1954. The Changing Character of a Hindu Festival. In: *American Anthropologist* 56, 74-86.

Barth, Frederik. (ed.). 1969. *Ethnic Groups and Boundaries. The Social Organisation of Cultural Difference*. Boston: Little Brown.

Basu, Amrita 1996. Mass Movement or Elite Conspiracy? The Puzzle of Hindu Nationalism. In: David Ludden (ed.): *Making India Hindu*. Delhi: Oxford University Press.

Basu, Tapan, Pradip Datta, Sumit Sarkar, Tanika Sarkar and Sambuddha Sen. 1993. *Khaki Shorts Saffron Flags*. Delhi: Orient Longman.

Bauman, Richard 1989. *Story, Performance, and Event. Contextual Studies of Oral Narrative.* Cambridge: Cambridge University Press.

Bauman, Zygmunt. 1973. *Culture as Praxis*. London: Routledge and Kegan.

——— 1992. *Intimations of Postmodernity*. London: Routledge.

Baumann, Gerd. 1996. *Contesting Culture. Discourses of Identity in Multi-Ethnic London*. Cambridge: Cambridge University Press.

Bayly, C.A. 1985. The Pre-History of Communalism? Religious Conflict in India 1700-1860. *Modern Asian Studies* 19, 177-203.

Bayly, Susan. 1984. Hindu Kingship and the Origin of Community. Religion, State and Society in Kerala 1750-1850. *Modern Asian Studies* 18, 177-213.

Bell, Daniel. 1977. The Return of the Sacred? *British Journal of Sociology* 28.

Benedict, Ruth. 1934. *Patterns of Culture*. Boston: Houghton Mifflin.

Berg, Eberhard and Martin Fuchs (eds.). 1993. *Kultur, soziale Praxis, Text. Die Krise der ethnographischen Repraesentation*. Frankfurt: Suhrkamp.

Béteille, André. 1965. Social Organisation of Temples in a Tanjore Village. *History of Religions* 5, 74-92.

——— 1992. Religion as a Subject for Sociology. *Economic and Political Weekly* 27, 1865-70.

——— 1994. Secularism and Intellectuals. *Economic and Political Weekly* 28, 559-66.

Bhadakariya, Shyamlal. 1958. *Suryavansha 360 Gotriya Kshatriya Vanshavala*. Gwalior: Royal Printing Press.

Bhargava, R. 1994. Giving Secularism its Due. *Economic and Political Weekly* 29, 1784-1791.

______ (ed.). 1998. *Secularism and its Critics*. Delhi: OUP.

Bhattacharyya, N.N. 1977. *The Indian Mother Goddess*. Delhi: Manohar.

Bilgrami, A. 1994. Two Concepts of Secularism. Reason, Modernity and Archimedean Ideal. *Economic and Political Weekly* 29, 1749-61.

Bird, John, Bary Curtis, Tim Punam, George Robertson and Lisa Tickner (eds.). 1993. *Mapping the Futures. Local Cultures, Global Change*. London: Routledge.

Blackburn, S.H. and A.K. Ramanujan (eds.). 1986. *Another Harmony. New Essays on the Folklore of India*. Delhi: Oxford University Press.

Blau, Peter M. 1964. *Exchange and Power in Social Life*. New York: John Wiley and Sons.

Borden, Carla M. (ed.). 1989. *Contemporary Indian Tradition. Voices on Culture, Nature and the Challenge of Change*. Washington: Smithsonian Institution Press.

Bourdieu, Pierre. 1977. *Outline of a Theory of Practice*. Cambridge: Cambridge University Press.

______ 1980. *Le Sense Pratique*. Paris: Les éditions de Minuit.

______ 1984. Espace Social et Genese de 'Classe'. *Actes de la Recherche en Sciences Sociales*, 52/53.

______ 1987: *Sozialer Sinn*. Frankfurt: Suhrkamp.

______ 1991. Physischer, Sozialer und Angeigneter Physischer Raum. In: Martin Wentz (ed.): *Stadt-Raeume*. Frankfurt: Campus.

Brass, Paul R. 1998. *Theft of an Idol. Text and Context in the Representation of Collective Violence*. Calcutta: Seagull.

Breckenridge, C.A. 1978. From Protector to Litigant. In: Burton Stein (ed.): *South Indian Temples. An Analytical Reconsideration*. Delhi: Vikas.

Brown, P. 1959. *Indian Architecture. Buddhist and Hindu Periods*. Bombay: B.D. Taraporevala and Sons.

Brown, Richard Harvey. 1996. Cultural Representation and State Formation. Discourses of Ethnicity, Nationality, and Political Community. *Dialectical Anthropology* 21, 265-97.

Brubaker, Richard L. 1979. Barbers, Washermen, and Other Priests. Servants of the South Indian Village and its Goddess. *History of Religions* 19, 128-52.

Brueckner, Heidrun, Lothar Lutze and Aditya Malik (eds.). 1993. *Flags of Fame. Studies in South Asian Folk Culture*. Delhi: Manohar.

Butler, Judith. 1997. *Excitable Speech. A Politics of the Performance*. New York: Routledge.

Cashman, Richard. 1970. The Politic Recruitment of God Ganapati. *Indian Economic and Social History Review* 7, 347-73.

______ 1975. *The Myth of the Lokamanya Tilak and Mass Politics in Maharashtra*. Berkeley: University of California Press.

Census of India of 1981. Series II, Madhya Pradesh Part II-A. General Population Tables. K.C. Dubey (ed.): 174.

Chakrabarty, Bidyut (ed.). 1990. *Secularism and Indian Polity*. Delhi: Segment.

Chakrabarty, Dipesh. 1989. *Rethinking Working-Class History. Bengal 1890-1940*. Princeton: Princeton University Press.

Chandra, Bipan. 1984. *Communalism in Modern India*. Delhi: Vikas.

——— 1991. Communalism and the Struggle against Communalism. In: P.N. Panikkar (ed.): *Communalism in India. History, Politics and Culture*. Delhi: Manohar.

Chatterjee, Partha. 1989. Caste and Subaltern Consciousness. In: Ranajit Guha (ed.): *Subaltern Studies VI. Writings on South Asian history and Society*. Delhi: Oxford University Press.

——— 1994. *The Nation and its Fragments. Colonial and Postcolonial History*. Delhi: Oxford University Press.

——— 1994. Secularism and Toleration. *Economic and Political Weekly* 29, 1768-77.

——— 1997. *A Possible India. Essays in Political Criticism*. Delhi: Oxford University Press.

Clifford, James and George E. Marcus (eds.). 1986. *Writing Culture. The Poetics and Politics of Ethnography*. Berkeley: University of California Press.

Coburn, Thomas B. 1984. Consort of None, Sakti of All. The Vision of the Devi-Mahatmya. In: John Stratton Hawley and Donna Marie Wulff (eds.): *The Divine Consort. Radha and the Goddesses of India*. Delhi: Motilal Banarsidass.

Cohen, Anthony P. 1985. *The Symbolic Construction of Community*. London: Routledge.

Cohen, Bernhard S. 1961. *The Development and Impact of British Administration in India*. Delhi: The Indian Institute of Public Administration.

——— 1968. Notes on the History of the Study of Indian Society and Culture. In: Milton Singer and Bernhard S. Cohen (eds.): *Structure and Change in Indian Society*. Chicago: Aldine Press.

——— 1975. Changing Traditions of a Low Caste. In: Milton Singer (ed.): *Traditional India. Structure and Change*. Jaipur: Rawat.

Comaroff, John and Jean Comaroff. 1992. *Ethnography and the Historical Imagination*. Boulder, Colorado: Westview Press.

Csordas, Thomas J. 1996. The Rhetoric of Transformation in Ritual Healing. In: Carol Laderman and Mariana Rosenman (eds.): *The Performance of Healing*. London: Routledge.

Dalmia, Vasudha and Heinrich von Stietencron (eds.) 1995. *Hinduism Represented*. Delhi: Sage.

Dalmia-Luederitz, Vasudha. 1991. Television and Tradition. Some Observations on the Serialization of the Ramayana. In: Monika Thiel-Horstmann (ed.): *Ramayana and Ramayanas*. Wiesbaden: Harrassowitz.

Das, Veena. 1989. Difference and Division as Design for Life. In: C.M. Borden (ed.): *Contemporary Indian Tradition. Voices on Culture, Nature and the Challenge of Change*. Washington.

——— (ed.). 1989. *Subaltern as Perspective*. In: Ranajit Guha (ed.): *Subaltern Studies VI*. Delhi: Oxford University Press.

Das, Veena (ed.). 1990a. *Mirrors of Violence. Communities, Riots, Survivors. The South Asian Experience*. Delhi: Oxford University Press.

______ 1990b. Our Work to Cry. Your Work to Listen. In: Veena Das (ed.): *Mirrors of Violence. Communities, Riots and Survivors in South Asia*. Delhi: Oxford University Press.

______ 1995. *Critical Events. An Anthropological Perspective on Contemporary India*. Delhi: Oxford University Press.

Davis, Richard H. 1995a. Introduction. In: Donald S. Lopez Jr. (ed.): *Religions of India in Practice*. Princeton, Princeton University Press.

______ 1995b. The Rebuilding of a Hindu Temple. In: Donald S. Lopez Jr. (ed.): *Religions of India in Practice*. Princeton, Princeton University Press.

______ 1996. The Iconography of Rama's Chariot. In: David Ludden (ed.): *Making India Hindu*. Delhi: Oxford University Press.

Derrett, J. Duncan M. 1966. The Reform of Hindu Religious Endowments. In: Donald Eugene Smith (ed.): *South Asian Politics and Religion*. Princeton: Princeton University Press.

Desai, A.R. 1984a. Caste and Communal Violence in the Post Partition Indian Union. In: Asghar Ali Engineer (ed.): *Communal Riots in Post-Independence India*. Bombay: Sangam Books.

______ 1984b. Congress (I), Communist Parties and Communalism. *Economic and Political Weekly*, 19, 1196-97.

Deshpande, G.P. 1993. Polity and Culture in the Wake of Ayodhya. *Economic and Political Weekly* 28, 215-18.

Diehl, Carl Gustav. 1956. *Instrument and Purposes. Studies on Rites and Rituals in South India*. Lund: CWK Geerup.

Dirks, Nicholas B. 1987. *The Hollow Crown. Ethnohistory of an Indian Kingdom*. Cambridge: Cambridge University Press.

______ 1976. Political Authority and Structural Change in Early South Indian History. *Indian Economic and Social History Review* 13, 125-58.

______ 1989a. The Invention of Caste. Civil Society in Colonial India. *Social Analysis (Special Issue Series)* 25, 42-52.

______ 1989b. The Original Caste. Power, History and Hierarchy in South Asia. In: *Contributions to Indian Sociology* 23, 59-79.

Dreyfus, Hubert L. and Paul Rabinow (eds.). 1983. *Michel Foucault: Beyond Structuralism and Hermeneutics*. Chicago: University of Chicago Press.

Dumont, Louis. 1970. Nationalism and Communalism. In: Louis Dumont (ed.): *Religion/Politics and History in India*. Paris: Mouton.

______ 1970. *Religion, Politics and History in India*. The Hague: Mouton.

______ 1972. *Homo Hierachicus*. London: Paladin.

Durkheim, Emil. 1971 [1915]. *The Elementary Forms of the Religious Life*. London: George Allen and Unwin.

Eade, John (ed.). 1997. *Living the Global City. Globalization as Local Process*. London: Routledge.

Eck, Diana L. 1981. *Darshan. Seeing the Divine Image in India*. Chambersbury: Anima.

______ 1986. Darshan of the Image. *India International Centre Quarterly* 13.

______ (ed.). 1991. *Devotion Divine. Bhakti Traditions from the Religions of India. Studies in Honour of Charlotte Vaudeville*. Groningen: Forsten.

Eliade, Mircea. 1991 [French org. 1965]. *Das Heilige und das Profane. Vom Wesen des Religioesen*. Frankfurt: Suhrkamp.

Engineer, Asghar Ali. 1984. *Communal Riots in Post-Independence India*. Hyderabad: Sangam Books.

______ (ed.). 1990. *Babri-Masjid Ramjanambhoomi Controversy*. Delhi: Ajanta.

Engineer, Asghar Ali and Moin Shahir (eds.). 1985. *Communalism in India*. Delhi: Ajanta.

Erndl, Kathleen M. 1993. *Victory of the Mother. The Hindu Goddess of Northwest India in Myth, Ritual, and Symbol*. New York: Oxford University Press.

Eschmann, Anncharlott, Hermann Kulke and Gaya Charan Tripathi (eds.). 1978. *The Cult of Jagannath and the Regional Tradition of Orissa*. Delhi: Manohar.

Fardon, Richard. 1990. General Introduction. In: Richard Fardon (ed.): Localizing *Strategies. Regional Traditions of Ethnographic Writing*. Edinburgh: Scottish Academic Press.

Fardon, R. (ed.). 1995. *Counterworks. Managing the Diversity of Knowledge*. London: Routledge.

Featherstone, Mike (ed.). 1990. *Global Culture. Nationalism, Globalization and Modernity*. London: Sage.

Fergusson, J. 1910. *History of Indian and Eastern Architecture*. London: J. Murray.

Fortes, Mayer. 1953. The Structure of Unilineal Descent Groups. *American Anthropologist*, 55, 17-51.

Foucault, Michel. 1972. *The Archaeology of Knowledge and the Discourse on Language*. New York: Pantheon.

______ 1979. *Discipline and Punish. The Birth of the Prison*. New York: Vintage/ Random House.

______ 1980. *Power/Knowledge. Selected Interviews and Other Writings 1972-1977*. Sussex: Harvester Press.

______ 1981. Is it Useless to Revolt? *Philosophy and Social Criticism* 8, 5-9.

______ 1983. The Subject and Power. In: Hubert L. Dreyfus and Paul Rabinow: *Michel Foucault. Beyond Structuralism and Hermeneutics*. Chicago: University of Chicago Press.

______ 1998 [1976]. *The Will to Knowledge. The History of Sexuality, Volume I*. London: Penguin Books.

Freeman, James M. 1986. The Consciousness of Freedom Among India's Untouchables. In: Dilip K. Basu and Richard Sisson (eds.): *Social and Economic Development in India*. Delhi: Sage.

Freitag, Sandria B. 1980. Sacred Symbol as Mobilizing Ideology. The North Indian Search for a 'Hindu' Community. In: *Comparative Studies in Society and History* 22, 597-625.

______ 1989. *Collective Action and Community. Public Areas and the Emergence of Communalism in North India*: California University Press.

______ 1991. Enactment of Ram's Story and the Changing Nature of 'the Public' in British India. *South Asia* 14, 65-90.

Friedman, Jonathan. 1997. Global Crisis, the Struggle for Cultural Identity and Intellectual Porkbarrelling. Cosmopolitans Versus Locals, Ethnics and

Nationals in an Era of De-Hegemonisation. In: Pnina Werbner and Tariq Modood (eds.): *Debating Cultural Hybridity. Multi-Cultural Identities and the Politics of Anti-Racism*. London: Zed Books.

Frykenberg, R.E. 1987. The Concept of Majority as a Devilish Force in the Politics of Modern India. *Journal of Commonwealth and Comparative Politics* 25, 267-74.

______ 1989. The Emergence of Modern 'Hinduism' as a Concept and as an Institution. A Reappraisal with Special Reference to South India. In: Guenther D. Sontheimer and Hermann Kulke (eds.): *Hinduism Reconsidered*. Delhi: Manohar.

Fuller, C.J. 1982. The Attempted Reform of South Indian Temple Hinduism. In: J. Davis (ed.): *Religious Organization and Religious Experience*. London: Academic Press.

______ 1984a. *Servants of the Goddess. The Priest of the South Indian Temple*. Cambridge: Cambridge University Press.

______ 1984b. The Government and the Temple. The Madurai Minakshi Temple Priests, 1937-1980. In: Kenneth Ballhatchet and David Taylor (eds.): *Changing South Asia. Religion and Society*. London: Sian Research Service, SOAS.

______ 1988. The Hindu Temple in Indian Society. In: Michael V. Fox (ed.): *The Temple in Society*. Winona Lake: Eisenbaum.

______ 1992. *The Camphor Flame. Popular Hinduism and Society in India*. Delhi: Penguin Books India.

______ (ed.). 1997. *Caste Today*. Delhi: Oxford University Press.

Gazetteer of India. Madhya Pradesh. Bhopal State. 1995 [1908]. Bhopal: Gazetteer Unit, Directorate of Rajbhasha and Culture, Government of Madhya Pradesh, Bhopal.

______ Madhya Pradesh. Sehore and Bhopal. 1989. Bhopal: Directorate of Gazetteers, Department of Culture, Madhya Pradesh, Bhopal.

Geertz, Clifford. 1966. *Anthropological Approaches to the Study of Religion*. London: Tavistock.

______ (ed.). 1963. *Old Societies and New States*. New York.

______ 1973. Deep Play. Notes on the Balinese Cockfight. In: Clifford Geertz: *The Interpretation of Cultures*. Clifford Geertz. New York: Harper.

______ 1988. *Works and Lives. The Anthropologist as Author*. Cambridge: Polity Press.

Giddens, Anthony. 1990. *The Consequences of Modernity*. Cambridge: Polity Press.

______ 1994. Living in a Post-Traditional Society. In: Ulrich Beck, Anthony Giddens and Scott Lash: *Reflexive Modernization. Politics, Tradition and Aesthetics in the Modern Social Order*. Oxford: Polity Press.

Gluckman, Max. 1954. *Rituals of Rebellion in South-East Africa*. Manchester: Manchester University Press.

______ 1963. Gossip and Scandal. *Current Anthropology* 4.

______ 1968. *Analysis of a Social Situation in Modern Zululand*. Manchester: Manchester University Press.

Gnanambal, K. 1967. *Festivals of India*. Calcutta: Government of India.

Golwalkar, M.S. 1945. *We or Our Nationhood Defined*. Nagpur.

Good, Anthony. 1987. The Religious, Economic and Social Organisation of a South Indian Temple. *Quarterly Journal of Social Affairs* 3, 1-25.

Gopal, Sarvepalli (ed.). 1991. *Anatomy of a Confrontation. The Babri Masjid—Ram Janmabhumi Issue*. Delhi: Penguin Books.

Gore, M.S. 1990. Secularism and Equal Regard (*Sarba Dharma Sambhav*) for all Religions. In: Bidyut Chakrabarty (ed.): *Secularism and Indian Polity*. Delhi: Segment.

Gouldner, Alvin. 1970. *The Coming of Crisis of Western Sociology*. New York: Basic Books.

Goyal, Gulabchandre. 1996. *The M.P. Public Trust Act, 1951*. Indore: Indian Publishing Company.

Graham, B.D. 1990. *Hindu Nationalism and Indian Politics. The Origins and Development of the BJP*. Cambridge: Cambridge University Press.

Gravely, F.H. 1936. *An Outline of Indian Temple Architecture*. Madras: Govt. Press.

Guha, Ranajit (ed.). 1982. *Subaltern Studies I*. Delhi: Oxford University Press.

______ (ed.). 1984. *Subaltern Studies III*. Delhi: Oxford University Press.

______ 1989. Dominance Without Hegemony and its Historiography. In: Ranajit Guha (ed.): *Subaltern Studies VI*. Delhi: Oxford University Press.

______ 1996. The Small Voice of History. In: Shahid Amin and Dipesh Chakrabarty (eds.): *Subaltern Studies IX*. Delhi: Oxford University Press.

Gupta, Charu. 1998. Articulating Hindu Masculinity and Femininity. 'Shuddhi' and 'Sangathan' Movements in United Provinces. *Economic and Political Weekly* 33, 720-6.

Gupta, Dipankar. 1982. *Nativism in a Metropolis. Shiv Sena in Bombay*. Delhi: Manohar.

______ 1991. Continuous Hierarchies and Discrete Castes. Dipankar Gupta: *Social Stratification*. Delhi: Oxford University Press.

Gupte, Rau Bahadur B.A. 1919. *Hindu Holidays and Ceremonials*. Calcutta: Thacker, Spink.

Habermas, Juergen. 1981. *Theorie des kommunikativen Handelns. Bd. 1: Handlungsrationalitaet und gesellschaftliche Rationalisierung*. Frankfurt: Suhrkamp

Handelman, Don. 1994. Critiques of Anthropology. Literary Turns, Slippery Bends. *Poetics Today* 15, 341-81.

Hannerz, Ulf. 1980. *Exploring the City. Inquiries Toward an Urban Anthropology*. New York: Columbia University Press.

Hansen, Thomas Blom. 2001. *Urban Violence in India*. Delhi: Permanent Black.

Harding, Elizabeth. 1993. *Kali. The Black Goddess of Dakshinewar*. York Beach, Maine: Nicolas-Hays.

Hassan, S.S. n.d. *The Castes and Tribes of HEN. The Nizam's Dominions*.

Hasan, Zoya. 1991. Changing Orientation of the State and the Emergence of Majoritarianism in the 1980s. In: K.N. Panikkar (ed.): *Communalism in India. History, Politics and Culture*. Delhi: Manohar.

Hastrup, Kerstin. 1995. *A Passage to Anthropology. Between Experience and Theory*. London: Routledge.

Hawley, J.S. and D. Wulff (eds.). 1996. *Devi. The Goddess in India*. Berkeley: University of California Press.

Hein, Norvin. 1972. *The Miracle Plays of Mathura*. New Haven: Yale University Press.

______ 1975. The Ram Lila. In: Milton Singer (ed.): *Traditional India. Structure and Change*. Jaipur: Rawat.

Hellman, Eva. 1996. Dynamic Hinduism. Towards a New Hindu Nation. In: D. Westerlund (ed.): *Questioning the Secular State.* London: Hurst.

Herrenschmidt, Oliver. 1989. *Les Meilleurs Dieu y Sont Hindous*. Paris: L'Age d'homme.

Hess, Linda. 1983. Ram Lila. The Audience Experience. In: Monika Thiel-Horstmann (ed.): *Bhakti in Current Research, 1979-1982.* Berlin: Reimer.

Heuze, Gerard. 1992. Shiv Sena and 'National' Hinduism. *Economic and Political Weekly* 27, 2189-95.

Hobsbawm, Eric and Terence Ranger (eds.). 1983. *The Invention of Tradition.* Cambridge: Cambridge University Press.

Holmstroem, M. 1971. Religious Change in an Industrial City in South India. *Journal of the Royal Asiatic Society* (1971), 28-40.

______ 1972. Caste and Status in an Indian City. *Economic and Political Weekly* 7, 769-74.

Hoy, David Couzens (ed.). 1986. *Foucault: A Critical Reader*. Oxford: Brasil Blackwell.

Hubert, H. and M. Mauss. 1981 [1964]. *Sacrifice. Its Nature and Functions.* Chicago: University Press.

Humphrey, Caroline and James Laidlaw. 1994. *The Archetypal Actions of Ritual. A Theory of Ritual Illustrated by the Jain Rite of Worship*. Oxford: Clarendon Press.

Hutdson, Dennis D. 1995. How to Worship at Siva's Temple. In: Donald S. Lopez, Jr (ed.): *Religions of India in Practice*. Princeton: Princeton University Press.

Ilaiah, Kancha. 1996. *Why I Am Not a Hindu. A Sudra Critique of Hindutva Philosophy, Culture and Political Economy*. Calcutta: Samya.

Ivy, Marilyn. 1995. *Discourses of the Vanishing*. Chicago: University of Chicago Press.

Jaffrelot, Christophe. 1996. *The Hindu Nationalist Movement and Indian Politics 1925 to the 1990s. Strategies of Identity-Building, Implantation and Mobilisation*. Delhi: Viking.

______ 1998. The Politics of Processions and Hindu-Muslim Riots. In: A. Basu and A. Kohli (eds.): *Community Conflicts and the State in India*. Delhi: Oxford University Press.

Jain, Randhir B. 1990. The Role of Bureaucracy in Policy Development and Implementation in India. In: *International Social Science Journal* 42, 31-47.

James, Wendy (eds.). 1995. *The Pursuit of Certainty. Religious and Cultural Formulations*. London: Routledge.

Jenks, Chris. 1993. *Culture*. London: Routledge.

Kakar, Sudhir. 1995. *The Colours of Violence*. Delhi: Viking.

Kane, P.V. 1974. *History of Dharmasastra (Ancient and Medieval Religious and Civil Law)*. Poona: Bhandarkar Oriental Research Institute.

Kannabiran, Vasantha and K. Lalitha. 1990. That Magic Time. In: Kumkum Sangari and Suresh Vaid (eds.): *Recasting Women*. New Brundwick, New Jersey: Rutgers University Press.

Kapferer, Bruce. 1983. *A Celebration of Demons. Exorcism and the Aesthetics of Healing in Sri Lanka*. Bloomington: Indiana University Press.

______ 1987. The Anthropology of Max Gluckman. In: *Social Analysis* 22, 3-21.

______ 1997. *The Feast of the Sorcerer. Practices of Consciousness and Power*. Chicago: University of Chicago Press.

Kapp, Robert A. 1980. Introduction. Review Symposium. Edward Said's Orientalism. *Journal of Asian Studies* 39, 481-4.

Kapur, Anuradha. 1984. Actors, Pilgrims, King and Gods. The Ramlila at Ramnagar. *Contribution to Indian Sociology* 19, 57-74.

______ 1991. Raja and Praja. Presentational Conventions in the Ramlila at Ramnagar. In: Monika Thiel-Horstmann (ed.): *Ramayana and Ramayanas*. Wiesbaden: Harrassowitz.

______ 1993. Deity to Crusader. The Changing Iconography of Ram. In: Gyandendra Pandey (ed.): *Hindus and Others*. Delhi: Oxford University Pr.

Kapur, Gita. 1991. Place of the Modern in Indian Cultural Practice. *Economic and Political Weekly* 26, 2803-6.

Karna, M.N. 1993. Meaning of Ayodhya. *Seminar* 402, 31-4.

Katzenstein, Mary Fainsod. 1979. *Ethnicity and Equality. The Shiv Sena Party and Preferential Polities in Bombay*. Ithaca: Cornell University Press.

Katzenstein, Mary Fainsod, Uday Singh Mehta and Usha Thakkar. 1998. The Rebirth of Shiv Sena in Maharashtra. The Symbiosis of Discursive and Institutional Power. In: Amrita Basu and Atul Kohli (eds.): *Community Conflicts and the State in India*. Delhi: Oxford University Press.

Kaviraj, Sudipta. 1990. On the Discourse of Secularism. In: Bidyut Chakrabarty (ed.): *Secularism and Indian Polity*. Delhi: Segment.

______ 1992. The Imaginary Institution of India. In: Partha Chatterjee and Gyanendra Pandey (eds.): *Subaltern Studies VII. Writings on South Asian History and Society*. Delhi: Oxford University Press.

______ *On the Construction of Colonial Power. Structure, Discourse, Hegemony* (Occasional Papers on History and Society, Second Series 35). Delhi.

Kendall, Laurel. 1996. Initiating Performances. The Story of Chini, a Korean Shaman. In: C. Laderman and M. Roseman (eds.): *The Performance of Healing*. London: Routledge.

Kennedy, Richard. 1974. Status and Control of Temples in Tamil Nadu. *Indian Economic and Social History Review* 11, 260-90.

Kertzer, David I. 1988. *Ritual, Politics and Power*. New Haven.

Kinsley, David. 1984. Blood and Death out of Place. Reflections on the Goddess Kali. In: John Stratton Hawley and Donna Mane Wulff (eds.): *The Divine Consort. Radha and the Goddesses of India*. Delhi: Motilal Banarsidass.

______ 1986. *Hindu Goddesses. Visions of the Divine Feminine in the Hindu Religious Tradition*. Berkeley: University of California Press.

Koepping, Klaus-Peter. 1977. Von der Rhetorik des Schreibens zum Eros der Begegnung in der Ethnographischen Praxis—Gibt es einen Weg zurueck? *Zeitschrift fuer Ethnologie* 122, 45-71.

Koepping, Klaus-Peter. 1987. Authentizitaet als Selbstfindung durch den anderen. Ethnologie zwischen Engagement und Reflexion, zwischen Leben und Wissenschaft. In: Hans-Peter Duerr (ed.): *Authentizitaet und Betrug in der Ethnologie*. Frankfurt: Surhkamp.

——— 1994a. Ethics in Ethnographic Practice. Contextual Pluralism and Solidarity of Research Partners. *Anthropological Journal on European Cultures* 3, 21-38.

——— 1994b. Ethik in einer loechrigen Welt. Zweideutigkeiten in Ethnologischer Praxis und Repraesentation. *Anthropolitan* 2, 5-38.

——— 1998. Religion in the Contemporary World. The Meeting of Cultures and Religious Acculturation. *The Journal of Oriental Studies* 8, 81-105.

——— 2002. Seduced Seducer. In: K.-P. Koepping: *Shattering Frames. Transgression and Transformations in Anthropological Discourse and Practice*. Berlin: Reimer.

Koepping, Klaus-Peter and Ursula Rao. 2001. Macht und Ohnmacht des Mediums—Transformationen individueller und kollektiver Wahrnehmung durch religioese Performanz. In: Fischer Lichte et al. (eds.): *Wahrnehmung und Medialitaet*. Tuebingen: Francke.

——— (2003). Erwartungen an das Unerwartet. In: Erika Fischer Lichte et al. (eds.): *Ereignis und Performativitaet*. Tuebingen: Francke.

Kothari, Rajni. 1988a. *State Against Democracy*. Delhi: Ajanta, 240-53.

——— 1988b. *Rethinking Development. In Search of Humane Alternatives*. Delhi: Ajanta.

——— 1992. Crisis and Catharsis. *Mainstream* 26.12.1992, 2-5.

Kramrisch, Stella. 1976 [1946]. *The Hindu Temple*. Delhi: Motilal Banarsidass.

Kulke, Hermann. 1974. Kings Without a Kingdom. The Raja of Khurda and the Jagannath Cult. *South Asia* 4, 60-77.

Laermans, Rudi, Bryan Wilson and Jaak Billiet (eds.). 1998. *Secularization and Social Integration. Papers in Honor of Karel Dobbelaere*. Leuven: Leuven University Press.

Leeds, Anthony. 1976. Institution. In: David E. Hunter and Phillip Whitten (eds.): *Encyclopaedia of Anthropology*. New York: Harper and Row.

Lele, Jayant. 1995. *Hindutva. The Emergence of the Right*. Madras: Earthworm Books.

Lepenies, Wolf. 1976. *Das Ende der Naturgeschichte*. Muenchen: Carl Hauser.

Lewandowski, S.J. 1980. The Hindu Temple in South India. In: A.D. King. (ed.): *Buildings and Society. Essays on the Social Development of the Built Environment*. London: Routledge.

Linkenbach, Antje. 1986. *Opake Gestalten des Denkens. Juergen Habermas und die Rationalitaet fremder Lebensformen*. Muenchen: Wilhelm Fink Verlag.

Lopez, D.S. (ed.). 1995. *Religions of India in Practice*. Princeton: Princeton University Press.

Lorenzen, David N. (ed.). 1995. *Bhakti Religion in North India. Community Identity and Political Action*. Albany, NY: State of Univ of New York Press.

Luckmann, T. 1991. *Die unsichtbare Religion*. Frankfurt: Suhrkamp.

Ludden, David (ed.). 1996. *Making India Hindu. Religion, Community, and the Politics of Democracy in India*. Delhi: Oxford University Press.

Luedtke, Alf (ed.). 1991. Einleitung. In: Alf Luedtke (ed.): *Herrschaft als soziale Praxis*. Goettingen: von der Hoeck Ruprecht.

Lukes, Steven. 1977 [1973]. *Émil Durkheim. His Life and Work: A Historical and Critical Study*. Middlesex: Penguin.

Lutgendorf, P. 1991. The 'Great Sacrifice' of Ramayana Recitation. Ritual Performance of the Ramacaritmanas. In: Monika Thiel-Horstmann (ed.): *Ramayana and Ramayanas*. Wiesbaden: Harrassowitz.

______ 1992. Words Made Flesh. The Banaras Ramalila as Epic Commentary. In: Joyce Burkhalter Flueckiger and Laurie J. Sears (eds.): *Boundaries of the Text*. Ann Arbor: The University of Michigan.

______ 1994. *The Life of Text. Performing Ramachariatmanas of Tulsidas*. Delhi: Oxford University Press.

Luett, Juergen. 1970. *Hindu-Nationalismus in Uttar Pradesh 1867-1900*. Stuttgart: Klett.

______ 1985. Die regionalen Wurzeln der Hindu Mahasabha. In: Hermann Kulke and Dietmar Rothermund (eds.): *Religioese Traditionen in Suedasien*. Stuttgart: Steiner.

______ 1991. Der Hinduismus auf der Suche nach einem Fundament. In: P.H. Kochanek (ed.): *Die verdraengte Freiheit*. Freiburg: Herder.

Lynch, G.M. 1981. Rioting as a Rational Action. An Interpretation of April 1978 Riots in Agra. *Economic and Political Weekly* 16, 1951-6.

Lynch, Owen M. 1969. *The Politics of Untouchability*. New York: Columbia University Press.

Madan, T.N. 1987. Secularism in its Place. *Journal of Asian Studies* 46.

______ 1991. *Religion in India*. Delhi: Oxford University Press.

______ 1994. Secularism and the Intellectuals. *Economic and Political Weekly* 29, 1095-6.

______ 1997. *Modern Myths, Locked Minds. Secularism and Fundamentalism in India*. Delhi: Oxford University Press.

Malhotra, P.C. 1964. *Socio-Economic Survey of Bhopal City and Bairagarh*. London: Asia Publishing House.

Malinar, Angelika. 1995. The Bhagavadgita in the Mahabharata TV Serial. Domestic Drama and Dharmic Solutions. In: Vasudha Dalmia and Heinrich von Stietencron (eds.): *Representing Hinduism. The Construction of Religious Traditions and National Identity*. Delhi: Sage.

Malinowski, Bronislaw. 1961 [1922]. *Argonauts of the Western Pacific. An Account of Native Enterprise and Adventure in the Archipelagoes of Melanesian New Guinea*. New York: Dutton.

Maljoniya, Bhagvan Das. 1984. *Jay Kshatrana* (Victory to Kshatrani). Bhopal: no publisher.

Mani, Lata. 1987. Contentious Traditions. The Debate on Sati in Colonial India. *Cultural Critique*, 119-56.

Marriott, McKim 1969. *Village India. Studies in the Little Community*. Chicago. Chicago University Press.

Masilamani-Meyer, Eveline and Cornelia Vogelsanger. 1993. Parvati, Kali, Mari—Verschiedene Formen der Devi. In: Cornelia Mallebrein (ed.): *Die Anderen Goetter. Volks- und Stammesbronzen aus Indien*. Koeln: Braus.

Mauss, Marcel. 1969 [1950]. *The Gift. Forms and Functions of Exchange in Archaic Societies*. London: Cohen and West.

McCutchion, David J. 1972. *Late Medieval Temples of Bengal*. Calcutta: The Asiatic Society.

McDermott, Rachel Fell. 1995. Bengali Songs to Kali. In: Donald S. Lopez, Jr (ed.): *Religions of India in Practice*. Princeton: Princeton University Press.

______ 1996. Popular Attitude Towards Kali and her Poetry Tradition. Interviewing Saktas in Bengal. In: Axel Michaels, Cornelia Vogelsanger and Annette Wilke (eds.): *Wild Goddesses in India and Nepal. Proceedings of an International Symposium, Bern and Zurich, November 1994*. Bern: Peter Lang.

McKean, Lise. 1996. *Divine Enterprise. Gurus and the Hindu Nationalist Movement*. Chicago: University of Chicago Press.

Mearns, David James. 1995. *Shiva's Other Children. Religion and Social Identity Amongst Overseas Indians*. Delhi: Sage.

Mead, Margaret 1974 [1928]. *Coming of Age in Samoa*. New York: Morrow.

Mehta, Kalpana. 1964. The Temple in the Politics of Village Bariapur. In: A.H. Somjee (ed.): *Politics in a Periurban Community in India*. London: Asian Publ. House.

Mencher, Joan P. 1991. The Caste System Upside Down. In: D. Gupta (ed.): *Social Stratification*. Delhi: Oxford University Press.

Mendelsohn, Oliver and Marika Vicziany. 1998. *The Untouchables. Subordination, Poverty and the State in Modern India*. Delhi: Cambridge University Press.

Michell, George. 1977. *The Hindu Temple. An Introduction to its Meaning and Form*. London: Paul Eck.

Miller, Daniel. 1995. *Worlds Apart. Modernity Through the Prism of the Local*. London: Routledge.

Miller, Donald F. 1987. Six Thesis on the Question of Religion and Politics in India Today. *Economic and Political Weekly* 22, PE-57-PE-63.

Mines, Mattison and Gourishankar Vijayalaksmi. 1990. Leadership and Individuality in South Asia. *Journal of Asian Studies* 49, 761-86.

______ 1996. *Public Faces, Private Voices. Community and Individuality in South India*. Delhi: Oxford University Press.

Mio, Minora. 1999. Faith, Identity and Communal Discourse. Some Ethnological Considerations on the Conflicts over the Administration of a Sufi Saint's Mausoleum in Rajasthan. In: N.a.F.o.C.i.c.S.A. Steering Committee of the Research Project Institutions (ed.): *Rituals as Popular Culture. Towards Historico-Anthropological Understanding of Modern Indian Society*. Tokyo: Printworld Tanne.

Mitchell, J.C. 1956. *The Kalela Dance. Aspects of Social Relationships Among Urban African in Northern Rhodesia*. Rhode-Livingstone Papers, No. 27. Manchester: Manchester University Press.

______ 1983. Case and Situational Analysis. *The Sociological Review* 31, 187-211.

Mittal, Kamla. 1990. *History of Bhopal State*. Delhi: Munshiram Manoharlal.

Mohanty, Manoranjan. 1989. Secularism. Hegemonic and Democratic. *Economic and Political Weekly* 24, 1219-20.

Mookerjee, Ajit. 1988. *Kali. The Feminine Force*. London: Thames and Hudson.

Moore, Sally Falk. 1987. Explaining the Present. Theoretical Dilemmas in Processual Anthropology. *American Ethnologist* 14, 727-36.

Mukerjee, A. 1988. *Kali the Feminine Force*. London: Thames and Hudson.

Nandy, A. 1984. Culture, State and the Rediscovery of Indian Politics. *Economic and Political Weekly* 19, 2078-83.

Nandy, Ashis. 1985. An Anti-Secularist Manifesto. *Seminar* 314, 14-23.

______ 1987a. Cultural Frames for Social Transformation. A Credo. *Alternatives* 12, 113-23.

______ 1987b. *Tradition, Tyranny and Utopia*. Delhi: Oxoford University Press.

______ (ed.). 1988. *Science, Hegemony and Violence*. Delhi: Oxford University Press.

______ 1990. The Politics of Secularism and the Recovery of Religious Tolerance. In: Veena Das (ed.): *Mirrors of Violence*. Delhi: Oxford University Press.

______ 1993. Three Positions. *Seminar* 402, 15-17.

______ Shikha Trivedy, Shail Mayaram and Achyut Yagnik. 1995. *Creating a Nationality. The Ramjanmabhumi Movement and Fear of the Self*. Delhi: Oxford University Press.

Narayan, Kirin. 1993. On Nose Cutters, Gurus, and Storytellers. In: Smadar Lavie, Kirin Narayan and Renato Rosaldo (eds.): *Creativity/Anthropology*. Ithaca: Cornell University Press.

Nawab Shahjahan, H.H., Begam of Bhopal. 1976. *The History of Bhopal*. Calcutta: Thacker, Spink and Co.

Niehus, H. 1905. Das Ram-Festspiel Nordindiens. *Globus* 87, 58-61.

Nuariya, Anil. 1989. Relationship Between State and Religion. *Economic and Political Weekly* 24, 405-6.

Nye, Malory. 1995. *A Place for our Gods*. Surrey: Curzon Press.

Omvedt, Gail. 1990. Hinduism and Politics. *Economic and Political Weekly*, 724-9.

Oestoer, Akos. 1980. *The Play of the Gods. Locality Ideology, Structure and Time in the Festival of a Bengali Town.* Chicago: Chicago University Press.

______ 1982. *Puja in Society.* Lucknow: Ethnographic and Folk Culture Society.

Oxford Dictionary of Current English. 1964. (eds.) H.W. Fowler, F.G. Fowler. Oxford: Oxford University Press. 5th edn.

Pande, Sumita. 1982. *Birth of Bhakti in Indian Religions and Art*. Delhi: Books and Books.

Pandey, Gyanendra. 1983. Rallying Round the Cow. In: Ranajit Guha (ed.): *Subaltern Studies II*. Delhi: Oxford University Press.

______ 1990. *The Construction of Communalism in Colonial North India*. Bombay: Oxford University Press.

______ 1991a. Hindus and Others. *Economic and Political Weekly* 26.

______ 1991b. In Defence of the Fragment. Writing about Hindu-Muslim Riots in India Today. *Economic and Political Weekly* 26, 559-72.

______ (ed.). 1993. *Hindus and Others. The Question of Identity in India Today*. Delhi: Viking.

Panikkar, K.N. (ed.). 1991. *Communalism in India. History Politics and Culture*. Delhi: Manohar.

Panikkar, K.N. 1999. Introduction. Defining the Nation. In: K.N. Panikkar (ed.): *The Concerned Indian's Guide to Communalism*. Delhi: Viking.

Parish, Steven M. 1996. *Hierarchy and its Discontents. Culture and the Politics of Consciousness in Caste Society*. Philadelphia: University of Pennsylvania Press.

Parkin, David. 1992. Ritual as Spatial Direction and Bodily Division. In: Daniel de Coppet (ed.): *Understanding Rituals*. London: Routledge.

Patel, Priyavadan. 1985. Recent History and Politics of Communalism and Communal Riots in Gujarat. In: Ashghar Ali Engineer and Moin Shakir (eds.): *Communalism in India*. Delhi: Ajanta.

Pavarala, Vindo. 1996. *Interpreting Corruption. Elite Perspectives in India*. Delhi: Sage.

Pile, Steve and Michael Keith (eds.). 1997. *Geographies of Resistance*. London: Routledge.

Pintchman, Tracy. 1994. *The Rise of the Goddess in Hindu Tradition*. Albany: State University of New York.

Prakash, Gyanendra. 1990. Writing Post-Orientalist Histories of the Third World. Perspectives from Indian Historiography. *Comparative Studies in Society and History* 32, 383-408.

______ 1994. Subaltern Studies as Postcolonial Criticism. *American Historical Review* 99, 1475-90.

Presler, Franklin A. 1978. The Legitimation of Religious Policy in Tamil Nadu. A Study of the 1970 Archaka Legislation. In: Bardwell L. Smith (ed.): *Religion and the Legitimation of Power in South Asia*. Leiden: Brill.

______ 1987. *Religion and Bureaucracy. Policy and Administration for Hindu Temples*. Cambridge: Cambridge University Press.

Preston, James J. 1980. *Cult of the Goddess. Social and Religious Change in a Hindu Temple*. Delhi: Vikas.

Quigley, D. 1993. *The Interpretation of Caste*. Oxford: Clarendon Press.

Rabe, Michael D. 1995. Royal Temple Dedications. In: *Religions of India in Practice*. (ed.) Donald S. Lopez, Jr. Princeton, Princeton University Press.

Rabinow, Paul. 1990 [1986]. Representations are Social Facts. Modernity and Post-Modernity in Anthropology. In: James Clifford and George E. Marcus (eds.): *Writing Culture. The Poetics and Politics of Ethnography*. Delhi: Oxford University Press.

Radcliffe-Brown, A.R. 1959 [1952]. *Structure and Function in Primitive Society*. London: Cohen and West.

Radin, Paul. 1957 [1937]. *Primitve Religion. Its Nature and Origin*. New York: Dover.

Rai, Alok. 1990. Addled Only in Parts. The Strange Case of Indian Secularism. In: Bidyut Chakrabarty (ed.): *Secularism and Indian Polity*. Delhi: Segment.

______ 1993. Religious Conversions and the Crisis of Brahminical Hinduism. In: Gyanendra Pandey (ed.): *Hindus and Others. The Question of Identity in India Today* Delhi: Viking.

Rao, Ursula. 2000. Regeln in Bewegung. Die Gestaltung indischer Tempelrituale zwischen Formalitaet und Offenheit. In: Klaus Peter Koepping and Ursula Rao (eds): *Im Rausch des Rituals. Gestaltung und Transformation der Wirklichkeit in koerperlicher Performanz*. Muenster: Lit.

Rao, Ursula. 2002a. Assessing the Past in Search for a Future: The Changing of Caste and the Writing of Caste History in Contemporary Urban India. In: Axel Harneit-Sievers (ed.): *A Place in the World. New Local Historiographies from Africa and South-Asia.* Leiden: Brill.

______ 2002b: How to Prove Divinities? Experiencing and Defending Divine Agency in a Modern Urban Indian Space. In: *Religion* 32(1): 3-11.

______ 2003: Kommunalismus im unabhängigen Indien. Eine Darstellung der wissenschaftlichen Diskussion über Hindu-Moslem Konflikte. Halle: Universitaet Halle.

Redfield, Robert. 1955/56. The Social Organization of Tradition. *The Far Eastern Quarterly* 15, 23-36.

Richards, Paul. 1993. Cultivation. Knowledge or Performance? In: Mark Hobart (ed.): *An Anthropological Critique of Development. The Growth of Ignorance.* London: Routledge.

Robertson, Roland. 1992. *Globalization*. London: Sage.

Rodman, Margaret C. 1992. Empowering Place: Multilocality and Multicocality. *American Anthropologist* 94, 640-56.

Roesel, Jakob. 1980. *Der Palast des Herrn der Welt. Eine Untersuchung der indischen Tempel und Pilgerstadt Puri in Orissa*. Muenchen: Weltforum Verlag.

Rorty, Richard. 1991. *Objectivity, Relativism, and Truth*. Cambridge: Cambridge University Press.

Rudolph, Lloyd I. and Susanne H. Rudolph. 1960. The Political Role of India's Caste Associations. In: *Pacific Affairs* 33, 5-22.

______ 1967. *The Modernity of Tradition. Political Development in India*. Chicago: University of Chicago Press.

Rumsey, A. 1994. The Dreaming, Human Agency and Inscriptive Practice. *Oceania* 65, 116-30.

Russel, R.V. 1975 [1916]. *The Tribes and Castes of the Central Provinces*. Delhi: Cosmo.

Saberwal, Satish. 1981. Elements of Communalism. *Mainstream*, Part I: 21.3.81, 27-30, Part II: 28.3.81, 15-19.

Sallnow, M.J. 1981. Communitas Reconsidered. The Sociology of the Andean Pilgrimage. *Man* 16, 163-82.

Samanta, D.K. 1997. *Sacred Complex of Ujjain*. Delhi: D.K. Printworld.

Sarkar, Tanika. 1993. The Rashtrasevika Samiti and Ramjanmabhoomi. In: Gyanendra Pandey (ed:): *Hindus and Others. The Question of Identity in India Today*. Delhi: Viking.

Sarkar, Tanikar and Urvashi Butalia. 1995. *Women and the Hindu Right*. Delhi: Kali for Women.

Sathyamurthy, T.V. (ed.). 1996. *Region, Religion, Caste, Gender, and Culture in Contemporary India* (Social change and politcal discourse in India. Structures of power, movements of resistance III). Delhi: Oxford University Press.

Savarkar, Vinayak Damodar. 1949 [1923]. *Who is a Hindu? Essential of Hindutva*. Poona: Bharat Mudranalaya.

Sax, William S. 1991. *Mountain Goddess. Gender and Politics in a Himalayan Pilgrimage.* New York: Oxford University Press.

Schieffelin, Edward. 1996. On Failure and Performance. Throwing the Medium Out of the Seance. In: C. Laderman and M. Roseman (ed.): *The Performance of Healing*. London: Routledge.

Schiffauer, Werner. 1997a. *Fremde in der Stadt*. Frankfurt: Suhrkamp.

______ 1997b. Kulturdynamik und Selbstinszenierung. *taz*, 4.3.1997.

Schroeder, Ralph. 1992. *Max Weber and the Sociology of Culture*. London: Sage.

Searle-Chatterjee, Mary and Ursula Sharma (eds.). 1994. *Contextualising Caste. Post-Dumontian Approaches*. Oxford: Blackwell.

Sethi, Krishanlal. 1996. *Commentary on M.P. Public Trust Act*. Indore: Lawyers Home.

Shah, A.B. 1981. *Religion and Society in India*. Bombay: Somaiya Publications.

Shah, A.M. and I.P. Desai. 1988. *Division and Hierarchy. An Overview of Caste in Gujarat*. Delhi: Hindustan.

Shakir, Moin. 1984. An Analytical View of Communal Violence. In: Asghar Ali Engineer (ed.): *Communal Riots in Post-Independence India*. Bombay: Sangam Books.

Shrinivastav, P.N. and S.D. Guru. 1989. *Madhya Pradesh District Gazetters. Sehore and Bhopal*. Bhopal: Directorate of Gazetteers, Department of Culture, Madhya Pradesh.

Singer, Milton. 1972. *When a Great Tradition Modernizes*. New York: Praeger.

Singh, Bhupinder and S.L. Batra. 1995. *Management of Lands with Religious and Charitable Institutions*. Delhi: Har-Anand.

Singh, J.P. 1994. *Central India. Resources and Development*. Bhopal: Bhaskar.

Singh, K.S. 1993. *People of India. National Series Volume II. The Scheduled Castes*. Delhi. Oxford University Press.

Singh, S.B. 1989. *Fairs and Festivals in Rural India. A Geospatial Study of Belief Systems*. Varanasi: Tara Book Agency.

Sontheimer, Guenther D. and Hermann Kulke (eds.). 1989. *Hinduism Reconsidered*. Delhi: Manohar.

Spencer, George W. 1968. Temple, Money Lending and Livestock Redistribution in Early Tanjore. *Indian Economic and Social History Review* 5, 279-93.

______ 1969. Religious Network and Royal Influence in Eleventh Century South India. *Journal of Economic and Social History of the Orient* 2, 42-56.

______ 1978. Crisis of Authority in a Hindu Temple Under the Impact of Islam. Srirangam in the Fourteenth Century. In: B.L. Smith (ed.): *Religion and the Legitimation of Power in South Asia*. Leiden: Brill.

Spencer, Jonathan. 1989. Anthropology as a Kind of Writing. *Man*, 24, 145-64.

Srinivas, M.N. 1952. *Religion and Society Among the Coorgs of South India*. Oxford.

______ 1955/56. A Note on Sanskritization and Westernization. *Far Eastern Quarterly* 15, 481-96.

______ 1962. *Caste in Modern India and Other Essays*. Bombay: Asia Publishing House.

Stein, Burton. 1960. The Economic Function of a Medieval South Indian Temple. *Journal of Asian Studies* 19, 163-76.

Stein, Burton (ed.). 1978. *South Indian Temples. An Analytical Reconsideration*. Delhi: Vikas.

Stietencron, Heinrich von. 1989. Hinduism. On the Proper Use of a Descriptive

Term. In: Guenther D. Sontheimer and Hermann Kulke (eds.): *Hinduism Reconsidered*. Delhi: Manohar.

Strathern, Marilyn (ed.). 1995. *Shifting Contexts*. London: Routledge.

Stutley, Margaret and James Stutley. 1977. *A Dictionary of Hinduism. Its Mythology, Folklore and Development 1500 B.C.-A.D. 1500*. London: Routledge.

Sundarayya, P. 1972. *Telangana People's Struggle and its Lessons*. Calcutta: Communist Party of India (Marxist).

Tambiah, Stanley, J. 1979. A Performative Approach to Ritual. *Proceedings of the British Academy* 65: 113-69.

——— 1985. *Culture, Thought and Social Action. An Anthropological Perspective*. Cambridge: Harvard University Press.

——— 1990. *Magic, Science, Religion, and the Scope of Rationality*. Cambridge: Cambridge University Press.

Tedlock, Barbara. 1991. From Participant Observation to the Observation of Participation. The Emergence of Narrative Ethnography. *Journal of Anthropological Research* 47, 69-94.

Thapar, Romila. 1985. Syndicated Moksha. *Seminar* 313, 14-22.

——— 1989a. 'Imagined Communities'? Ancient History and the Modern Search for a Hindu Identity. *Modern Asian Studies* 23, 209-31.

——— 1989b. The Ramayana Syndrome. *Seminar* 353, 71-5.

——— 1991. Communalism and the Historical Legacy. Some Facets. In: K.N. Panikkar (ed.): *Communalism in India*. Delhi: Manohar.

Thapar, Romila, Harbans Mukhia and Bipan Chandra. 1977. *Communalism and the Writing of Indian History*. Delhi: People's Publishing House.

Thiel-Horstmann, Monika (ed.). 1983. *Bhakti in Current Research, 1979-1982*. Berlin: Reimer.

Thiel-Horstmann, Monika. 1985. *Naechtliches Wachen. Eine Form indischen Gottesdienstes*. Bonn: Indica et Tibetica.

——— 1991. *Ramayana and Ramayanas*. Wiesbaden: Harrassowitz.

Thomas, P. 1984. *Festivals and Holidays of India*. Bombay: Taraporevala.

Turner, Victor. 1957. *Schism and Continuity in an African Society*. Manchester: Manchester Universirt Press.

——— 1967. *The Forest of Symbols. Aspects of Ndembu Ritual*. Ithaca: Cornell University Press.

——— 1969. *The Ritual Process. Structure and Anti-Structure*. Chicago: Aldine.

Tyabji, Nasir. 1994. Political Economy of Secularism. Rediscovery of India. *Economic and Political Weekly* 29, 1798-1802.

Tylor, E.B. 1958. *Primitive Culture*. New York: Harper and Row.

Tyler, Steven A. 1990 [1986]. Post-Modern Ethnography. From Document of the Occult to Occult Document. In: James Clifford and George E. Marus (eds.): *Writing Culture. The Poetics and Politics of Ethnography*. Delhi: Oxford University Press.

Upadhyaya, Prakash Chandra. 1992. The Politics of Indian Secularism. *Modern Asian Studies* 26, 815-53.

van de Veer, Peter. 1987. 'God must be Liberated!' A Hindu Liberation Movement in Ayodhya. *Modern Asian Studies* 21(2): 283-301.

——— 1991. Life as Theatre. Performing the Ramayana in Ayodhya. In: Monika

Thiel-Horstman (ed.): *Ramayana and Ramayanas*. Wiesbaden: Harrassowitz.

______ 1994. *Religious Nationalism. Hindus and Muslims in India*. Berkeley: University of California Press.

van Velsen, J. 1967. The Extended-Case Method and Situational Analysis. In: A.L. Epstein (ed.): *The Craft of Social Anthropology*. London: Tavistock.

Vanaik, Achin. 1997. *Communalism Contested. Religion, Modernity and Secularization*. Delhi: Vistaar.

Varshney, Ashutosh 1993. Contested Meanings. India's National Identity. Hindu Nationalism, and the Politics of Anxiety. *Dredalus* 122, 227-61.

Verma, Rajendra. 1984. *The Freedom Struggle in the Bhopal State*. Delhi: Intellectual.

Verma, S.L. 1985. Reformulation of Indian Secularism. *Indian Journal of Political Science* 46, 32-48.

Vidal, Denis. 1996. When the Gods Drink Milk. Empiricism and Belief in Contemporary Hinduism. Paper presented to the 14th Conference on Modern South Asian Studies, Copenhagen, 23.8.1996.

Vidyarthi, L.P. 1960. Thinking about a Sarced City. *The Eastern Anthropologist* 13, 203-15.

Weber, Max. 1949. *The Methodology of the Social Sciences*. Glencoe, Ill.: Free Press.

Webster's Third New International Dictionary of the English Language. 1971. Chicago: Helen Hemingway Benton Publication.

Weiner, Myron. 1978. *Sons of the Soil. Migration and Ethnic Conflict in India*. Princeton: Princeton University Press.

Weiß, Christian, Tom Weichert, Evelin Hust and Harald Fischer-Tiné (eds.). 1996. *Religion—Macht—Gewalt. Religioeser 'Fundamentalismus' und Hindu-Moslem—Konflikte in Suedasien*. Frankfurt: IKO.

Werbner, Pnina and H. Basu (eds.). 1998. *Embodying Charisma. Modernity, Locality and the Performance of Emotion in Sufi Cults*. London: Routledge.

Werner, Karel (ed.). 1993. *Love Divine. Studies in Bhakti and Devotional Mysticism*. Richmond Surrey: Curzon Press.

Wikan, Unni. 1993. Beyond the Words. The Power of Resonance. In: Gísli Pálsson (ed:): *Beyond Boundaries. Understanding, Translation and Anthropological Discourse*. Oxford: Berg.

Wolf, Kurt H. 1976. *Surrender and Catch*. Dordrecht: Reidel.

Wrong, Dennis. 1999. Where Darwin Meets Durkheim. In: *The Times Literary Supplement*.

Yang, Ananda. 1980. Sacred Symbol and Sacred Space in Rural India. *Comparative Studies in Society and History* 22, 576-96.

Index